Classical Economic Theory and the Modern
Economy

Classical Economic Theory and the Modern Economy

Steven Kates

Honorary Professor, School of Economics, Finance and Marketing, RMIT University, Melbourne, Australia

Edward Elgar
PUBLISHING

Cheltenham, UK • Northampton, MA, USA

Published by
Edward Elgar Publishing Limited
The Lypiatts
15 Lansdown Road
Cheltenham
Glos GL50 2JA
UK

Edward Elgar Publishing, Inc.
William Pratt House
9 Dewey Court
Northampton
Massachusetts 01060
USA

A catalogue record for this book
is available from the British Library

Library of Congress Control Number: 2020932133

This book is available electronically in the **Elgar**online
Economics subject collection
DOI 10.4337/9781786433572

ISBN 978 1 78643 356 5 (cased)
ISBN 978 1 78643 357 2 (eBook)
Printed and bound by CPI Group (UK) Ltd, Croydon, CR0 4YY

Contents

1. Introduction

Writing this book was an odd experience, since the premise of everything found within the rest of this book is that just about the whole of modern economic theory is perniciously wrong, that other than here and there, such as in its opposition to rent controls, there is virtually nothing useful one can learn from a modern economics text in how to manage an economy.

And while you are reading this introduction first, it was written last. I started the book recognizing how absurd it is to be saying what I say and believing what I believe, yet the further into the book I went, the more it felt accurate and the less I felt I was in the territory of the economically absurd. If I am wrong, it must be for others to explain to me why.

What, then, is the premise of the book? It is that economic theory reached its peak level of understanding with the nineteenth-century classical school, and, in particular, with the economic theory presented in John Stuart Mill's *Principles of Political Economy*, whose first edition was published in 1848, and whose final statement may be found in the last edition published during his lifetime, the seventh edition, published in 1871.

Almost nothing from Mill's time remains alive in economics. Virtually all has been purged. The two economic revolutions since that time – the marginal revolution of the 1870s and the Keynesian revolution of the 1930s – have left behind almost nothing that was taught and discussed within the classical school.

Let me emphasize this to the fullest extent. It is J.S. Mill and his contemporaries that I refer to as the proponents of classical economic principles in their final and fullest extent. Others before, such as Adam Smith and David Ricardo, helped lay the groundwork that would finally reach its full flowering with Mill. It is not an argument against anything written in this book to refer to any economist who had written before Mill had published his *Principles*. Mill took from them those elements he had agreed with and reformulated the rest.

The notion that economic theory has gone in such a misguided direction, and has done so since the end of the nineteenth century with little to correct it other than this book written a century and a half later, is, I agree, a very odd idea. Yet, such is as it is. Therefore, a brief summary of all that follows in the rest of the text will give you the reader some guidance on whether to continue or just abandon going further. So, here below is what you will find argued in the coming chapters.

A SUMMARY

Classical economics saw an economy run on the basis of entrepreneurial decision making, where non-value-adding forms of production were rapidly culled to prevent them using up an economy's resources. It was an entirely supply-side theory of the operation of an economy. The supply side, as represented by entrepreneurs (usually referred to as capitalists) would seek to earn a living by working out what others wished to buy, and those who succeeded in finding profit-making activities would prosper, even while others would enter the market to compete. The theory of value that developed during classical times was based on the costs of production. Although the labour theory of value had had some attraction early on among the very first of the major classical economists – Adam Smith and David Ricardo being the most notable – by the middle of the nineteenth century, a theory of value based on production costs represented the approach that dominated economics. The focus was on the role of relative prices in the adjustment of an economy. Demand and utility had an important place but were seen as peripheral to a full and complete understanding of how an economy functioned.

None of this prevented governments from filling in gaps where the private sector had not produced as much as the market sought or had not produced anything at all. Government regulation and oversight were also recognized as essential for the operation of a market economy. It was also the role of governments to provide welfare where needed. *Laissez-faire* was in no sense a feature of economic theory. A role for government was absolutely recognized, although strict limits on government intervention were seen as essential. Understanding those limits was also a major aspect of economic theory.

The shift away from the supply-side focus began with the marginal revolution. The reason for placing marginal utility at the core of the theory of value had a number of motivations behind it, with developing a counterargument to the Marxist labour theory of value high on the list. Whatever the reason, the focus on utility redirected attention to the demand side of the economy as the driving force in giving an economy direction, rather than finding the direction through entrepreneurial activity.

And while much of the classical theory of the market was maintained by the early marginalists as part of their unstated presuppositions, over time these faded into the deep background. And with the marginal revolution, certain intrinsic attributes of the classical approach faded, notably the important distinction between productive and unproductive economic actions, as well as the distinction between value in use versus value in exchange. What had been a study of the operation of the economy as a whole was whittled down to a study of the individual actions of buyers. The macroeconomic perspective shrivelled into a much narrower focus on microeconomic adjustment.

The further effect of the marginal revolution was to shift economic theory from a philosophical study of markets into a mathematical study of equations. Economists had recognized mathematics as a useful background tool for clarifying concepts. The introduction of mathematical models would then, over time, replace the more conceptual approach, turning economic theory into a social scientist's form of physics.

Not until the 1930s, however, some 60 years after the marginal revolution began, was there a full flowering of the use of diagrams to explain the operation of an economy. As with the introduction of mathematics, diagrams shifted economic theory even further from the kind of subject matter on which abstract thought would be applied to market adjustment. Instead, economic theory became a subject matter in which the operation of an economy was presented via a string of static two-dimensional diagrams. Possibly the most damaging has been the diagrams showing price determination to occur where marginal revenue is equal to marginal cost. Since no seller ever knows the position and shape of the demand curve for any product being sold, the reality was that economic theory became more detached from an actual representation of market processes led by entrepreneurial decision making since there was no means to calculate marginal revenue.

The next stage in shifting economics into its present dead end was the Keynesian revolution, which began with the publication of John Maynard Keynes's *General Theory of Employment, Interest and Money* in 1936 (Keynes, *Collected Writings* [1936] 1981, VII). Published after the Great Depression had ended, never actually applied to the circumstances of any economy until the 1960s, Keynesian theory completely stormed the citadels of economic theory, so that by the end of the 1940s it had entirely replaced the classical theory of the business cycle across the academic world, and would therefore soon after replace the framework used by policy makers in dealing with unemployment and recessions.

Keynesian theory was introduced on the premise (now almost entirely forgotten) that economists did not until then even have a theory of recession and mass unemployment. Keynes's purpose, therefore, was to provide economists with just such a theory, and the theory that was then introduced into economics was the theory of demand failure (or overproduction) as the cause of recession. This remains the central theory adopted by policy makers ever since, which has led to attempts to regenerate growth following a downturn using measures to increase demand, usually with higher levels of public spending and often through lowering interest rates.

One further result of the Keynesian revolution is that virtually no economist any longer knows what the classical theory of the business cycle was. And far from classical economists having had no such theory, they had had many. But the one aspect of classical theory upon which there was virtual unanimity was that an economic downturn would never be caused by a deficiency of demand. The causes of recession inevitably stemmed from structural dislocations that could occur for any number of reasons but were often caused by some kind of failure within the credit creation system. This was a theory that had been developed over more than a century since the start of the nineteenth century, but which has entirely disappeared from economic discourse and from within the considerations of policy makers.

In relation to unemployment and the level of economic activity, the clearest statement of the conclusions that had been drawn by classical economists was from John Stuart Mill, who wrote in his *Principles*, 'demand for commodities is not demand for labour'. His meaning was clear during the whole of the classical period, but since then has become almost incomprehensible. His point was that the number of jobs in an economy is unrelated to the level of demand for goods and services. That is the actual meaning of Say's Law, and it was this proposition that Keynes very successfully displaced. It is a proposition that is, for all that, absolutely correct both in theory and also from the evidence of every attempt to use a stimulus to increase the level of employment.

The arguments developed within this volume are mainly, but not entirely, based on the theoretical writings of John Stuart Mill in the seventh edition of his *Principles of Political Economy* published in 1871, the last edition published before his death. The first edition had been published in 1848, and while there were many changes to the book, which is near 1000 pages in length, had not changed substantially in that time, but had mostly been refined and updated as circumstances had changed. Although other economists are brought into the argument, all are self-identified followers of the economics of John Stuart Mill, many of whom were writing well into the twentieth century.

THE STRUCTURE OF THE BOOK

Let me explain how this book is structured in detail so that the contours of the argument are set out more completely.

Chapter 2 deals with why only I could have written this book but also why I was able to. I was able to write the book because I had independently discovered the actual meaning of Say's Law on my own, not knowing it was Say's Law I had discovered, and then found the identical argument I had formulated in Mill's *Principles*. Having found the argument in Mill, only then did I discover that what I had stumbled across was what we now think of as Say's Law. Having discovered that Say's Law – properly understood – is not only valid but essential for understanding the operation of an economy, I proceeded to write my doctoral thesis in an attempt to explain all this to others. The PhD was then published as *Say's Law and the Keynesian Revolution* in 1998. As part of my work on Say's Law, I continued my research into the economics of John Stuart Mill and the entire late classical school, in which I discovered an understanding of the operation of an economy that is not only superior to what is taught today but also an understanding that has completely disappeared from the ways in which economics is taught in the modern world.

Beyond that, working in a political environment as the chief economist of Australia's national employers' association, I had endless opportunities to put classical economic theory to a real-world test. (Let me also mention parenthetically that I do find it interesting that for 24 years I was the economist for the Australian Chamber of Commerce in the same way that Ludwig von Mises had been the economist for the Austrian Chamber of Commerce, and also for 24 years.) In my work for the Chamber, I found that applying classical theory to modern economic circumstances never failed me on any occasion to make sense of economic events and allowed me to forecast what would follow the applications of particular policies. The economics of Mill in particular, and the classics in general, always and inevitably provided the correct judgement in every instance. Since everything I have written and said on the economy since that time is on public record, and this goes back to 1982 when I discovered Say's Law and Mill, it can all be verified, including from my work in industry as well as my published academic work, which includes books and articles. There are also any number of submissions and news commentaries that will also demonstrate the accuracy of my economic judgements made since that time. Much of this is discussed in Chapter 2. How to substantiate beyond that the accuracy of classical theory I do not know, other than for others to recognize how badly served we have all been by the application of Keynesian policies since that time. The invitation I offer in the writing of this book is for others to apply classical theory in making sense of the economic events they come across themselves.

Chapter 3 outlines the shifts in economic theory that have occurred since classical times, with an emphasis on the disappearance of the classical theory of the business cycle and its replacement with Keynesian macro. Crucial to understanding the economics of another time are the presuppositions that saturate all attempts to discuss economic management. At any moment there are belief systems and beliefs in general that dominate virtually all discourse on any philosophical and political topic. There is a surrounding world in which things are done in particular ways. An important part of the value in using the economics of John Stuart Mill as the standard for classical theory is that Mill was more than just an economic theorist, but was also possibly the most important political philosopher of his time. His *On Liberty* was a core text in outlining the political philosophy of his time, with the focus on individualism and personal responsibility. While Mill self-identified as a 'socialist', the meaning of socialist in 1848 was far different from the meaning and connotations the word would take on in later times.

The chapter goes to some length in discussing the advent of Keynesian theory, which was summarized by Paul Krugman in his introduction to the 2006 edition of *The General Theory*, 70 years after Keynes's original publication in 1936:

> Stripped down, the conclusions of *The General Theory* might be expressed as four bullet [sic] points:
>
> 1. Economies can and often do suffer from an overall lack of demand, which leads to involuntary unemployment
> 2. The economy's automatic tendency to correct shortfalls in demand, if it exists at all, operates slowly and painfully
> 3. Government policies to increase demand, by contrast, can reduce unemployment quickly
> 4. Sometimes increasing the money supply will not be enough to persuade the private sector to spend more, and government spending must step into the breach
>
> To a modern practitioner of economic policy, none of this – except, possibly, the last point – sounds startling or even especially controversial. But these ideas weren't just radical when Keynes proposed them; they were very nearly unthinkable. And the great achievement of *The General Theory* was precisely to make them thinkable. (Reprinted from DeLong, 2006)

There is no question that Keynes did indeed make each of these more than just thinkable. He was able to turn these propositions into the mainstream where virtually every economist has accepted them ever since. It is classical economic theory that has now become unthinkable. The result of the Keynesian revolution has left things such that the classical alternative is not just no longer contemplated by anyone within the mainstream of economic theory, but that no one within the mainstream even knows what that alternative is.

Chapter 4 introduces classical economic theory in contrast to modern macroeconomics. Modern macro is, for all practical purposes, entirely a descendent of the Keynesian economics that followed from the publication of *The General Theory* in 1936. Keynesian theory has not in any significant way been transcended, although much has been added since that time. The central division between classical and modern remains whether economies can and do go into recession because of a lack of demand, and following from that, whether a demand stimulus is capable of bringing an economy into recovery. Classical economists denied that recessions, which were frequent, were ever caused by oversaving and a lack of demand and that increased public spending could hasten a recovery. Modern economic theory and policy since 1936 has emphasized demand deficiency as the major, if not the sole cause of recessions, and that an increase in public spending not only can, but is also necessary to generate recovery, as specifically noted by Krugman.

The chapter further discusses how Keynes stitched together his arguments. Discussed, in particular, are the origins of the term 'Say's Law' and the phrase, 'supply creates its own demand'. Their origins are virtually unknown among economists, given how discrediting to the Keynesian mythology they are. 'Say's Law' was a term invented by the American economist, Fred Manville Taylor, and is entirely twentieth century in origin. It became part of the discourse among economists with the official publication of Taylor's introductory text in 1921, having originally been used as in-house university publication since 1911. The phrase 'supply creates its own demand' was formulated by another American economist, Harlan Linneus McCracken, in a book published in 1933, and is thus also twentieth century in origin. There are other elements in the creation myth of how Keynes came to write *The General Theory* that are utterly unknown and can be found only in this text, as well as in other books and articles I have previously published. The mythology on the steps taken between his *Treatise on Money* and *The General Theory* is bogus.

Chapter 5 provides the essential guide if one is to understand how economists became cut off from their classical past. There have been so many changes in terminology and definitions that it is impossible for a modern economist to read a classical text and follow its meaning. There are many, many such changes, with perhaps the most insidious being the definitions of capital and saving. The classical definitions are more fruitful if one is to understand how economies operate, but in the end, definitions are only definitions. If one is to follow modern theory, then only the definitions used within modern theory can be applied if one is to make coherent sense of what is being said. The same must apply to making sense of classical theory. What is important, however, is that if one applies modern terminology when reading a classical text, it becomes impossible to understand properly what is being said. To follow a classical text, the terms used must be understood in the sense they are being applied. This chapter explains the terminology of classical theory so that the classical perspective can be brought to the surface.

Beyond that, it is important to appreciate the changed presuppositions between those that existed during the classical period and those that existed in the 1930s. During classical times, the emergence out of the poverty of the entire human past and into a sudden burst of wealth was everywhere to be seen. The incredible growth in personal and communal wealth occurred before their eyes, since this was the generation that had lived through the astonishing transformation of the world's economy that followed the Industrial Revolution. This was in sharp contrast with the presuppositions that surrounded discussions of the economy in the 1930s, which were taking place well after the secret of economic growth and prosperity had been unlocked. Economic growth was by then an old story. The result was that by the 1930s, the general presumption, even among economists, was that, as far as the economy was concerned, everything would only keep getting better. This is only the first of the changes made in the state of mind between individuals who lived in the two eras. The aim of this chapter is to allow a modern economist to make sense of a classical text in the way it was meant to be understood.

Chapter 6 discusses the classical theory of value and, in addition, Mill's conception of the steady state. It has not just the classical theory of the business cycle that has been overturned. The micro side of classical theory has completely disappeared as well. To follow these shifts, however, it is necessary to return to the marginal revolution and examine the displacement of the classical theory of value to see the effects this has caused. Everyone assumes that marginal analysis replaced the labour theory of value (LTV). Certainly, the LTV had been at the core of Adam Smith's and David Ricardo's theory of value. The LTV had, however, disappeared from classical theory by the mid-nineteenth century. Mill had a list of 17 elements in his theory of value, of which the second of the 17 was how prices are in the first instance determined by supply and demand. Beyond that is a more sophisticated depiction of the forces that affect the price level and encompass every possible combination of circumstances that might be imagined. There is, no doubt, more to it than can be presented in a single chapter, as Mill acknowledged, but marginal cost equals marginal revenue was not the missing element. The LTV was not embodied in Mill's theory of value, although the cost of labour quite rightly was one part, but only one part of total production costs.

The steady state, as envisaged by Mill, was not a theory of secular stagnation. In 1848, in the long, long run, it was conceivable that the economy would eventually settle into a steady-state equilibrium, which far from any notion of a period of stagnation, was one in which everyone had more than enough of worldly goods to settle into a period of idyllic contentment. That rapid growth and unimaginable levels of innovation would occur instead was recognized as an ongoing possibility, but the extent to which it would and did occur was only dimly seen as a living possibility. We no longer think of the steady state as a realistic potential, but this possibility should be distinguished from the recessionary state that occurs from time to time in every economy.

Chapter 7 discusses the way in which Keynesian theory overran the classics. The Keynesian revolution is a phenomenon unique within the sciences, even from within the social sciences. *The General Theory* was published in 1936 and within a decade had entirely conquered the economics profession. That is not to say that those who had been educated within the classical tradition were converted to Keynesian macro. There were, in fact, virtually no converts whatsoever. What did happen, however, was that so overwhelming was the Keynesian tide that no other approach to economic issues could stand in its way. By war's end in 1946, if there were still non-Keynesians left in teaching roles, they kept their views to themselves. New modern Keynesian textbooks replaced the old. There may have been a few sporadic skirmishes here and there, but as far as the profession was concerned, the battles, to the extent there had even been any battles, had all come to an end.

The chapter therefore goes through the main staging posts in the step-by-step progress from the publication of a book that many had looked forward to in anticipation, but which virtually no one could make coherent sense of when it was finally published, through to the publication of the first Keynesian introductory texts and the disappearance of virtually all dissenting voices. The result is that while there has been elaboration of the Keynesian IS–LM (investment-saving–liquidity preference-money supply) model developed by Hicks, or the Samuelson $I = S$ (investment = saving) and aggregate demand 45-degree-line diagrams, these remain completely orthodox in both the teaching of economic theory and in the development of policy. The equilibrium between aggregate supply and aggregate demand carries on this tradition.

Chapter 8 delves more deeply into the reasons for Keynes's success. Keynes was certainly the best-known economist in the world in his time, and amongst the most well-known public intellectuals. His early fame came from the publication of *The Economic Consequences of the Peace* (Keynes, *Collected Writings* [1919] 1981, II), an international bestseller in which he had attacked the Treaty of Versailles that followed World War I. He was also internationally recognized because of his frequent media commentaries and his various books, some professional and others more popular, that made him very well known. In addition, he was the editor of *The Economic Journal*, at the time the most prestigious economics journal in the world, where he was able to publish articles that dealt with *The General Theory* and in which he was able to post his own replies to others, adding to his ability to control the debate.

Beyond his own fame and respectability, there were the various channels in which economic discussion was conducted in the period after 1936. Of crucial importance was the complete dominance of the 'neoclassical synthesis', which was the name given to the ways in which Keynesian theory was expanded outwards in the post-war economies. Keynesian terms and forms of analysis dominated the way theory was discussed and policy options were analysed. The national accounts were structured along the lines of Keynesian theory. Not only were the data being collected in conformity with the primitive classroom models that had been developed following the theories outlined in Keynesian texts, these primitive models were expanded into massive econometric models that were fitted to the data sets that were being simultaneously developed. Public sector and university economics departments found it relatively easy to design programmes to test the various Keynesian propositions being developed by a more mathematically oriented economics community.

The simplicity of the Keynesian model also made it easy both for policy makers and the community to fathom, or to believe they had fathomed, the intricacies of economic theory and policy. Fiscal expansion seemed to make sense. An absence of demand had always been the first port of call for anyone observing a recession. There had to be a reason in a world of scarcity for the failure of everything being offered for sale not to find buyers. The simplistic answers had turned to demand-side failures for an answer. Keynesian theory provided just that answer, and not just answers from anywhere, but from within Cambridge University, possibly the most prestigious university of its time. And with any critical response to this apparently obvious argument needing to be much more complex, and in need of a major effort to comprehend, it became an answer that easily fitted the public mood and allowed governments to undertake public sector expansions with less regard for concerns about the potential for inflation that would have accompanied such fiscal policies in pre-Keynesian times. This was all the more the case since it could be argued that the world's economies had been brought out of the Great Depression by the increases in demand that had occurred during the war when unemployment reached low levels that had not by then been experienced for many years.

Chapter 9 is a response to the common belief that classical economic theory was in essence *laissez-faire*, that among the major shifts that followed the Keynesian revolution was a more robust effort to use the resources of governments to assist individuals to deal with the fallout from adverse economic conditions. Such government actions, whether specific to themselves – such as in providing assistance during periods of unemployment – or more general – such as in providing education and healthcare to the entire community – were seen as opening up new possibilities for enlightened public policy. The fact that there were fewer resources available to governments during the nineteenth and early twentieth centuries was seldom recognized as the impediment it had been. But more important was the belief that what had changed was the willingness of economists to argue that a greater role for government was appropriate, and that these beliefs were in contrast to the beliefs that were common within the classical school. The recognition among economists that there was a significant role for government involvement in economic matters had existed throughout classical times, and in particular is absolutely spelled out in John Stuart Mill's *Principles*.

There has always been a need to ensure that such assistance is affordable, or that expenditure programmes do not defeat their own purpose by reducing the willingness of members of the community from undertaking productive work. Within these constraints, there were no limitations on the perceived role of governments in assisting the community. The last 200 pages of Mill's 1000-page *Principles* – the entire Book V, 'On the Influence of Government' – outlines both the proper means for governments to raise revenue and the various roles the government should take upon itself in undertaking these efforts. Classical economists were not characterized by an automatic *laissez-faire* attitude to the role of government in managing an economy.

Chapter 10 examines Austrian economic theory and its differences from the classical theory out of which it emerged, with the crucial difference being the demand-side approach that would become indelibly embedded within Austrian theory because of its focus on utility and marginal analysis. This focus on utility has obscured the classical presuppositions that were silently embedded within Austrian theory. Austrian economists to a large extent assume the whole of the classical supply-side understanding of the operation of a market economy without explicitly drawing out its implications. They are just there, understated and often unstated, with Say's Law almost universally ignored.

Among the problems in such an examination are the different historical roots of Austrian theory, which are continental in their background and scope, different from the classical school that was the province of the English-speaking nations – in particular, the United States and Great Britain. The particular differences that will be examined are, first, the theory of value, which in Austrian theory focuses on utility – a demand-side concept – while in classical theory the focus was on cost of production, obviously supply-side in its orientation. The Austrian tradition in many respects denies even the existence of a macroeconomic sphere, where the entire economy is looked at as a single unit. 'Methodological individualism' is the term often applied to the Austrian approach. From this perspective, economic outcomes are often left unexamined in relation to various economic aggregates, such as employment as a whole.

In many ways, the Austrian school took for granted the presuppositions of the classical school and assumed these would always be there as the background. In addition, and possibly for this reason, there was no anti-Keynesian attack on *The General Theory* when it was published, which has unfortunately remained the Austrian attitude ever since. There is no lack of criticisms from Austrian theorists of mainstream macroeconomics, but such criticisms are not frontal assaults and have seldom made an attack on Keynes's version of Say's Law a core element.

The second difference relates to the emphasis on an active role for governments that was embedded within classical economic theory and policy. Classical theory saw an important role for governments. Indeed, much of the reason for the development of economic theory was to determine the kinds of policies that would benefit the community in general, but also to identify the kinds of policies that would do more harm than good. There may have been cautions that needed to be observed, but there was nothing within classical theory that attempted to deny a key role for government involvement. In contrast, among Austrian economists, there has been a tradition where government efforts to involve itself with economic outcomes are either left unsupported or are instead often criticized in principle. No effort is made in this chapter to settle these differences, but there is a need to recognize that these differences exist.

Finally, the Austrian theory of the business cycle needs to be seen as merely one version of the classical theory of the business cycle, which explained the downturn in the cycle as due to disharmonies in the structure of production that were often, but not necessarily, brought on by upheavals in the credit creation process.

Chapter 11 presents a very brief overview of classical economic theory and outlines in modern terms not only why classical economists had reached the conclusions they had, but also why they had been right to reach those conclusions.

The chapter will focus on the consequences of the two revolutionary periods in economic theory, the marginal revolution and the Keynesian revolution, and the ways in which these first obscured and then finally all but obliterated the classical perspective on virtually every issue of consequence. The marginal revolution took the focus away from aggregates and the economy in general and reduced the perspective to the individual as the core decision maker. Marginal utility is the perspective of a sole individual, which was the foundation for a demand-side microeconomic perspective. The Keynesian revolution then furthered this demand-side perspective by introducing a macroeconomics that was based on aggregate demand. These individually and together almost entirely removed the supply side of the economy from economic analysis.

Classical theory was almost in its entirety based on a supply-side perspective that revolved around the role of the entrepreneur. That entrepreneurial activity was based on seeking to produce what others will buy, at prices that covered all their costs of production, was the core of classical thought. But, entrenched within theory was the recognition that everyone, in attempting to meet the demands of others, could only work their way forward in almost complete blindness to what others would really buy, and in almost complete ignorance of what others would attempt to supply in competition with what they were producing themselves. We now use the word 'uncertainty' to describe what is in reality and inevitably an almost complete lack of knowledge about the future.

Within this, it was recognized that the economic system would only work productively if individual entrepreneurs were almost entirely left to make their own decisions without being overburdened by government regulations, onerous taxation and high levels of non-productive publicly subsidized expenditures that did not repay their costs in an increased volume of goods and services. In these kinds of circumstances, entrepreneurs would be more cautious and, therefore, would also be more likely to make productive decisions, since to do otherwise would come at great personal cost. In addition, the price system had to be left on its own to determine relative prices, not only of final goods and services, but of all the inputs that went into the production process.

An analysis of the business cycle was also an integral feature of classical theory. The Keynesian mythology that *The General Theory* introduced the first such theory into economics is absurd, and should be recognized as absurd. What was absolutely true, however, was that among all the many different explanations for recession, the one that was universally rejected was any theory that attributed an economic downturn to an absence of demand. Ultimately, but not until the start of the twentieth century, was this principle given a name: 'Say's Law'. It stated that demand deficiency did not cause recessions and that public spending could not bring a recession to an end. This principle is not, it should be emphasized, J.-B. Say's *loi des débouchés*. We will come back to this issue in much greater detail, but, in short, the sequence of events leading to the origins of the term 'Say's Law' and its coming into common usage across the economics profession is described in Box 1.1. Crucially, Say's Law is fundamentally different in meaning and implications from the nineteenth century's *loi des débouchés*, which is properly attributed to Say.

BOX 1.1   SAY'S *LOI* VERSUS SAY'S LAW

1. In 1803, J.-B. Say published the first edition of his *Treatise*, in which he argued that recessions are not due to a shortage of money. His argument was that *demand is constituted by supply*. A shortage of money is never the cause of a lack of demand. The demand for goods and services in total is made up of the goods and services supplied to the market in total. A shortage of money, according to Say, had nothing to do with the totality of the amounts exchanged. This is Say's *loi des débouchés*.

2. In 1808, James Mill used Say's argument to help demonstrate that *an economy can never suffer from a lack of overall demand*. This principle ultimately became known as "Say's Law" but not for more than 100 years. Until then, although unnamed, this principle became the orthodox position across economic theory.

3. This principle had become particularly important after the 'General Glut' debate that followed the publication of Robert Malthus's *Principles* in 1820. Malthus had argued that recessions were caused by too much saving, which led to overproduction and demand deficiency. James Mill in the early 1820s had, among many others, written books and papers to argue that Malthus was completely wrong on this.

4. At the conclusion of the General Glut debate, an absolute denial of the proposition that demand deficiency of goods and services in total across

an entire economy was even possible became the universally accepted proposition. This remained accepted across the whole of mainstream economic theory, especially in the English-speaking world, through until the publication of *The General Theory*.

5. J.-B. Say wrote in agreement with Mill – first when he revised the second edition of his *Treatise* in 1812, in which he revised his entire chapter on the *loi des débouchés* to bring it into conformity with Mill's argument, and then in more detail when he wrote his book-length reply to Malthus, published in French in 1820 and in English in 1821. But, the principle denying the possibility of deficient total demand was first stated by James Mill and not Say. Importantly, this principle, having been stated and adopted across the whole of economic theory, had no specific name associated with this consensus position until the start of the twentieth century.

6. First in a brief paper published in 1909, then in a textbook used only by his own students at the University of Michigan as an in-house text published in 1911, and then, in his more broadly distributed textbook first published in 1921, the economist Fred Taylor noted that the principle denying the possibility of overproduction and demand deficiency did not have a name. To emphasize its importance, he supplied that name, calling it 'Say's Law' after J.-B. Say. 'Say's Law' is, however, not Say's *loi des débouchés*.

7. Following the wider publication of Taylor's text in 1921, 'Say's Law' becomes somewhat controversial in the United States in regard to the nature of the business cycle. The question raised was whether the denial of overproduction across the whole of an economy was a valid argument.

8. Keynes in the early 1930s comes across both the name 'Say's Law' and also the arguments over the possibility of demand deficiency as a cause of recession. At the same time, he came across the definition of Say's Law in the writings of another American economist, Harlan McCracken: 'supply creates its own demand.' As a result, Say's Law becomes the core of Keynes's *General Theory* in which he rejects the conclusions that follow from Say's Law in Taylor's sense, arguing that demand deficiency is not only possible, but the single most important cause of recession and unemployment. Keynes also adopted McCracken's phrase as the definition of Say's Law.

9. The rejection of Say's Law has remained the single most important element in modern macroeconomic theory, differentiating modern macroeconomics from classical theory, with its emphasis on demand deficiency as the cause of recession, with demand stimulation remain-

ing at the core of the policy of employment creation when high unemployment occurs.

10. The importance in understanding the origins of the term 'Say's Law' is because unless one understands the Taylor definition one cannot follow Keynes's own arguments. Keynes was not trying to deny that demand is constituted by supply. He was denying that economies never enter recession because of a deficiency of demand. Unless this distinction is kept firmly in mind, it is impossible to understand what occurred during the Keynesian Revolution.

The actual cause of recessions was a dislocation in the structure of production. For some reason, the capital structure that had been built up through entrepreneurial decisions turned out to have been misdirected because the world did not turn out to be the world that had been expected to come into existence when these investment decisions had been made. The only effective solution to such misdirected production decisions was to allow the economy to readjust by allowing entrepreneurs to find new forms of production that would pay their way in the world of demand as it actually was. Public spending to 'create jobs' would only divert productive activity into areas in which the capital that was put in place would not repay their costs of production.

The core element in the theory of employment stated, as found in Mill, that 'the demand for commodities is not the demand for labour'. Producing goods and services would not lead to the creation of a higher number of jobs. As an expression of the classical perspective delivered as late as 1929, there is a discussion of Winston Churchill's budget speech as UK treasurer in May 1929, delivered well before the Great Depression began that October. It is clear that Churchill was surprised to find that orthodox theory correctly understood how an economy worked, but surprised or not, discovered that their forecast of no effect of public spending on employment had been accurate:

> Churchill pointed to recent government expenditure on public works such as housing, roads, telephones, electricity supply, and agricultural development, and concluded that, although expenditure for these purposes had been justified:
>
>> for the purposes of curing unemployment the results have certainly been disappointing. They are, in fact, so meagre as to lend considerable colour to the orthodox Treasury doctrine which has been steadfastly held that, whatever might be the political or social advantages, very little additional employment and no permanent additional employment can in fact and as a general rule be created by State borrowing and State expenditure. (Peden, 1996, pp. 69–70)

This entire passage in relation to Churchill and his surprise in finding that the 'Treasury View' had turned out to be an accurate summary of the effects of public spending on employment will be repeated in full later on in the book and more than once, in both Chapters 8 and 9. Mill and classical economists had not just observed that this classical conclusion was borne out in reality, but more importantly had also explained the reason. By 1929, it was more than 80 years since Mill had discussed why the demand for commodities was not the demand for labour, a conclusion that to Churchill, as well as to Keynes a few years later, seemed inexplicable, in just the same way that this conclusion is inexplicable to virtually every economist today, although not to the British Treasury back then. What makes Churchill's observation so especially notable is that the government to which he had belonged had attempted to encourage employment through a series of public works, every one of which appears highly productive, and yet discovered that these expenditures had not led to an increase in employment. He was thus more than an unbiased observer. The government he was a member of had tried to lower unemployment through public spending and had undoubtedly hoped the policy would work. He had nothing to gain by admitting that the policy of encouraging higher employment through increased public spending had been a failure.

The most important reverse example of the lack of any connection between the level of public spending and the level of national employment occurred at the end of World War II in 1945 when the Truman administration in the United States immediately balanced the budget, less than a decade since the Great Depression had come to an end. This was in the face of the tens of millions of Americans who had suddenly become 'unemployed', having lost their 'jobs', both in the armed forces and throughout the armaments industries that had shut down across the country. Yet, this massive cut to public spending and the elimination of the huge deficits that had continued throughout the war began the greatest period of expansion in world history, which continued with virtually no let up until the 1970s.

The insights into the operation of an economy that were discovered by classical economists and thoroughly discussed by Mill and his contemporaries have now disappeared. It is the aim of this book to bring the classical understanding of the operation of an economy to a wider audience. Economists know nothing whatsoever about the analytical depth of the classical economists, among whom John Stuart Mill was the greatest of them all, and who is arguably the greatest who has ever lived.

2. The purpose of this book and why only I could write it

My aim in writing this book is to explain why classical economics is vastly superior to modern economic theory. And in attempting to demonstrate that this is so, I will explain how a classical economist understood the operation of the economy. But, in outlining the classical approach to economic analysis, I begin with the recognition that anyone who has already been taught modern economics will be virtually incapable of understanding classical economic theory.

I will therefore start with a personal explanation of why I believe I am almost uniquely placed to explain classical economic theory and why it is important that we do so. It will be argued that the disappearance of classical economic theory has led to an enormous loss in our ability to understand what needs to be understood if we are to make sense of how an economy works.

Modern economic theory is a labyrinth. Perhaps all theory is like that. Once one enters its precincts it becomes virtually impossible to escape other than by accident. I will therefore explain how I accidentally found my way out as perhaps a way to help others do the same.

And even as I begin, I will acknowledge how obscure I am within the world of economics. I have published papers and books. I have attended conferences and meetings of economic societies around the world. And in all this time, I have come across virtually no one who sees things as I do. There are a handful of others, but our numbers are trivially small. So, to my story.

HOW I DISCOVERED SAY'S LAW FOR MYSELF

I was educated in the usual way, with Keynesian economics at the core of macroeconomics and marginal analysis at the core of micro. Every element of all this instruction I accepted as perfectly plain and obvious. But in 1980, I became the economist for the Confederation of Australian Industry (CAI then, now the Australian Chamber of Commerce and Industry), which had the most profound effect on my intellectual destiny.

In Australia, there is an annual court case to determine whether there should be an adjustment made to the minimum wage, and if so, how much that adjustment should be. In 1980, I was writing the economic submission on behalf of employers and had to deal with what was already by then an antique argument from the union side:

> Raising wages will stimulate economic activity and therefore increase the level of employment because it will increase the demand for goods and services.

Keynesian though I was, I found this argument instantly without merit. If you compel employers to give employees an extra $100 by making them pay an extra $100, but without any additional output produced, prices must then rise by enough to cover the extra wage payments if job losses are not to occur. There is therefore no stimulus to demand.

Around the same time as I was writing this submission, I picked up a copy of John Stuart Mill's *Principles of Political Economy*, which I read purely out of interest, with no other motivation in mind. The book starts with chapter-length discussions of the factors of production, something no modern economics text now does, focusing first on labour and then on capital. I was breezing through the book, caught up in the sweep of its argument, when I came to Chapter V: 'Fundamental Propositions Respecting Capital'. And then, within this chapter, I came upon Mill's Fourth Proposition, which instantly changed my understanding of how an economy works. This is the short-form version that has attracted a continuous thread of commentary from some of the greatest economists who have ever lived. This is what Mill wrote:[1]

> Demand for commodities is not demand for labour. (Mill, *Principles* [1871] 1921, p. 79)

This was not to me at that moment some ancient proposition from a long-discarded text. This was John Stuart Mill arguing along the same lines I had been arguing myself during the wage case. It was not identical, but similar enough that it made me read further on what Mill had written. Where I then went next was to Mill's second essay in his *Essays on Some Unsettled Questions in Economics*, 'Of the Influence of Production on Consumption' (see Appendix A for the opening paragraphs of the essay), where I came upon this. Mill obviously found this argument patently absurd:

> The man who steals money out of a shop, provided he expends it all again at the same shop, is a benefactor to the tradesman whom he robs, and that the same operation, repeated sufficiently often, would make the tradesman's fortune. (Mill, [1844] 1974, p. 263)

This was almost identical to the argument I had crafted myself. Rather than it being theft, the process was a legal mandate on employers to pay higher wages, which was supported with the argument that paying these higher wages would be beneficial to the businesses that had been made to pay these higher wages.

The text then went on to explain why, using modern terminology, an increase in aggregate demand would not lead to an increase in the demand for labour. The argument, which will be discussed in subsequent chapters, struck me as so obviously correct that I could not believe it was not obvious to everyone.

I recall speaking to an economics colleague in the very week I had come across this argument and saying to him something that was absolutely true: that in the very instant that I read Mill's words I stopped being a Keynesian. More than that, I instantly understood why Keynesian economic theory was false and that a Keynesian policy would only do harm.

What I did not know, which would take a year or two before I fully realized this, was that what I had come across in Mill was what we today refer to as Say's Law. I had thus discovered Say's Law for myself and on my own.

RICARDO'S DOCTRINE

Keynes had muddled the definition, rendering it as, 'supply creates its own demand', which does not, on its own, make any coherent statement of economic principle. The actual economic theory Keynes was trying to refute he described in *The General Theory* as 'Ricardo's doctrine':

> The idea that we can safely neglect the aggregate demand function is fundamental to the Ricardian economics, which underlie what we have been taught for more than a century. Malthus, indeed, had vehemently opposed **Ricardo's doctrine** that it was impossible for effective demand to be deficient; but vainly. (Keynes, *Collected Writings* [1936] 1981, VII, p. 32; bold emphasis added)

On this, Keynes was absolutely correct. Ricardo, along with virtually all his contemporaries, denied that recessions could be due to a deficiency of demand. What he did not deny was that recessions accompanied by high levels of unemployment might from time to time occur.

That this is indeed Ricardo's own doctrine can be seen in this reply from Ricardo to Malthus in a letter sent in 1820, just after Malthus had published his own *Principles of Political Economy*. Malthus had argued that the recessions that had followed the Napoleonic Wars had been caused by there being too little demand. Ricardo in his reply to Malthus therefore wrote:

> Men err in their productions, there is no deficiency of demand. (Ricardo, [1819–21] 1973, VIII, p. 277)

Ricardo thus does not deny there might be recessions and abnormally high levels of unemployment. How could any classical economist deny it? How could any economist anywhere at any time deny it? What Ricardo did deny, however, along with the entire mainstream of the economics community through until 1936, was that the cause of high unemployment was a deficiency of demand. And with this I had discovered a subject of such immense personal interest that, although having a full-time job, I eventually made it the subject of my doctoral thesis, which was completed in 1996 and published in 1998 as, *Say's Law and the Keynesian Revolution* (Kates, 1998).

SAY'S LAW IS CENTRAL TO UNDERSTANDING THE OPERATION OF AN ECONOMY

In writing this thesis, my research required me to read a vast expanse of the classical economic literature from the time of Adam Smith until the publication of *The General Theory*. And as a side note, while working on my research, rather than owning up that I was looking into the notoriously infamous Say's Law, I would tell others I was working on the classical theory of the business cycle, which ironically was absolutely true, since Say's Law, properly understood, is an essential element in the explanation of the cycle.

But what was of more consequence at the time was that while still the chief economist of Australia's national employer association, I remained in the midst of our national debate on economic issues, beyond questions on wages policy, but involved with every aspect of economic policy of every kind. I was also, moreover, a frequent delegate at international conferences at the Organisation for Economic Co-operation and Development (OECD), the International Labour Organization (ILO) and other international meetings of economists. And in writing submissions and commenting on economic events and policy, I followed a 100 per cent strictly classical approach, in which the guiding light was my growing understanding of classical theory in general and Say's Law in particular.

In so doing, over a period of 24 years I never made a single wrong call on the economy or the effects of public policy on economic outcomes both domestically and internationally. Economic events and the results of public policy, both in Australia and across the world, became so obvious that I simply became used to seeing things work out just as I thought they would, while others, using conventional economic analysis, would see these things in a completely different way. I will provide a few instances to indicate how contrary to the modern received wisdom my economic policy prescriptions were, yet how accurate they always turned out to be. For myself, understanding the grip of Keynesian theory on others, I could see what they were doing and why they thought the measures they took would succeed. But because I understood things from a classical perspective, things always looked very different to me. I will provide a number of instances that for the most part have an international dimension, so that they do not entirely require a knowledge of Australia's economic history.

FORECASTER OF THE YEAR

The first example led me to become *The Australian Financial Review* (AFR) (our *Wall Street Journal*) Forecaster of the Year following the worldwide share market collapse in October 1987. The finance editor of the AFR spoke to economists across the economy to ask how likely they thought it was that a recession would occur due to the collapse of share market prices, since to quite a few it looked like a replay of the start of the Great Depression in 1929.

With the government having gone into panic mode, it had behaved in perfect accord with classical economic policy. It had balanced the budget, in the same way that across the world others had, for a change, acted in a sober and sensible way, proving that policy makers really do know what needs to be done to make an economy hum. So, while others rated the prospect of recession as high, upwards of a 50 per cent probability, I said that the likelihood was effectively zero, given how well, for a change, our economies were being managed. When 1988 turned out to be one of the best years on record economically, I was named the Forecaster of the Year, although I am not by trade a forecaster at all. The only remnant I can find on the net of my forecasting is this passage from the *Industrial Review*, the CAI newsletter that I wrote, which was quoted extensively in the press at the time, such as, for example, here:

> 'An Australian economic miracle, a truly Lazarus-like recovery is now a clear possibility', says the Confederation of Australian Industry (CAI) in a newsletter this month. (*Sydney Morning Herald,* 14 April 1988, p. 4)

The economy actually ended up bursting at the seams, as did economies everywhere due to the careful economic management that occurred at the time. This unfortunately led to an absolute overkill response across the developed world, with massive increases in official interest rates that finally drove economies around the world into deep recession that began two to three years later. I did everything I could to persuade our central bank, along with central banks everywhere else, not to murder this astonishing recovery in its tracks, but nothing could be done. Across the world, economies were said to be 'overheating' and down they would eventually crash due to a ridiculous policy of high interest rates designed to kill off economic growth to forestall an inflation that was never even remotely possible. I even said as much to Janet Yellen, during a meeting I attended at the OECD at the time, well before she would become the Chair of the Federal Reserve many years later.

That recession eventually and inevitably arrived in 1991–92. In 1991, before the dam finally broke while economic conditions were still seemingly positive, the head of the OECD came to visit Australia, and came to visit us, as we were the peak employer association in the country. I told him of our grave concerns for the economy and he, who was French, went on a quite funny rap in his charming French accent, about how employers always remind him of French farmers. You ask them one year how things are and they complain there is too much rain. Then you ask them the next year and they complain again, but this time that there is not enough rain. You employers are just like French farmers, never satisfied, always complaining. And then the downturn came, and then the very next year, when the world's economy was somewhere near the trough, he came back to Australia and specifically came to see us to apologize for what he had said the year before.

AUSTRALIAN BALANCED BUDGET ON THE WAY TO ACHIEVING ZERO GOVERNMENT DEBT

The second instance of a stand-alone policy understanding occurred in 1996 with the election of an Australian government that immediately proceeded not only to cut spending in the midst of a mild recession in order to balance the budget, but as it turned out, during what is now referred to as the Asian Financial Crisis. Moreover, the succeeding years of public sector restraint led to Australia becoming, as far as I know, the only nation anywhere since the end of World War II where the government achieved an entirely debt-free economy. CAI (with me driving the response) again, uniquely, supported these policies and from the start. The result was a succession of years of rapid uninterrupted growth, and a continuously falling rate of unemployment. Eventually, others would subscribe to the policy, since it is hard to argue with success. But only someone with a classical non-Keynesian view of the operation of an economy could see that massive cuts to public spending in the midst of a recession would lead to a rekindling of economic growth and a fall in unemployment. Obvious if you understand the classics. Mystifying if you are a student of modern macro.

Here I might append that at the start of 1993 I was sat next to someone at a lunch who was a major economic official in Japan (possibly its Treasury head) just as they were about to start their reflation of the Japanese economy through a massive fiscal stimulus. So, I said to him that it would be a huge mistake to undertake this spending programme, to which he replied, 'Don't you care about the unemployed?' There our conversation on economic matters ended, but the Japanese economy has been dead in the water ever since. No one understands why the Japanese economy has performed so poorly since those times, although many explanations have been cobbled together to provide one.

The answers are, however, clear enough if you take your policy from a classical economics text.

THE RESPONSE TO THE GLOBAL FINANCIAL CRISIS

The third instance was my unrelenting public opposition to the fiscal stimulus packages that were introduced across the world following the Global Financial Crisis in 2008–09. Most supported these stimulus programmes, and those who did not focused on the likelihood that the result would be an increased and uncontrollable level of debt. Few argued that the stimulus packages would not lead to recovery and actually make conditions worse. For myself, nothing was less likely than that large increases in public spending would lead to recovery. The following was part of an article published in March 2009 titled, 'The Dangerous Return of Keynesian Economics':

> Just as the causes of this downturn cannot be charted through a Keynesian demand deficiency model, neither can the solution. The world's economies are not suffering from a lack of demand and the right policy response is not a demand stimulus. Increased public sector spending will only add to the market confusions that already exist.
>   What is potentially catastrophic would be to try to spend our way to recovery. The recession that will follow will be deep, prolonged and potentially take years to overcome. (Kates, 2009)

I maintain a classical definition of recession that is identified by much higher than normal rates of unemployment and much slower than normal rates of economic growth. In relation to this definition, there is no question the world's economies operated well below potential during the entire period following the introduction of the stimulus packages. No economy recovered other than in the most anaemic fashion. Strong rates of economic growth remained elusive.

That all this was on the public record is also clear from this question I was asked by Senator Doug Cameron at an Australian Senate Economic References Committee on 21 September 2009, after I had provided testimony arguing against the introduction of a stimulus package:

> Why have the IMF, the OECD, the ILO, the treasuries of every advanced economy, the Treasury in Australia, the business economists around the world, why have they got it so wrong and yet you in your ivory tower have got it so right?

That was exactly the right question. Why was I able to get it right when all others got it so wrong? That is just what this book is attempting to explain.

In Appendix B at the end of this chapter is an article published in March 2019, ten years following the earlier warning written in March 2009 about what I saw as the certain negative consequences of using a Keynesian stimulus package to reverse the recession that began following the Global Financial Crisis (GFC). What is perhaps of particular note is that in this article is an explanation for the GFC in completely classical terms, providing a description taken directly from Walter Bagehot's 1873 *Lombard Street*. No modern discussion provides as natural an explanation for what took place than the one set down by Bagehot 135 years before the GFC had actually occurred.

FREE MARKET ECONOMICS: AN INTRODUCTION

Beyond writing this article on how mistaken a public sector stimulus would be, I completely revised the introductory course in economics I had been teaching. It was a graduate course in which I had over the years reshaped what I taught towards a somewhat more classical approach. But given the nature of every single textbook on the market, I could not shift very far from the standard macro/micro that made my students cardboard cut-outs of students everywhere else. That immediately came to a halt.

I spoke to my Head of School, the woman who was my co-teacher on the course, and to the students I was teaching, advising them that there would be no course text available in the first semester of 2009 (which in Australia begins in February). Instead, I would write my own textbook, completing a chapter a week over the succeeding 12 weeks of the course, in which I would outline economics as I thought it ought to be taught. Because it was a graduate course, half the students had already undertaken economics as part of their undergraduate training. To those students I provided a straight-out warning, that if they thought that they could pass this course based on what they had already studied, they would be very sadly mistaken. Because what I set out to do was write my own classical economics text for the twenty-first century right down to an inclusion of Mill's 'Four Propositions Respecting Capital', the first time, as far as I know, they had been included in an economics text since Mill had written them himself.

The first edition was published in 2011 under the title, *Free Market Economics: An Introduction for the General Reader* (Kates, 2011a). To appreciate what the text was attempting to achieve, this is from the Preface to the second edition written in 2014, reproduced in the third edition:

> The book is my update for the twenty-first century of two of economic theory's great classics, John Stuart Mill's *Principles of Political Economy* published in 1848, and Henry Clay's *Economics: An Introduction for the General Reader* published in 1916 and from which I adopted the title.[2] They knew nothing of Keynesian economics other than its being a common but at the time an unnamed fallacy that economists had to refute continuously. Keynesian economics is now, however, the mainstream. If you would like to understand what is wrong with Keynesian theory and much

else, as well as understanding how to view the economy and economic issues from a classical perspective, this book is the place to start. (Kates, 2017, p. ix)

This is the entire Preface to the third edition:

> The major change made in the third edition is to introduce a model of an economy that explains the difference between the modern theory of recession on the one hand, and the classical theory of the business cycle on the other. Mainstream theory continues to revolve around demand deficiency with the resulting policies to return an economy to rapid growth and full employment dependent on increases in aggregate demand. The theory has thus maintained its place in spite of the failure of increased public spending to achieve a recovery anywhere in the world at any time in history. Aggregate demand will eventually disappear from economics, although when that will be is hard to say. Bad theory does seem to persist for an unconscionably long period of time.
>
> The model introduced in a new Chapter 15 explains the causes of recession in relation to distortions in the structure of supply through the use of a simple graphical model. Although the explanation in this new chapter provides greater clarity, it is only a summary statement of the arguments that were already present in the first and second editions. The model is based on the economics of John Stuart Mill and Henry Clay, as is almost the entire book and as were both the first and second editions, which is why the new cover continues to display a water mill made of clay. (Kates, 2017, p. xi)

The text is a restatement of the economics of John Stuart Mill, as best as I was able. I think of Mill's *Principles* as the greatest economics text ever written. But I am also aware how difficult he is to read, with his 150-word sentences, endlessly complex examples to explain the simplest ideas, and a formality of language that has now all but disappeared. I therefore did what I could, by writing this text, to reintroduce classical economic theory to the modern world.

KEYNESIAN ECONOMICS AND ITS FAILINGS

Beyond this text, I put together three book-length collections of specially commissioned articles to document how incompetent modern economic theory is in dealing with our economic problems. The first, published in 2010, was titled, *Macroeconomic Theory and Its Failings: Alternative Perspectives on the Global Financial Crisis* (Kates, 2010a), and then a year later *The Global Financial Crisis: What Have We Learnt?* (Kates, 2011b) was published. There was then a third volume, *What's Wrong with Keynesian Economic Theory?* (Kates, 2016b), which gathered together a sampling from every contemporary anti-Keynesian economist I could find, of which there are very few.

My assumption in all this was that the failure of Keynesian policies to regenerate growth would lead to a re-examination of modern macroeconomic theory, with these books being part of the reconsideration that would then go on. And with no doubt whatsoever, aside from the United States since 2017 (a very important exception), no economy even a decade later had had the robust recovery that typically follows a downturn. As with Japan, in the period after its Keynesian stimulus during the 1980s, virtually no one blamed the anaemic recovery on the prior Keynesian policies that had been adopted to hasten the return to normal conditions. Instead, growth rates remained low, unemployment did not fall back to previous levels, while real wages growth slowed if not actually fell back. Ad hoc explanations were available at every turn to explain what had been an unexpected turn of events, but was an inevitable series of outcomes if one begins from a classical economic perspective.

There were also two articles in particular, among a number of others, that were published in which I tried to explain these issues to others. The first was written and published in the *Journal of the History of Economic Thought* (JHET) in 2015. The second was an extended interview focused on Say's Law, published in the journal of the Coase Society, *Man and the Economy*, in 2016. These are discussed in the next two sections.

MILL'S FOURTH PROPOSITION ON CAPITAL – THE KEY TO CLASSICAL THEORY

The JHET article was titled, 'Mill's Fourth Fundamental Proposition on Capital: A Paradox Explained'. This is its abstract:

> John Stuart Mill's Fourth Proposition on Capital, first stated in 1848, had become an enigma well before the nineteenth century had come to an end. Described in 1876 as 'the best test of a sound economist' and never challenged in Mill's own lifetime, it is now a statement that not only fails to find others in agreement but fails even to find an internally consistent interpretation that would make clear why Mill found it of such fundamental importance. Yet the Fourth Proposition should be easily understood as a continuation and extension of the General Glut debate. Economists led by Malthus had argued, contra Say's Law, that demand deficiency was the cause of recession and that a body of unproductive consumers was needed to raise the level of demand if everyone who wished to work was to find employment. Mill's answer to such economists was to argue that to buy goods and services would not lead to an increase in employment, or in Mill's own words, that the demand for commodities was not the demand for labour. (Kates, 2015a, p. 39)

While it can hardly be said that its publication has risen to the level of becoming a controversy, the article nevertheless attracted a number of published comments, for the most part, and unsurprisingly, critical. What the article does, however, is restate Mill's Fourth Proposition in a way that provides its meaning with a clarity that has been missing since the 1870s, because, for the first time since then, an interpretation has been written by someone who agrees with Mill completely. As I point out in the article, there is a deep mystery about this proposition, which is why it has continued to attract such attention:

> John Stuart Mill's Fourth Proposition in respect of capital has in many respects the same mystery about it that 'Fermat's Last Theorem' had in mathematics. It is a statement found in an ancient text of the highest reputation, yet it is statement that can no longer be explained in a way that makes clear why Mill found this Fourth Proposition of such fundamental importance. (Ibid., p. 39n.)

If you would like to see Mill's Fourth Proposition on capital clearly explained by someone who believes it is valid, go to this article.

SAY'S LAW IN THE COASE SOCIETY JOURNAL

The second article was an interview with me conducted by journalist Grégoire Canlorbe for the journal *Man and the Economy*, which continues for 30 pages and runs to almost 15 000 words, published under the title, 'Say's Law, Between Classical, Keynesian and Austrian Interpretations' (Canlorbe, 2016). It was about as comprehensive as any such interview can be. The interviewer had spent almost two years himself researching these issues so that his questions would elicit answers as illuminating as possible. Here is part of one of his questions along with the beginning of my answer:

> **GC**: [James] Mill did not contend that a general glut could only occur as a consequence of entrepreneurial miscalculations. His point was that a general glut could simply never occur: while some definite goods might be overproduced at some time, such mistakes could never affect the whole of production simultaneously.
> **SK**: Let me first repeat James Mill's perfectly pitched statement, but also at the same time add in the date of publication: first edition 1807:
>
>> It may be necessary, however, to remark, that a nation may easily have more than enough of any one commodity, though she can never have more than enough of commodities in general. The quantity of any one commodity may easily be carried beyond its due proportion; but by that very circumstance is implied that some other commodity is not provided in sufficient proportion. What indeed is meant by a commodity's exceeding the market? Is it not that there is a portion of it for which there is nothing that can be had in exchange. But of those other things then the proportion is too small. A part of the means of production which had been applied to the preparation of this superabundant commodity, should have been applied to the preparation of those other commodities till the balance between them had been established.
>
> Here he is stating the standard argument of classical economists: that you can have a particular glut of individual goods or services even while a general glut is impossible. You can never produce so much that a community will run out of demands. Think how much more abundant goods and services are today compared with the start of the nineteenth century, and even so what he wrote then would apply just as

much to the present and to any imaginable future we might contemplate. You have to be compulsorily mis-educated into accepting Keynesian theory to believe that demand deficiency is a realistic possibility.

All this and more seems perfectly obvious to me, yet it causes virtually no one to stop and think about any of it. Had Keynes taught, as I have, at some obscure university on the far side of the globe, nothing he had written would have made the slightest ripple in the firmament. Instead, he was the single most famous economist in the world, possibly the single most influential public intellectual of his time, and what he wrote mattered. He was at Cambridge, he was the editor of the *Economic Journal*, and he was surrounded by many young and bright students who took up his message and spread it across the world.

THE HISTORY OF IDEAS

But beyond even his name and his position, there must have been something extraordinary about what Keynes wrote that fit in with the times in which he published. Unlike the other 'general theory', that one by Einstein, there was no radical experiment available to test the validity of the theory, no 'transit of Venus' moment that could confirm the validity of Keynesian economics. Whatever it was, Keynesian theory found its moment and is now established to such an extent that it seems almost impossible to imagine a set of circumstances that will reverse the direction of macroeconomic theory towards the re-establishment of classical economics.

The rapidity of the transformation is astonishing. In imagining a transition in the opposite direction, it is instructive to look at a comparison of a number of other revolutionary moments in the past. Notorious among economists is the misfortune that was visited upon the economies of the world because of Aristotle's observation in around 400 BC that money is barren so that charging interest on loans was unproductive. How long has it taken to unwind this observation, and moral attitudes towards 'usury' and the charging of interest? It is a moral attitude that is still by no means fully unwound. Similarly, there are the issues that have never disappeared in relation to 'the just price', which is far different in concept from the equilibrium price. These are examples of economic doctrine that were established through authority, remaining unchallenged over not just centuries, but millennia. Of a similar caste are notions that are now so familiar in the sciences that it is almost unimaginable how difficult it was to establish certain ideas that are today absolute facts, universally accepted. Semmelweis died a broken man in poverty, having fought the medical establishment of his time to ensure that proper handwashing with antiseptics was undertaken following autopsies prior to assisting at births. William Harvey in the seventeenth century had to overturn an understanding that had originated in the second century AD to establish the circulation of the blood through the body, which until he wrote, was absolutely denied by everyone. And as recently as the end of the nineteenth century, Pasteur and Koch had to fight major battles amongst the medical establishment of their time to establish that diseases such as anthrax and cholera were caused by germs.

As Samuelson observed in his obituary for Keynes:

> And perhaps most important from the long-run standpoint, the Keynesian analysis has begun to filter down into the elementary textbooks; and as everybody knows once an idea gets into these, however bad it may be, it becomes practically immortal. (Samuelson, 1946, p. 189)

Keynesian economics, whether it is described as such or not, is found in all economics texts, and has all the appearance of immortality. Yet, classical economics, which was also in its time found in all the texts, has evaporated completely. There is scarcely anything left. It is Keynesian theory of aggregate demand that has taken its place, with no sign whatsoever that its grip is any less strong today than it has been since the 1960s at least, if not before.

THE STRUCTURE OF THE KEYNESIAN REVOLUTION

Although I have tended to be sceptical about Thomas Kuhn (1962) and his argument that scientific revolutions create such a discontinuity between a new paradigm and its older predecessor that it becomes impossible for those who have been raised with the new paradigm to comprehend what had existed before, my own experience has more than confirmed this conclusion over and again. Bear in mind that nothing I write is novel. Everything I discuss was the virtually unanimous position of classical economists from at least the time of Mill until the coming of the Keynesian revolution. Yet, it is clear to me, who was raised in one tradition but has adopted another out of conviction, that no one raised as a Keynesian is able to understand classical theory unless, for some reason, they make the effort to make sense of it for themselves, or else, through some accident of personal history, reach these conclusions on their own and then discover who had had these thoughts before.

The aim of the book is to make as comprehensible as possible the logic of classical theory that has required me to attempt to explain the different definitions that prevailed during classical times, as well as by trying to fill in the presuppositions that economists in those earlier times brought with them to their readings of classical theory. None of them were fools; all understood as a matter of certainty that recessions occurred, were frequent and had devastating consequences for the working population; and every one of them denied that demand deficiency was ever a cause of a downturn in the business cycle.

With this in mind, there is a possibility that you will end up understanding how a classical economist understood the operation of a market economy.

D.P. O'BRIEN: *THE CLASSICAL ECONOMISTS REVISITED*

The unfortunate reality is that virtually no one, not even the most authoritative economist of the modern day, has much of an idea of what a classical economist might or might not have believed. What I have therefore done is cite passages from Denis O'Brien's outstanding text *The Classical Economists Revisited* ([1975] 2004). These are provided so that there is at least this much corroboration of the points made in my own text that follows. I do not wish to implicate O'Brien in any of my own arguments. What I do wish to do is to provide some substantiation for the various positions I take myself, to show that they are not from out of left field but are standard judgements about the kinds of beliefs classical economists had. What follows below are quotes with page references to O'Brien's original text, which are preceded by a series of bullet points on where our views overlap. The aim in these citations is to demonstrate that my views on what classical economists argued is entirely mainstream among historians of economics even if not everyone agrees. My contribution is to explain not only how these views disappeared, but also that the classical views that disappeared are superior to the mainstream economic theory of today, both macro and micro. But while O'Brien and I agree on these background issues, I wish to emphasize that as far as the remainder of the book is concerned, these are not necessarily O'Brien's views, only my own. The citations are listed by subheading. No other organizing principle is involved. I will note that this section was added only after the entire book had been written. O'Brien and I see things in much the same way only because we both independently came to the same conclusions.

Below, in bullet points, is a list of areas that O'Brien and I see eye to eye on:

- Classical economists saw a major role for governments in regulating an economy and in providing welfare and financial assistance to members of the community.
- Classical economists cannot in any way be classified as *laissez-faire*.
- Classical economists were perfectly aware of the frequency of recessions.
- Classical economists universally understood that recessions were associated with high levels of involuntary unemployment.
- Classical economists did not, however, believe that increased public works expenditure would reduce the level of unemployment or increase the number of jobs.

- Classical economists argued that there were many reasons an economy might end up in recession but demand deficiency (more commonly referred to in classical times as overproduction) was never the reason why a recession would occur.
- Classical economists were virtually unanimous in arguing that it was impossible for there to be an insufficient level of investment opportunities.
- Say's Law specifically meant that an economy would not enter recession due to a deficiency of demand or an excess of saving, which was a proposition that was accepted by classical economists with near unanimity.
- The focus of classical economic theory was on what we would today classify as macroeconomic issues and the conditions that underpin economic growth, in contrast with 'the neoclassical synthesis' that largely focuses on microeconomic theories of resource allocation.
- Aggregate demand played no role in classical economic theory.
- There was a profound change in the nature of economic theory caused by the marginal revolution.
- The marginal revolution introduced utility into mainstream theory and diverted the focus from the supply side of the economy to the demand side and from the macroeconomy to micro with a focus on individual agents.
- The dynamic view of economic phenomena that was taken for granted by classical economists entirely disappeared following the marginal revolution of the 1870s.
- Classical economic theory was conceived in real terms, with the effects of money on the economy only examined after the role of the real adjustment process had been analysed.
- The discoordination caused by money and credit was only examined after the real adjustment process was first analysed.
- Classical economic theory was focused on policy formation – on how to create prosperity and economic growth.
- Classical economists agreed that 'demand for commodities was not demand for labour' – that public spending would not add to the level of employment across an economy.
- Classical concepts and the definitions of various terms, such as saving, investment, consumption, along with many others, are entirely different from their meaning in modern economic theory.
- The economics of John Stuart Mill is among the most important presentations of classical theory.
- Mill's theory of value provides a clear understanding of the analysis provided by classical theorists.
- Mill's theory of value began in the same way as modern economics, with an examination of supply and demand.

- Mill's economics is very different from the economics of Smith and Ricardo – later classical economic theory is profoundly different from the theory that had been forged by the early classical theorists.
- Money was not seen as neutral among classical economists.
- 'Productive versus unproductive' in relation to capital and labour were important distinctions.
- Private property was identified as the core to a productive and growing economy.
- Although Mill described himself as a 'socialist', what he meant was a socialism made up of competing decentralized productive groups of individual producers, and was not in any sense the centralized economic structure that the term has come to mean since his time.

The following direct quotes provide textual support for the above beliefs attributed to O'Brien ([1975] 2004). Most represent a significant difference with modern economic analysis and are different from the common judgements of mainstream economists over what classical economists believed. There were also many more differences than just these:

Presupposition on which classical economics was grounded

Classical economists wrote and worked through an explosion of economic growth for which there was no historical precedent, and which they were faced with explaining and analysing. (p. 16)

The profound differences between classical and modern economics

A dynamic view of economic phenomena, taken for granted in the Classical writings, disappeared from view with the marginal revolution of the 1870s. (p. 53)

Classical economics was structured in real terms

The rise of Classical economics ... marks a sharp shift in the balance of economic writing towards real as distinct from monetary analysis. (p. 33)

John Stuart Mill and the non-neutrality of money

Classical economists certainly did not regard money as neutral. The most striking case here is that of J.S. Mill. (p. 161)

The meaning of capital was conceived differently by classical economists as a stock of existing productive assets

Mill saw capital as a stock of previously accumulated products of labour affording a means to future production. (p. 220)

Demand for commodities is not demand for labour (demand failure does not cause recession)

Abstinence from consumption was the source of capital, and capital was demand for labour. … Starting from these positions we can understand J.S. Mill's famous fourth proposition on capital – that demand for commodities is not demand for labour. (p. 112)

Savings were conceived in real terms not money terms

Savings derive from decisions to postpone consumption by investing in production. (p. 33)

Say's Law

Say's Law – the denial of the possibility of a failure of effective demand – continued to rule throughout the Classical period. (p. 44)

The classical theory of value was not based on utility although Mill was himself a utilitarian

Mill advances a 'cost of production' theory of value. … He was not a subjective value theorist. … He treated utility as merely a condition of value. (p. 96)

Productive and unproductive labour and capital

This distinction between productive and unproductive activities has now passed out of economics. (p. 235)

Classical economists did not accept the principle of *laissez-faire*

The caricature of the Classical economists as the die-hard defenders of extreme *laissez-faire* is one which has proved extremely persistent. … Examination of the Classical writings on the role of government quickly reveals the misleading nature of the caricature. (p. 272)

Classical economists had a positive view of the role of government

> Classical writers ... were perfectly clear that [the market] could only operate within a framework of restrictions. Such restrictions were partly legal and partly religious, moral and conventional, and they were designed to ensure the coincidence of self and community interest. (p. 272)

Concern with the power of the state

> The Classical economists in general were concerned ... about the accretion of power to the State involving dangers to individual liberty. There was a danger in a democracy that everyone would try to increase the power of the State and use it to their own advantage. (p. 273)

Socialism

> The socialism which Mill had in mind was ... decentralized socialism with competition between producing co-operatives. ... He presciently forecast the effects of forced collectivisation. If he believed in socialism, he did not believe in centralization. (p. 277)

PRESUPPOSITIONS

The quotes from O'Brien highlight what many now automatically accept as the beliefs that classical economists held and the reality that is quite different. Bringing these differences to light is crucial if someone is to approach the older literature with the intention of understanding things as they were originally understood at the time these passages were written. These are, however, often differences in how the world was seen that are actually not very different from how economists see things today, such as the common ground over *laissez-faire*, which virtually no economist, then or now, accepted.

More difficult is ensuring that earlier presuppositions are identified and understood. Below is a quote from Friedrich Hayek, discussing the enormous importance of presuppositions in preventing a reader from properly understanding an earlier text. Nothing may make an examination of past economic discussions more difficult than the shifting through time of the underlying common grounds on which at the time everyone agreed so that none of it is brought into the debate:

> The discussions of every age are filled with the issues on which its leading schools of thought differ. But the general intellectual atmosphere of the time is always determined by the views on which its opposing schools agree. They become the unspoken presuppositions of all thought, and common and unquestioned accepted foundations on which all discussion proceeds. (Hayek, [1971] 2013, p. 367)

Classical economists would have taken train travel in their stride as we take air travel. No economic examples of presuppositions are given, precisely because it is so difficult to predict what someone in the future will find inexplicable because we assume that is how things are, whereas someone in the future will find our presuppositions foreign and will be misled by the unstated assumptions we make. This is one of the uncertainties that exist in knowing that one's book will be read by others at a different time who will hold different presuppositions from those we hold today. Having said this, it is an uncertainty that no one can anticipate and therefore provide for, other than by alerting you the reader that such presuppositions exist in everyone's writings that will make reading an older literature more difficult to understand. This is so even though the meaning was obviously there, right on the surface, at the time these words were written. It is obvious when reading Shakespeare. It is less obvious reading economics. With Shakespeare, that is what is expected. With economic theory it is not expected at all, but has the potential to leave a later reader misunderstanding the point that was being made.

NOTES

1. This is the full passage from *The Principles*:

    We now pass to a fourth fundamental theorem respecting Capital, which is, perhaps, oftener overlooked or misconceived than even any of the foregoing. What supports and employs productive labour, is the capital expended in setting it to work, and not the demand of purchasers for the produce of the labour when completed. *Demand for commodities is not demand for labour.* The demand for commodities determines in what particular branch of production the labour and capital shall be employed; it determines the direction of the labour; but not the more or less of the labour itself, or of the maintenance or payment of the labour. These depend on the amount of the capital, or other funds directly devoted to the sustenance and remuneration of labour. (Mill, *Principles* [1871] 1921, p. 79; italics emphasis added)

2. I have also published an article on Clay's text (Clay, 1916) on the 100th anniversary of its publication (Kates, 2016a), which is subtitled 'The Best Introduction to Economics Ever Written'.

APPENDIX A: JOHN STUART MILL, 'OF THE INFLUENCE OF PRODUCTION ON CONSUMPTION'

[*This was written in 1829 and first published in 1844. These were Mill's opening paragraphs in his first attempt to explain why overproduction, otherwise referred to, especially since the publication of* The General Theory, *as demand deficiency, never occurs and is never an appropriate explanation for recessions. As he states in the first paragraph below, such beliefs are 'completely erroneous'. He also makes clear why a public sector stimulus will never lead an economy into recovery.*]

Before the appearance of those great writers whose discoveries have given to political economy its present comparatively scientific character, the ideas universally entertained both by theorists and by practical men, on the causes of national wealth, were grounded upon certain general views, which almost all who have given any considerable attention to the subject now justly hold to be completely erroneous.

Among the mistakes which were most pernicious in their direct consequences, and tended in the greatest degree to prevent a just conception of the objects of the science, or of the test to be applied to the solution of the questions which it presents, was the immense importance attached to consumption. The great end of legislation in matters of national wealth, according to the prevalent opinion, was to create consumers. A great and rapid consumption was what the producers, of all classes and denominations, wanted, to enrich themselves and the country. This object, under the varying names of an extensive demand, a brisk circulation, a great expenditure of money, and sometimes *totidem verbis* a large consumption, was conceived to be the great condition of prosperity.

It is not necessary, in the present state of the science, to contest this doctrine in the most flagrantly absurd of its forms or of its applications. The utility of a large government expenditure, for the purpose of encouraging industry, is no longer maintained. Taxes are not now esteemed to be "like the dews of heaven, which return again in prolific showers". It is no longer supposed that you benefit the producer by taking his money, provided you give it to him again in exchange for his goods. There is nothing which impresses a person of reflection with a stronger sense of the shallowness of the political reasonings of the last two centuries, than the general reception so long given to a doctrine which, if it proves anything, proves that the more you take from the pockets of the people to spend on your own pleasures, the richer they grow; that **the man who steals money out of a shop, provided he expends it all again at the same shop, is a benefactor to the tradesman whom he robs, and that the same operation, repeated sufficiently often, would make the tradesman's fortune**.

In opposition to these palpable absurdities, it was triumphantly established by political economists, that consumption never needs encouragement. All which is produced is already consumed, either for the purpose of reproduction or of enjoyment. The person who saves his income is no less a consumer than he who spends it: he consumes it in a different way; it supplies food and clothing to be consumed, tools and materials to be used, by productive labourers. Consumption, therefore, already takes place to the greatest extent which the amount of production admits of; but, of the two kinds of consumption, reproductive and unproductive, the former alone adds to the national wealth, the latter impairs it. What is consumed for mere enjoyment, is gone; what is consumed for reproduction, leaves commodities of equal value, commonly with the addition of a profit. The usual effect of the attempts of government to encourage consumption, is merely to prevent saving; that is, to promote unproductive consumption at the expense of reproductive, and diminish the national wealth by the very means which were intended to increase it.

What a country wants to make it richer, is never consumption, but production. Where there is the latter, we may be sure that there is no want of the former. To produce, implies that the producer desires to consume; why else should he give himself useless labour? He may not wish to consume what he himself produces, but his motive for producing and selling is the desire to buy. Therefore, if the producers generally produce and sell more and more, they certainly also buy more and more. Each may not want more of what he himself produces, but each wants more of what some other produces; and, by producing what the other wants, hopes to obtain what the other produces. There will never, therefore, be a greater quantity produced, of commodities in general, than there are consumers for. But there may be, and always are, abundance of persons who have the inclination to become consumers of some commodity, but are unable to satisfy their wish, because they have not the means of producing either that, or anything to give in exchange for it. The legislator, therefore, needs not give himself any concern about consumption. There will always be consumption for everything which can be produced, until the wants of all who possess the means of producing are completely satisfied, and then production will not increase any farther. The legislator has to look solely to two points: that no obstacle shall exist to prevent those who have the means of producing, from employing those means as they find most for their interest; and that those who have not at present the means of producing, to the extent of their desire to consume, shall have every facility afforded to their acquiring the means, that, becoming producers, they may be enabled to consume.

These general principles are now well understood by almost all who profess to have studied the subject, and are disputed by few except those who ostentatiously proclaim their contempt for such studies. We touch upon the question, not in the hope of rendering these fundamental truths clearer than they already are, but to perform a task, so useful and needful, that it is to be wished it were oftener deemed part of the business of those who direct their assaults against ancient prejudices,— that of seeing that no scattered particles of important truth are buried and lost in the ruins of exploded error. Every prejudice, which has long and extensively prevailed among the educated and intelligent, must certainly be borne out by some strong appearance of evidence; and when it is found that the evidence does not prove the received conclusion, it is of the highest importance to see what it does prove. If this be thought not worth inquiring into, an error conformable to appearances is often merely exchanged for an error contrary to appearances; while, even if the result be truth, it is paradoxical truth, and will have difficulty in obtaining credence while the false appearances remain. (Mill, [1844] 1974; bold emphasis added)

APPENDIX B: THE DANGEROUS PERSISTENCE OF KEYNESIAN ECONOMICS

[*Reprinted with permission from* Quadrant *magazine – March 2019. This is a ten-years-after follow-up on an article published, also by* Quadrant, *in March 2009, which had discussed why a Keynesian stimulus would not achieve its intended ends, but would, in fact, make conditions even worse and delay recovery for a significant period of time. Italic text in the original.*]

> *Just as the causes of this downturn cannot be charted through a Keynesian demand deficiency model, neither can the solution. The world's economies are not suffering from a lack of demand and the right policy response is not a demand stimulus. Increased public sector spending will only add to the market confusions that already exist.*
>
> *What is potentially catastrophic would be to try to spend our way to recovery. The recession that will follow will be deep, prolonged and potentially take years to overcome.*
> **–Steven Kates,** *Quadrant,* **March 2009**

> *Why have the IMF, the OECD, the ILO, the treasuries of every advanced economy, the Treasury in Australia, the business economists around the world, why have they got it so wrong and yet you in your ivory tower at RMIT have got it so right?*
> **–Question to Steven Kates from Senator Doug Cameron, Senate Economic References Committee, September 21, 2009**

Outside the United States, no economy has fully recovered from the downturn that followed the Global Financial Crisis in 2008–09. The crisis came and went within half a year, but just about every economy continues to have problems generating growth, increasing employment and raising real incomes. As I was writing my article on 'The Dangerous Return to Keynesian Economics' in 2009, I commenced working on an economic textbook, now in its third edition, to explain why modern macroeconomic theory is utterly useless, why no one using these economic models as a guide to policy would ever succeed. And here we are, ten years later, and everything discussed in that earlier article, explained in far more detail in that text, has come to pass.

Why did I get it so right? Because nearly everyone else thinks economies are made to grow through increases in demand, while in reality, as was once universally understood, economies can only be made to grow through improvements in supply-side conditions. Demand has absolutely nothing to do with making an economy grow. Demand of course is crucial to how many units of any particular good or service will sell, but has nothing whatsoever to do with how fast an economy in total will grow, or how many workers will be employed. The underlying principle is known as 'Say's Law', which since 1936 has been the grand villain of economic theory.

Say's Law
The following were the opening paragraphs of my 2009 article published exactly ten years ago:

> The Great Depression, in most places, began with the share market crash in 1929 and by the end of 1933 was already receding into history. In 1936, well after the

Great Depression had reached its lowest point and recovery had begun, a book was published that remains to this day the most influential economics treatise written during the whole of the twentieth century.

The book was *The General Theory of Employment, Interest and Money*. The author was John Maynard Keynes. And his book overturned a tradition in economic thought that had already by then stretched back for more than a hundred years.

The importance of these dates is important. The economics which Keynes's writings had overturned is today called 'classical theory', yet it was the application of this self-same classical theory that had brought the Great Depression to its end everywhere but in the United States, where something else was tried instead. And at the centre of classical thought was a proposition that Keynes made it his ambition to see disappear absolutely from economics. It was an ambition in which he was wildly successful.

Following a lead set by Keynes, this proposition is now almost invariably referred to as Say's Law. It is a proposition that since 1936 every economist has been explicitly taught to reject as the most certain obstacle to clear thinking and sound policy. Economists have thus been taught to ignore the one principle most necessary for understanding the causes of recessions and their cures. Worse still, they have been taught to apply the very measures to remedy downturns that are most likely, from the classical perspective, to push them into an even steeper downward spiral …

Keynes wrote that Say's Law meant that 'supply creates its own demand'. In his interpretation of this supposedly classical proposition, everything produced would automatically find a buyer. Aggregate demand would always equal aggregate supply. Recessions would therefore never occur and full employment was always a certainty. That economists have accepted as fact the proposition that the entire mainstream of the profession prior to 1936 had believed recessions could never occur when in fact they regularly did shows the power of authority in allowing people to believe three impossible things before breakfast.

But what was important were the policy implications of Keynes's message. These may be reduced to two. First, the problem of recessions is due to a deficiency of aggregate demand. The symptoms of recession were its actual cause. And then, second, an economy in recession cannot be expected to recover on its own, and certainly not within a reasonable time, without the assistance of high levels of public spending and the liberal use of deficit finance.

The missing ingredient in classical economic theory, Keynes wrote, had been the absence of any discussion of aggregate demand. It was this missing ingredient that Keynes made it his mission to put in place.

No economy at any time in history has had a recovery occur as a result of an increase in aggregate demand. Not one, not ever. Yet it is the same Keynesian nonsense that remains the staple across the entire economics profession, taught to this very day and in virtually every mainstream text as the basis for understanding what must be done to lift an economy out of recession.

Supply-side Economics
What does work are measures that allow and encourage businesses to produce, employ and invest. Many changes can lead to these outcomes: lower taxes, less-onerous regulations, reduced public spending, increased competition. Anything

that transfers resources into the hands of the most productive entrepreneurs and allows profits to be earned will do the trick. These are the policies that were at the heart of the economic policies adopted by Ronald Reagan in the 1980s and are the self-same policies adopted in the United States by Donald Trump. Larry Kudlow, Trump's principal economic advisor, on January 4 this year [2019], following the release of a series of economic indicators showing an unmistakeable return to rapid rates of growth in the American economy and a large increase in employment:

> *I just want to note that we are in a boom. We had this blockbuster jobs number today. There is no inflation. There is no inflation. More growth, more people working does not cause inflation.*
>
> *These old Federal Reserve models are outdated and have proven to be incorrect. Right now the inflation rate is probably less than one and a half percent even while unemployment is low and jobs are soaring and we are growing at three per cent. ...*
>
> *This is supply side revolution. We're creating more goods and services. We're increasing the capital stock and business investment and that's what creates incomes and jobs.*
>
> *I'm sure you remember Jean-Baptiste Say. He wrote in the early part of the nineteenth century. He was a French economic philosopher ...*
>
> *Say's Law: supply creates its own demand. This is not government spending from the demand side, this is lower tax rates from the supply side, and it is businesses that ultimately drive the economy.*
>
> *I would like Jay Powell* [the Chairman of the US Federal Reserve] *to hear that argument from President Trump who knows the argument very well. ...*

The principles that underpin Say's Law are explicitly recognised as having made the difference. And in spite of what is believed by just about every economist today, it is not possible to understand the nature of recession and the business cycle unless one has first understood the principles behind Say's Law.

Classical Theory of the Business Cycle

Since the start of the Industrial Revolution, there have been periodic episodes when an economy in full flight has suddenly found itself in the midst of a downturn, with an abnormally large number of businesses closing and many more workers than usual losing their jobs. In even the best of times businesses close and workers lose jobs, but in a downturn the number of business closures and the number of workers becoming unemployed rapidly rise.

Eventually, four phases of the cycle were recognised. These could be listed in any order since each phase leads into the next; but begin with the most dramatic moment, the *crisis* when, almost out of the blue, the economy suddenly falls apart. Things had been brewing for a while, but beneath the surface. And then, seemingly from nowhere, businesses are closing and employees are being let go. There is wholesale panic, during which uncertainty grows and the future looks black.

The crisis lasts a few months at most, after which disintegration comes to an end, those businesses doomed to close have closed, while most of those employees who will lose their jobs have lost those jobs. Conditions settle at a lower level of activity but at least things are no longer getting worse. The economy has entered into the next phase of the cycle, the period of *recession.*

Recessions are periods when those who have seen their businesses close, or their jobs disappear, begin finding other ways to earn their living. These losses represent a small proportion of firms and jobs across the economy, but cause immense anxiety everywhere since no one can know who might be affected next.

The lost jobs represent lost incomes and can cause serious hardship. The lost businesses also leave their proprietors without an income, and they often find themselves facing a mountain of debt. Looked at from the perspective of the economy as a whole, the downturn represents a major loss in productive activity and a fall in the real level of output.

Eventually, as time goes by, after perhaps a year, a *trough* is reached where the economy is at the lowest point. From that point the *recovery* commences.

The recovery phase is what most people think of as 'normal', being the way most people would like to see an economy work. And this is the way an economy does work most of the time. New businesses open while others expand. Employment levels rise so that if a job is lost in one place another is soon found somewhere else. Real incomes pick up, with stability the apparent reality.

But eventually at some stage, the economy reaches another crisis, when again, apparently out of the blue, the entire cycle repeats itself: crisis-recession-trough-recovery. All with this added feature: the level of real incomes at the end of each recovery phase is higher than it had been at the peak of the previous recovery.

Why Is There a Cycle?

Why is there a business cycle at all? Why is it that in some years the economy is bursting at the seams, and in others business conditions are dead? It is obvious enough that in bad times there is less demand for the goods and services produced while in good times demand is growing and businesses can hardly keep up. But while increased demand may seem to be driving the economy forward, one should never confuse the symptoms for the cause.

What triggers the eventual downturn is that a larger proportion of businesses than usual find they are producing goods and services that cannot be sold at prices that cover production costs. Not all businesses; not even most businesses. But more businesses than usual find themselves unable to earn a profitable return on the goods and services they put up for sale.

If during a normal year, let us say 15 per cent of firms find themselves forced to close, then during a crisis the proportion may have risen to 20 per cent, so that suddenly an untypically large number of firms find themselves closing and many more individuals than usual find themselves out of work. The structure of supply – the actual composition of goods and services produced – is no longer synchronised with the structure of demand – the composition of goods and services buyers wish to buy with the incomes they have. It is not the *level* of demand that matters but its *structure*.

And then, beyond that, the initial downturn in activity creates so much additional uncertainty that fewer business are commenced, while existing businesses that might in normal times have expanded, not only slow their operations but halt further expansion. Their owners wait till things clear up, contracting even further the number of jobs created and the flow of output onto the market.

And beyond even that, the flow of credit not only seizes up, but the demand for funding intensifies among firms failing to sell as much as they had expected. Thus, just as the demand for funds increases, the supply of funding recedes. Eventually, there is a revival of entrepreneurial interest in production and growth, and in the willingness of those with funds to increase their lending. Recovery gathers momentum and continues until something once again brings this upturn to a halt.

The Dynamics of the GFC

The Global Financial Crisis was an absolutely classical recession in every respect. In no sensible way could the GFC be described using a Keynesian macro model. What did not happen is that collectively across the world buyers decided they no longer needed to buy as much as they previously were buying and had chosen to save instead. A Keynesian explanation for the GFC is an absurdity.

What did happen was that a *structural* imbalance in the American economy led to a financial meltdown across the world. The American economy was being driven by its housing market, which was itself being driven by the supply of credit. Here is the Wikipedia explanation, as standard a depiction of the events as one could find:

> *The financial crisis of 2007–2008, also known as the global financial crisis and the 2008 financial crisis, is considered by many economists to have been the worst financial crisis since the Great Depression of the 1930s.*
>
> *It began in 2007 with a crisis in the subprime mortgage market in the United States, and developed into a full-blown international banking crisis with the collapse of the investment bank Lehman Brothers on September 15, 2008. Excessive risk-taking by banks such as Lehman Brothers helped to magnify the financial impact globally ... The European debt crisis, a crisis in the banking system of the European countries using the euro, followed later ...*
>
> *The precipitating factor for the Financial Crisis of 2007–2008 was a high default rate in the United States subprime home mortgage sector – the bursting of the 'subprime bubble'.*

For a variety of reasons, the housing market in the United States had been force-fed with borrowed funds to such an extent that an almost inevitable failure was locked in. When the underlying credit conditions fell apart, there was a collapse within the house-construction sector, followed by a fall in those sectors that supplied material to the housing sector, and then a further fall in demand for the goods and services previously purchased by those who had been employed in the housing sector, and then the secondary and tertiary effects on all purchases and sales across the economy.

At the same time, the supply of credit to all industries evaporated. No one knew who would be affected next so that even as the desire for finance intensified, the willingness to lend came to an almost complete halt.

The absolute necessity to turn the economy around was, first, to recognise the housing sector had been over-extended and needed to contract, while measures had to be taken to restore confidence in credit markets. The one absolute not required was a public-sector stimulus to try to revive the economy in the midst of a period of profound structural change. Which brings us back to this from 2009, already quoted above:

> *Just as the causes of this downturn cannot be charted through a Keynesian demand deficiency model, neither can the solution. The world's economies are not suffering from a lack of demand and the right policy response is not a demand stimulus. Increased public sector spending will only add to the market confusions that already exist.*
>
> *What is potentially catastrophic would be to try to spend our way to recovery. The recession that will follow will be deep, prolonged and potentially take years to overcome.*

Of course, living in the Keynesian world as we do, the only thoughts in the minds of policy-makers everywhere was to pursue a fiscal stimulus. Public spending was the near-universal response, with the near-universal consequence that economies across the world have continued to struggle.

One might argue whether our economies have been in 'recession' for the past decade, but there is no denying that the contours of the post-crisis recovery phase have been generally dismal. Nowhere had there been the kind of rapid upturn that normally follows a downturn. The crisis came and went, economies around the world settled into a prolonged period of growth below their long-term average, real incomes never recovered, and aside from the United States, the unemployment rate [as of 2019] has never returned to levels common before the onset of the GFC.

The Business Cycle Described
To bring home how much has been lost through the advent of Keynesian theory, I will end this with a discussion of the sixth chapter of Walter Bagehot's 1873 book *Lombard Street*, whose subtitle was, *A Description of the Money Market*. Chapter Six is a discussion of the business cycle in exactly the same terms described above.

Bagehot begins by asking why there is a cycle at all. He answers by providing two basic principles that underpin the performance of an economy. The second is particularly important, focusing on the need for the structure of supply to conform to the structure of demand. Businesses must find buyers for the specific goods and services they are trying to sell:

> *First. That as goods are produced to be exchanged, it is good that they should be exchanged as quickly as possible.*
> *Secondly. That as every producer is mainly occupied in producing what others want, and not what he wants himself, it is desirable that he should always be able to find, without effort, without delay, and without uncertainty, others who want what he can produce.*

How do these principles matter?

> *Taken together, they make the whole difference between times of brisk trade and great prosperity, and times of stagnant trade and great adversity ... If they are satisfied, everyone knows whom to work for, and what to make, and he can get immediately in exchange what he wants himself. There is no idle labour and no sluggish capital in the whole community, and, in consequence, all which can be produced is produced, the effectiveness of human industry is augmented, and both kinds of producers – both capitalists and labourers – are much richer than usual, because the amount to be divided between them is also much greater than usual.*

That is, if the structure of supply and demand conform, the economy just keeps ticking over. However, once a recession begins, where the structure of supply no longer conforms to the structure of supply, the effects cannot be contained:

> *There is a partnership in industries. No single large industry can be depressed without injury to other industries; still less can any great group of industries. Each industry when prosperous buys and consumes the produce probably of most (certainly of very many) other industries.*

The downturn can begin in any industry with further repercussions across the economy:

> *A great calamity to any great industry will tend to produce* [wide consequences],
> *but the fortunes of the industries on which the wages of labour are expended*
> *are much more important than those of all others, because they act much more*
> *quickly upon a larger mass of purchasers ... And far from its being at all natural*
> *that trade should develop constantly, steadily, and equably, it is plain, without*
> *going farther, from theory as well as from experience, that there are inevitably*
> *periods of rapid dilatation* [i.e., expansion], *and as inevitably periods of con-*
> *traction and of stagnation.*

There is one additional factor. In the passage below, let me note, I have changed the words from 'a good state of credit' to a 'bad state', then adjusted the remainder of the passage to conform to the point being made:

> *Credit – the disposition of one man to trust another – is singularly varying. In*
> *England, after a great calamity, everybody is suspicious of everybody. ... In*
> *a bad state of credit, goods lie on hand a much longer time than when credit is*
> *good; sales are slower; intermediate dealers borrow with difficulty to augment*
> *their trade, and so fewer and fewer goods are more slowly and less easily trans-*
> *mitted from the producer to the consumer.*

The same description and analysis of the business cycle is found throughout the nineteenth century and into the twentieth, but then, with the publication of *The General Theory*, they vanished. And with the disappearance of the theory, recognition that public spending cannot bring a recession to an end has also disappeared. This was the 'Treasury View', the universally accepted conclusion among the entire economics discipline during pre-Keynesian times: public spending would never lead to an upturn in employment. The quote below is a discussion of Winston Churchill's budget speech in May 1929, delivered well before the Great Depression began that October:

> *Churchill pointed to recent government expenditure on public works such as*
> *housing, roads, telephones, electricity supply, and agricultural development,*
> *and concluded that, although expenditure for these purposes had been justified:*
>
> > *for the purposes of curing unemployment the results have certainly been*
> > *disappointing. They are, in fact, so meagre as to lend considerable colour*
> > *to the orthodox Treasury doctrine which has been steadfastly held that,*
> > *whatever might be the political or social advantages, very little additional*
> > *employment and no permanent additional employment can in fact and as*
> > *a general rule be created by State borrowing and State expenditure. [Peden,*
> > *1996, pp. 69–70]*

Nothing has changed, other than the belief among economists that public sector spending will create jobs. It won't, just as it never has, just as it will not create jobs in the future when the next economic crisis eventually occurs, as it inevitably must.

3. The background

Classical economists observed the world they lived in, saw before their eyes the extraordinary explosion of wealth, and attempted to explain what they had seen and how it had occurred. Since then, economists – in fact, pretty well everyone – have just taken for granted everything that turns out to have mattered, which is why modern economic theory almost entirely leaves out the essentials of how an economy works.

The premise of this book is that the way a classical economist looked at the economy was superior and vastly more insightful than that of those who followed. So, who were these 'classical' economists and what did they believe? Who are modern economists, and what do they believe that is different?

Here is the problem. Modern economics is founded on classical fallacies of such an intricate nature and confounding depth that it is almost impossible to understand how it was ever different or to see the logic of the economics of the past. Nevertheless, that is the challenge for me – to somehow make the conceptual basis and superstructure of the economics of the classical economists clear to you.

But this is also the challenge for you. If you are interested in understanding the economics that once dominated economic discourse, the absolute requirement is to just take it all in without judgement, merely as an attempt to learn something new and different without at any stage bothering to think of it as actually valid. The danger for you is that at some stage you *might*, but let that pass for now. Here I am only hoping to provide enough understanding of the classical economists' view of the conceptual structure and operation of an economy that you will be able to look at the world through their eyes. Just think of it as following the sage advice given to Lewis Carroll's Alice in *Through the Looking Glass*:

> 'There's no use trying', she said: 'one can't believe impossible things'. 'I daresay you haven't had much practice', said the Queen. 'When I was your age, I always did it for half-an-hour a day. Why, sometimes I've believed as many as six impossible things before breakfast'.

I'm aware of how difficult this is because many years ago I went to a lecture given by someone who was trying to say the same as I am attempting to explain here in this text, and, at the end of his presentation, I told a friend that I had found it very interesting but really could not catch the point. As it happens, a few years later, and neither because of the lecturer nor his presentation, I ended up finally understanding all of it for myself and on my own. I now, therefore, look back at that moment with a kind of wonder at who I was then and how hard it was to break those intellectual habits of a lifetime. Yet, I was obviously susceptible to these arguments, since they eventually appealed to me, and I now hold them for myself.

WHO WERE THE CLASSICAL ECONOMISTS?

Who were these classical economists? In its own way, as the name 'classical' implies, they were economists of an earlier period, and the name was originally chosen as a form of condescension. Indeed, Karl Marx first applied the name to his mainstream economic contemporaries, in particular David Ricardo, and for none of whom, other than Ricardo himself, did Marx have any regard whatsoever. However, our modern usage of the term comes from the footnote in John Maynard Keynes's opening chapter of his *General Theory of Employment, Interest and Money*:

> 'The classical economists' was a name invented by Marx to cover Ricardo and James Mill and their *predecessors*, that is to say for the founders of the theory which culminated in the Ricardian economics. I have become accustomed, perhaps perpetrating a solecism, to include in 'the classical school' the *followers* of Ricardo, those, that is to say, who adopted and perfected the theory of the Ricardian economics, including (for example) J.S. Mill, Marshall, Edgeworth and Prof. Pigou. (Keynes, *Collected Writings* [1936] 1981, VII, p. 3n.; original emphasis)

You may be sure that Keynes meant to imply nothing respectful in categorizing every one of the economists from the time of Ricardo, that is, from 1817, when Ricardo published his *Principles*, through to his own contemporaries in 1936, as 'classical'. For Keynes, in spite of the enormous changes that had occurred within economics over more than a century between the writings of Ricardo and Pigou, all were lumped together, so that everything they had written could be discarded in a single bundle without having to pick through what each had written.

And while the negative connotations that have been associated with the 'classical' school have been slow to dissipate, dissipate they have. While it is not yet a term of veneration in most quarters, nevertheless, to be identified as within the classical tradition is seen as respectable if even still outside the bounds of modern thought. And there are some who take on the label as a personal form of branding. To be 'classical' places oneself outside the mainstream, but also with a particular view on how an economy works. It is no longer a term of abuse.

In its own way, Keynes's definition is in some ways accurate, since his term of intended abuse has become the general usage. 'Classical' is therefore in many ways equivalent to 'pre-Keynesian'. Yet, in most respects this is far too broad. While it provides a time dimension – all economists who had become established as part of the mainstream in the years before *The General Theory*'s publication – it says nothing about the actual economic beliefs of anyone described as 'classical'.

To some extent, Keynes had narrowed the definition by arguing that a classical economist had accepted some entity he referred to as 'Say's Law', which was defined as 'supply creates its own demand'. Yet that, too, is far too rough and inexact. No one could determine from anyone's writings whether they did or did not believe that 'supply created its own demand', since almost nothing concrete is conjured up by these words without additional instruction in what they mean.

WHAT MADE CLASSICAL ECONOMISTS CLASSICAL?

While a good deal more will be said about the belief system of a classical economist in the rest of this volume, a preliminary distinction will be made here. This is how to identify a classical economist:

> A classical economist is an economist who believes the economy should be largely left to run itself.

The emphasis should be placed on the word 'largely'. Virtually no one, least of all economists from the classical era, thought the economy should be left entirely on its own, without legislation, regulation, supervision or guidance. No one had accepted that whatever the outcomes thrown up by the unfolding of economic events, no effort should be made to modify the outcomes that were determined by the market process. This was stated in no uncertain terms by Keynes himself, in a discussion of economic theory since the time of Bastiat, that is, since the middle of the nineteenth century:

> From the time of John Stuart Mill, economists of authority have been in strong reaction against all such ideas. 'Scarcely a single English economist of repute', as Professor Cannan has expressed it, 'will join in a frontal attack upon Socialism in general', though, as he also adds, 'nearly every economist, whether of repute or not, is always ready to pick holes in most socialistic proposals'.[1] Economists no longer have any link with the theological or political philosophies out of which the dogma of social harmony was born, and their scientific analysis leads them to no such conclusions.
>
> Cairnes, in the introductory lecture on 'Political Economy and *Laissez-faire*', which he delivered at University College, London, in 1870, was perhaps the first orthodox economist to deliver a frontal attack upon *laissez-faire* in general. 'The

maxim of *laissez-faire*', he declared, 'has no scientific basis whatever, but is at best a mere handy rule of practice'.[2] This, for 50 years past, has been the view of all leading economists. Some of the most important work of Alfred Marshall – to take one instance – was directed to the elucidation of the leading cases in which private interest and social interest are *not* harmonious. (Keynes, *Collected Writings* [1936] 1981, VII, pp. 281–2; original emphasis)

But if no economist even in classical times believed that an economy should be left entirely to itself, how does one distinguish the classical view from what came later? And here there are two additions to economic theory that need to be identified, both of which are largely the result of the Keynesian revolution.

AGGREGATE DEMAND

The first of these changes has been endlessly noted, although seldom with the recognition of the damage that has been caused. This was Keynes's rejection of the principles that lay behind the invoking of 'Say's Law'. But in so doing, Keynes used a term that he had not himself invented, but worse, had chosen a near-meaningless definition in 'supply creates its own demand'. Yet, there is no doubting the principle Keynes had sought to reject, which was discussed under the heading, 'Ricardo's doctrine' found in the midst of the following passage:

> The idea that we can safely neglect the aggregate demand function is fundamental to the Ricardian economics, which underlie what we have been taught for more than a century. Malthus, indeed, had vehemently opposed **Ricardo's doctrine that it was impossible for effective demand to be deficient**; but vainly. For, since Malthus was unable to explain clearly (apart from an appeal to the facts of common observation) how and why effective demand could be deficient or excessive, he failed to furnish an alternative construction; and Ricardo conquered England as completely as the Holy Inquisition conquered Spain. Not only was his theory accepted by the city, by statesmen and by the academic world. But controversy ceased; the other point of view completely disappeared; it ceased to be discussed. The great puzzle of Effective Demand with which Malthus had wrestled vanished from economic literature. You will not find it mentioned even once in the whole works of Marshall, Edgeworth and Professor Pigou, from whose hands the classical theory has received its most mature embodiment. It could only live on furtively, below the surface, in the underworlds of Karl Marx, Silvio Gesell or Major Douglas. (Keynes, *Collected Writings* [1936] 1981, VII, p. 32; bold emphasis added)

It is from this passage that modern macroeconomics separates itself from the classical tradition. Keynes attributed the view to classical economists that they had denied the possibility that a recession could be due to a deficiency of aggregate demand. Whether this was the belief that lies beneath the words 'supply creates its own demand' can be debated endlessly but with no means for resolution. Yet, no one will deny that Keynes's aim and intent in writing *The General Theory* was to argue that deficient demand was not only a possible cause of recession but was also its most important cause.

And on this distinction Keynes was absolutely correct. Classical economists did indeed reject demand deficiency as a cause of recession. What they did not do, however, was reject the possibility of recessions. And in this we find the first of the major divisions between the modern view and the classical. Modern economists accept the possibility that recessions may be caused by a deficiency of demand. Classical economists not only rejected such a possibility, but declared the reasoning behind arguments in its favour utterly fallacious.

MONEY AND THE REAL ECONOMY

The second matter has entirely slipped the notice of economists, which in any case came as an aside while Keynes dwelt on the issue of deficient demand. To follow the argument, a series of passages from *The General Theory* are presented that are in sequence but in which the looseness of the argument has allowed a conclusion to slip in that is not even prefigured by the preceding logic. These are from pages 18–19, at the start of Section VI. Keynes is expanding on the issue of Say's Law:

> From the time of Say and Ricardo the classical economists have taught that supply creates its own demand; meaning by this in some significant, but not clearly defined, sense that the whole of the costs of production must necessarily be spent in the aggregate, directly or indirectly, on purchasing the product. (Keynes, [1936] 1981, VII, p. 18)

Economists, Keynes wrote, always assumed that everything produced would be bought. Demand deficiency was never therefore a potential problem. Keynes then reproduces a passage from John Stuart Mill to substantiate his claim.[3]

> In J.S. Mill's *Principles of Political Economy* the doctrine is expressly set forth:
>
> > What constitutes the means of payment for commodities is simply commodities. Each person's means of paying for the productions of other people consist of those which he himself possesses. All sellers are inevitably, and by the meaning of the word, buyers. Could we suddenly double the productive powers of the country, we should double the supply of commodities in every market; but we should, by the same stroke, double the purchasing power. Everybody would bring a double demand as well as supply; everybody would be able to buy twice as much, because every one would have twice as much to offer in exchange. [*Principles of Political Economy*, Book III, Chap. xiv. § 2.]. (Ibid.)

Keynes interprets Mill to be arguing that not spending one's money income and therefore saving does not mean that the spending will not occur. These savings will be spent, which Keynes then points out in the passage that follows his quote from Mill:

> As a corollary of the same doctrine, it has been supposed that any individual act of abstaining from consumption necessarily leads to, and amounts to the same thing as, causing the labour and commodities thus released from supplying consumption to be invested in the production of capital wealth. The following passage from Marshall's *Pure Theory of Domestic Values* illustrates the traditional approach:
>
> > The whole of a man's income is expended in the purchase of services and of commodities. It is indeed commonly said that a man spends some portion of his income and saves another. But it is a familiar economic axiom that a man purchases labour and commodities with that portion of his income which he saves just as much as he does with that he is said to spend. He is said to spend when he seeks to obtain present enjoyment from the services and commodities which he purchases. He is said to save when he causes the labour and the commodities which he purchases to be devoted to the production of wealth from which he expects to derive the means of enjoyment in the future. (Ibid., p. 19)

Saving is thus a form of expenditure, a way in which money is spent. This leads Keynes to make the following observation:

> It is true that it would not be easy to quote comparable passages from Marshall's later work or from Edgeworth or Professor Pigou. The doctrine is never stated today in this crude form. Nevertheless it still underlies the whole classical theory, which would collapse without it. Contemporary economists, who might hesitate to agree with Mill, do not hesitate to accept conclusions which require Mill's doctrine as their premise. (Ibid., pp. 19–20)

And here we come towards the pivotal issue, Mill's premise:

> The conviction, which runs, for example, through almost all Professor Pigou's work, that money makes no real difference except frictionally and that **the theory of production and employment can be worked out (like Mill's) as being based on 'real' exchanges with money introduced perfunctorily in a later chapter, is the modern version of the classical tradition.** (Ibid., p. 20; bold emphasis added)

And then these threads are tied up in the continuation of the same paragraph:

> Contemporary thought is still deeply steeped in the notion that if people do not spend their **money** in one way they will spend it in another. (Ibid.; bold emphasis added)

And with this, Keynes transformed the notion of saving from being a stock of potentially productive resources whose owners always sought to put to use in order to earn as high an income as possible, into a sum of money received as part of one's current income that might or might not be spent. And it did more. The entire classical approach, based as it was on the underlying real entities, was replaced by sums of money, and to the extent that those entities were to be referred to, they became an amount of money rather than a diverse array of specific items in an inventory across the economy.

DEFINITION OF SAVING

To a classical economist, investment and saving were equal because investment constituted that portion of the economy's existing resource base being used to maintain or to add on to the existing capital base of the economy. At the same time, that portion of the economy's existing resource base being used to add on to the existing capital base of the economy constituted national saving. They were always equal because they could not ever be anything else. They were the same thing, and thought of as a set of assets, not as a sum of money.

In a modern text, however, saving is the difference between current income and current consumption, which entirely loses conceptual clarity. The proportion of the resource base of the economy available for investment purposes is ignored and in its place is the difference during the present time period between total expenditure on consumer goods in comparison with the total level of production. Insofar as examining the state of the economy, there is virtually nothing in that calculation that provides the slightest insight into the nature of the economic system or how the economy is travelling or can be expected to travel.

But the problem goes deeper still. Where economic theory has landed is the reverse of Keynes's complaint that the theory of production and employment is worked out based on 'real' exchanges, with money introduced perfunctorily in a later chapter. What is now the mode of explanation is that production and employment are worked out based on money, with 'real' exchanges not introduced at all.

In macroeconomic theory's base equation, $Y = C + I + G + NX$, where Y is national income, C is total consumption, I is total private investment, G is total government expenditure and NX is net exports, everything is calculated as a sum of money. Even when calculated as 'real' variables, they are still thought of and conceived as sums of money. An increase in an amount of public spending is recorded as a positive contribution to output with no consideration or attempted measurement of the underlying net addition to economic value. The expectation is that the addition to spending will lead either to the maintenance of the level of employment or perhaps an increase. Whether what is produced actually raises the standard of living is assumed to be true, but is never examined and in many respects is seen as irrelevant, since the aim is to raise employment and not productivity.

Saving, in the meantime, as presently conceived, is a negative in an economy, because saving reduces the level of demand. Saving is not recognized as an unmitigated blessing, the provision of resources to the productive base of the economy. Saving is instead depicted as non-spending, as a reduction in the level of demand. This reduction in demand due to increased saving is of itself the problem, which must be made up for by additional purchases made by others, either by increased levels of investment, or higher levels of public spending. To the extent that saving is recognized as the feedstock of economic growth, it is no more than a side issue.

NEW CLASSICAL ECONOMICS IS NOT CLASSICAL

There is one further issue that must be dealt with and then put away. There is one additional issue that can confuse these issues if one is to understand classical economics as classical economists understood it. And that is that the one strand of economic theory that is unrelated to classical theory is what is now described as 'new classical economics'. This is a creation most closely associated with Robert Lucas and Thomas Sargeant and revolves around the notion of rational expectations. Lucas famously stated in 2003, that is, around half a decade before the Global Financial Crisis, that the 'central problem of depression-prevention has been solved, for all practical purposes, and has in fact been solved for many decades' (Lucas, 2003, p. 1).

New classical economic theory is, in fact, a model constructed from the straw-man caricature invented by Keynes in *The General Theory*. None of it is based on the views and writings of any of the pre-Keynesian economists. It was Keynes who had stated that classical economists had denied the possibility of involuntary unemployment and had only accepted the possibility of frictional unemployment (Keynes, *Collected Writings* [1936] 1981, VII, pp. 16, 26). The following passage is from *The General Theory* and is fully consistent with the new classical postulates of Lucas:

> Writers in the classical tradition, overlooking the special assumption underlying their theory, have been driven inevitably to the conclusion, perfectly logical on their assumption, that apparent unemployment (apart from the admitted exceptions) must be due at bottom to a refusal by the unemployed factors to accept a reward which corresponds to their marginal productivity. A classical economist may sympathise with labour in refusing to accept a cut in its money-wage, and he will admit that it may not be wise to make it to meet conditions which are temporary; but scientific integrity forces him to declare that this refusal is, nevertheless, at the bottom of the trouble. (Keynes, *Collected Writings* [1936] 1981, VII, p. 16)

Contrast this with Hoover's depiction of the origins of new classical economics:

> Although its name suggests a rejection of Keynesian economics and a revival of classical economics, the new classical macroeconomics began with Lucas's and Leonard Rapping's attempt to provide microfoundations for the Keynesian labor market. Lucas and Rapping applied the rule that equilibrium in a market occurs when quantity supplied equals quantity demanded. This turned out to be a radical step. Because involuntary unemployment is exactly the situation in which the amount of labor supplied exceeds the amount demanded, their analysis leaves no room at all for involuntary unemployment. (Hoover, 2007)

It is therefore crucial to distinguish classical economics proper, which is mainstream economic theory as it was prior to the publication of *The General Theory*, from New Classical economics, which was devised in the 1970s, and in many ways had come for a time to dominate economic theory, at least prior to the onset of the Global Financial Crisis. New Classical economics was given its name by those who had been taken in by Keynes's depiction of pre-Keynesian economic theory as essentially *laissez-faire*, with no role for public sector activity and in which mass unemployment never occurred other than as a brief blip in time before economic conditions righted themselves. It is also part of the 'rational economics' tradition that again assumes that in a market economy, where everyone makes decisions for themselves, that we live in the best of all possible economic worlds.

Following the GFC, this brand of economic thinking went into hibernation, but never fully disappears from among the different configurations that economists are prone to adopt. In spite of its name, however, New Classical economics should be understood to be absolutely unrelated to the classical economics that preceded the publication of *The General Theory*. There will therefore be no further discussion of new classical economics since it has nothing whatever to contribute to an understanding of classical economics properly understood.

AUSTRIAN ECONOMICS

The Austrian school presents a more difficult problem and in many ways is part of the traditional classical school. The Austrian approach, as its name suggests, developed within continental Europe. It is in many important respects different from the English classical school.

Austrian theory traces its own origins back to the marginal revolution, with the writings of Menger and Böhm von Bawerk its founding inspiration. It was the marginal revolution that at one time represented the dividing line between classical and modern. There were four effects of the marginal revolution that make the classical quite distinct from an Austrian approach:

1. The marginal revolution took the focus of economic theory away from 'macroeconomic' questions and replaced these with a theory of individual decision making. The classical preoccupation with the theory of growth in a dynamic setting was replaced with a theory of resource allocation in a static setting.
2. More importantly, the focus of analysis was switched from the supply side of the economy to the demand side. Marginal utility became the central frame of reference. In the way Austrians approached economic issues, supply would follow demand.
3. The marginal revolution also opened a pathway to a more mathematical approach to explaining economics even if almost all the elements in the theory of marginal utility were intrinsically unquantifiable.
4. The Austrian tradition almost entirely omits the fact that an economy is part and parcel of a larger society and must be seen within the political context of time and place. Austrian economics is therefore an austere abstract depiction of an economy, in which political considerations are largely removed. The classical tradition, by contrast, always understood that economic decisions were made within a political community whose existence and influence had to be taken into account in framing theory.

Chapter 10 will therefore be devoted to an examination of Austrian theory within the context of the classical tradition.

CLASSICAL THEORY IS SUPPLY-SIDE ECONOMICS

A classical economist believed that an economy was driven forward from the supply side, rather than demand, by real forces that were often severely affected by changes in the volume of credit and money. Given that classical economists argued that an economy was driven from the supply side, they believed an economy could only be understood by first examining real factors in isolation from money and credit. Money and credit could only be brought in separately, and only after the underlying real forces had been examined.

The classical and modern approaches to theory are, therefore, oceans apart. The deep abstractions required to make sense of an economy from a classical perspective are utterly foreign to the approach taken by modern economic theory, which uses aggregated money totals in place of conceptually itemized forms of production and consumption. The terms may have seemed aggregated, terms such as capital or saving, but the underlying conceptions were thought of as individual items with their individual characteristics. As a very rough analogy, the various elements that made up the economy were thought of as pieces on a chessboard that can only be understood in relation to each other, and where each piece has a value in relation to the entire array of pieces that happen to be left on the board. Capital was not just some totality explicable as a sum of money, but could only be understood as various existing items of produced means of production, each with its own particular characteristics, that could be moved about as their owners thought best. These were part of the economy's structure of production. An 'aggregate supply curve', being an aggregation, is thus in no sense equivalent to the conception that underlay the supply side of an economy as conceived by classical economic theory.

NOTES

1. Keynes's footnote to this quotation was as follows:

    Theories of Production and Distribution, p. 494.

2. Keynes's footnote here is as follows, quoting Cairnes:

    Cairnes well described the 'prevailing notion' in the following passage from the same lecture:

    > The prevailing notion is that P.E. [political economy] undertakes to show that wealth may be most rapidly accumulated and most fairly distributed; that is to say, that human well-being may be most effectually promoted by the simple process of leaving people to themselves; leaving individuals, that is to say, to follow the promptings of self-interest, unrestrained either by State or by the public opinion, so long as they abstain from force and fraud. This is the doctrine commonly known as *laissez-faire*; and accordingly political economy is, I think, very generally regarded as a sort of scientific rendering of this maxim – a vindication of freedom of individual enterprise and of contract as the one and sufficient solution of all industrial problems.

3. This is an entirely problematic passage for a number of reasons that will be noted but not dwelt on since it is irrelevant to the core issue. Nevertheless, it should be noted that the passage is not as written by Mill, but is in the form constructed by Marshall and then repeated, although again not exactly in the same form by Hobson and Mummery. And even then, it does not address the issue raised by Keynes, but is examining whether demand deficiency might arise from income not having been received by workers, rather than the possibility that incomes had been saved and not spent. Thus, the passage does not even address the issue that Keynes is attempting to prove (see Kates, 1998, pp. 218–19).

4. The Keynesian revolution and classical theory

The publication in 1936 of John Maynard Keynes's *General Theory* did indeed create a revolution within economics and political economy as well. The differences in both theory and policy since its publication have been immense, yet the transition was so rapid that almost no one any longer understands what had changed and what difference these changes have actually made. Indeed, the shift was so rapid that even those who lived through it at the time only barely understood what was taking place.

As a result, from around the 1950s, almost all that any economist would understand about the nature of the revolution that occurred in economic theory during the 1930s is that Keynes was able to refute some entity he referred to as 'Say's Law', which he defined as 'supply creates its own demand'. Because, according to Keynes, classical economists had accepted Say's Law, they had therefore ignored the possibility of aggregate demand failure, and therefore did not even have a theory to explain the existence of involuntary unemployment. In the view of the classical economists, according to economists ever since, a recession causing large-scale unemployment supposedly either could not occur or, if it did, would come rapidly to an end. Virtually all economists, both in Keynes's own time and now, have no idea how fallacious this characterization of classical economic theory is. Keynes was therefore able to effect a change in economic policy, which encouraged increased public spending, even entirely wasteful public spending, along with other measures to raise the level of aggregate demand in times of recession. This approach was in complete contrast to classical policy, which, Keynes argued, sought an entirely *laissez-faire* approach. Keynes indeed went further, alleging that recessions and prolonged periods of high unemployment were forbidden according to the classical economic theory of the time. These supposedly non-existent recessions, according to Keynes's version of classical theory, would be allowed to run their course to purge an economy of the loss-making parts of its overall economic structure.

What Keynes believed he had done was draw attention to the very fact of recession and involuntary unemployment, explaining for the first time why they occurred. With classical theory replaced by his own macroeconomic notions, a policy framework that would short-circuit the downturn could be put in place, therefore allowing a more rapid return to economic growth, and more importantly, a return to full employment. This is still more or less the mythology that surrounds the Keynesian revolution. It is overwhelmingly the mainstream position, with practically no dissent even to this day, challenged by almost no one. Yet, what will be argued here is that each of these elements in the Keynesian mythological history is false.

Classical economists were perfectly aware not only of the existence of recessions but also the devastation they caused. There was, moreover, never any doubt that involuntary unemployment was the certain companion of recession. Most importantly, the classical theory of the business cycle is superior to the macroeconomics that has replaced it, both in relation to understanding the causes of recession as well as the policy approach required to bring recessions to an end. Given the universal failure of a Keynesian fiscal stimulus to bring on a peacetime recovery on any occasion since 1936, there is no serious evidence that macroeconomic theory has actually captured the underlying dynamics of a market economy, or more to the point, there is widespread evidence that it does not.

However, to understand the nature of these criticisms, it is first necessary to examine the history, looking not only at the nature of Keynesian theory as it is today, but also at the classical theory that Keynesian macro replaced. The place one must begin is with the Keynesian revolution itself.

THE KEYNESIAN REVOLUTION

This is the central point made in *The General Theory*, which remains at the core of macroeconomic theory to this day:

> The mere existence of an insufficiency of effective demand may, and often will, bring the increase of employment to a standstill *before* a level of full employment has been reached. (Keynes, *Collected Writings* [1936] 1981, VII, pp. 30–31; original emphasis)

The central issue is employment and unemployment. The cause of high unemployment is insufficient demand. Macroeconomics, from the introductory level through to graduate school, starts from here – the need to maintain the level of aggregate demand if an economy is to grow and employment is to reach its maximum possible level. No economist educated any time since the 1940s would be unfamiliar with this core element of macroeconomic theory.

What is therefore important to recognize is what is neither part of a Keynesian analysis nor the economic theory in which it is embedded. Not discussed is how an economy actually operates. There is no aspect that explains how wealth is created, or the structures required to cause an economy to grow. Absent is any discussion of the market mechanism or the role of an entrepreneur. There is virtually no discussion of the price mechanism that is different from a discussion of supply and demand. The vestigial remains of the classical theory of the cycle have almost entirely disappeared. What had been the pre-Keynesian theoretical apparatus, built around the invisible hand, the price mechanism and entrepreneurial judgement, was replaced by a theoretical structure in which each of the three was no longer even discussed. Most of this is assumed away, presumably because it is seen as too obvious even to mention.

Pre-Keynesian economic analysis, in contrast, had been designed to explain how the spontaneous actions of individual entrepreneurs, reacting to the circumstances of the world as they found them, would produce and therefore employ as a means of creating goods and services as a means of earning an income. The owners of the factors of production (landlords, workers, capitalists) would make decisions where they expected their own highest returns were to be found. The entire structure of economic theory had been built around this conception of the nature of economic activity where the price system would co-ordinate the production decisions of individual entrepreneurs. Instead, classical theory was replaced by a theory of employment and unemployment, with the actual mechanisms of the economy placed in the deep background and largely ignored.

Associated with the classical theory of growth and adjustment was the theory of the business cycle. The grim experience of recessions and abnormally high unemployment required an explanation that had been provided and continuously developed from the early years of the nineteenth century. It was based on the theory of growth and adjustment, which explained recession as a natural occurrence in an economy where the future is unknown and entrepreneurial misjudgements are certain to occur.

THE CHANGE IN THE NATURE OF ECONOMIC THEORY

With the publication of *The General Theory*, the focus of economic theory at the aggregate level had been sharply shifted away from questions about how businesses come into existence, the role of innovation, the nature of entrepreneurial activity, the importance of the price mechanism, the significance of property rights and any number of other issues that determine the ability of an economy to respond to the wishes of the community. In their place was an analysis of what determines the level of employment across the economy as a whole, based on the level of aggregate demand.

This was a fundamental change in the nature of economic theory. Classical economic analysis had focused on 'the wealth of nations', that is, on how the level of per capita output could be raised to the highest level and then further increased over time. The high point of the classical school is found in the economics of John Stuart Mill in his *Principles of Political Economy*. This is from the second paragraph of Mill's *Principles*, on its very first page, explaining the purpose of studying economics:

> Writers on Political Economy profess to teach, or to investigate, the nature of Wealth, and the laws of its production and distribution: including, directly or remotely, the operation of all the causes by which the condition of mankind, or of any society of human beings, in respect to this universal object of human desire, is made prosperous or the reverse. Not that any treatise on Political Economy can discuss or even enumerate all these causes; but it undertakes to set forth as much as is known of the laws and principles according to which they operate. (Mill, *Principles* [1871] 1921, p. 1)

Keynes explains the purpose of *his* book in the Preface:

> This book ... has evolved into what is primarily a study of the forces which determine changes in the scale of output and employment as a whole. (Keynes, *Collected Writings* [1936] 1981, VII, p. vii)

He again explains his intent at the start of Chapter 2, following the brief one-page opening chapter that is mostly polemical in character and that says nothing about the nature of the text that was to come. Here, still in Chapter 2, Keynes again emphasizes that the book is concerned with the level of employment, not with the operation of an economy overall:

> The pure theory of what determines the *actual employment* of the available resources has seldom been examined in great detail. To say that it has not been examined at all would, of course, be absurd. For every discussion concerning fluctuations of employment, of which there have been many, has been concerned with it. I mean, not that the topic has been overlooked, but that the fundamental theory underlying it has been deemed so simple and obvious that it has received, at the most, a bare mention. (Ibid., pp. 4–5; original emphasis)

The General Theory was never intended as a theory of the economy as a whole, only as a theory of aggregate employment. That the theory invaded and immediately conquered the newly established subdiscipline of macroeconomics – the term having been first used in 1933 (see Haberler, 1941, p. 248n.) – led to the narrowing of macroeconomics as a study of the functioning of the entire economy and became instead a study of the forces of aggregate demand and employment. Output would merely follow the dictates set by the level of demand. The actual process in which particular economic entities came into existence, with production levels determined on the supply side of the economy through a chain of economic relationships determined through the price mechanism, disappeared almost entirely from within macroeconomic discussion. Classical economic theory had for all practical purposes been removed from within the body of economic thought.

To some extent, one may argue that these concepts were represented within microeconomic theory. Yet, even there, what remained was a much-weakened structure. With the classical theory of the economy as a whole now so restricted, microeconomics more than ever reverted to an examination of the individual entities within an economy, becoming a theory of utility and profit maximization structured on marginalist principles. Macro was seen as the entire economy looked at all at once. Micro was then a theory of the efficient allocation of resources. The question then arose in an attempt to work out the microfoundations of macroeconomics, a quest that has never succeeded, and may well have been abandoned (King, 2014).

Even on the microeconomics side, the marginal revolution had itself weakened the classical tradition. And while it may accurately be said that the marginal revolution was also focused on the requirements necessary to raise the level of value-adding output to the greatest extent, the shift in emphasis from the supply side of the economy to the demand side had itself led to a withering of the attention paid to production and the dynamics of growth. With the marginal revolution, the approach to wealth creation moved away from the supply side of the economy. Rather than concentrating on value-adding activities and the combinations of elements that were necessary to cause an economy to grow, there was a shift in focus towards the demand side of the economy and the allocation of resources within a static framework. Marginal utility became the single most important constituent of microeconomic analysis, with the supply side more or less expected to shape itself in the way most capable of providing the goods and services.

MACRO/MICRO

Yet, to understand classical theory it is imperative to appreciate that not only was there no macro/micro division, but almost the entire purpose of economic theory as it once was would have been classified as macroeconomic. The interest was in 'the wealth of nations'. The questions of interest centred on how living standards could be raised. Not just within the living memory of every classical economist, but right before their eyes, was an astonishing level of poverty side by side with the discovery of a social mechanism through which poverty could be reduced and living standards raised for the entire population. This is what drew scholars and philosophers to the study of how economies worked.

These mechanisms worked so well that even before the nineteenth century had come to an end, the newly discovered road to wealth creation was being taken for granted. The original questions that Smith and Ricardo had attempted to answer in relation to how prosperity could be extended were being super-seded by other issues about how to ensure that everyone shared in this new prosperity. By the end of the nineteenth century, attention was being given to relative income shares and the equity of the economic system. It was, in part, for this reason that the marginal revolution occurred, since much of it was driven by an attempt to seek answers to why income differences existed. Whether the wage was or was not equal to the marginal product of labour became an answer to those who had used the labour theory of value to argue that output was entirely the result of the workforce so that anything taken by the owners of capital was no better than theft.

In this way, an independent microeconomic sphere grew, almost totally outside the original issues raised by classical theory. Different kinds of questions came to the fore, in which a microeconomic orientation was more conducive to thinking through the issues. Classical theory, with its different kinds of questions, remained but retreated into the background. Sure, markets could produce high levels of output and an incredible array of new products and production techniques, but that was a problem that had been solved. Now the question being asked was whether there was a way not just to maintain this new prosperity but also share the wealth more evenly and more justly.

The economics of Smith and Mill did not disappear but faded into the back-ground. Marshall's *Principles of Economics* and other texts of the same kind took centre stage, in which macroeconomic issues fell into the background and were replaced by an almost entirely microeconomic perspective. Price determination and the theory of value were identified as the issues that needed to be understood. As just one example of the way in which economic theory had developed, the sixth edition of Richard Ely and Ralph Hess's *Outline of Economics*, published in 1937, had a mere 15 pages devoted to 'business cycles', in Chapter XXXVI. There was, of course, a well-developed theory of the business cycle, so that, until the Great Depression at the end of the 1920s, economists believed they had a theoretical understanding of every aspect of the economic system. This self-belief was undermined by the arrival of the Great Depression with its persistently high levels of unemployment.

Into the midst of this seeming vacuum in the ability of economists to make sense of, and deal with, the unemployment of the early 1930s, Keynes's *General Theory* was published. That it was published three years after the Great Depression had reached its depths and at a time when economies across the world had sharply reduced their levels of unemployment using a classical approach to policy, and recovery was well on its way, scarcely affected its impact.

Among the many consequences that have followed the publication of *The General Theory* has been a division of basic economics between macro-economic and microeconomic theory, which has persisted to this day. What has disappeared is the classical theory of the economy as a whole, which has been replaced by a theory of employment based on aggregates. It is not only a weaker and less comprehensive theoretical structure, but it remains fundamentally misguided even in the one area it was supposed to provide insight into – how an increase in the level of employment can be achieved by increasing the level of aggregate demand.

$Z = D$

Although we are now so used to the view behind the following statement from *The General Theory*, it really is peculiar, and is the direct opposite of the approach taken by classical economists:

> In a given situation of technique, resources and costs, income (both money-income and real income) depends on the volume of employment N. (Keynes, *Collected Writings* [1936] 1981, VII, p. 28)

In the short run of perhaps a year or two, where very little of significance in relation to the economy can be changed, the total income of wage earners is, according to Keynes, determined by the number of wage earners employed. The more wage earners employed, the greater is national output. The greater is national output, the more spending there will be. But the total level of output and employment is restricted by the level of aggregate demand. More explicitly, Keynes wrote:

> The volume of employment in equilibrium depends on (i) the aggregate supply function, ϕ [$\phi(N)$], (ii) the propensity to consume, χ [$\chi(N)$], and (iii) the volume of investment, $D2$. This is the essence of the General Theory of Employment. (Ibid., p. 29)

Both total aggregate supply and total aggregate demand are functions of the number of wage earners employed. Using Keynes's original notation, $D1$ is consumer demand and $D2$ is business investment. Add $D1$ and $D2$ to arrive at D, which is total revenue received. In equilibrium, the total amount received in revenue (which Keynes calls Z) must equal the total amount spent. That is, in equilibrium, $Z = D1 + D2$, or $Z = D$.

The level of employment is what it is, which may employ everyone who wishes to work, or there may be a large number unemployed. But with the equilibrium determined in a world in which the resource base including capital has insufficient time to adjust, whatever unemployment there may be remains what it is. Figure 4.1 shows the Z and D lines meeting at a point where employment is Ne, while full employment would be at Nf.

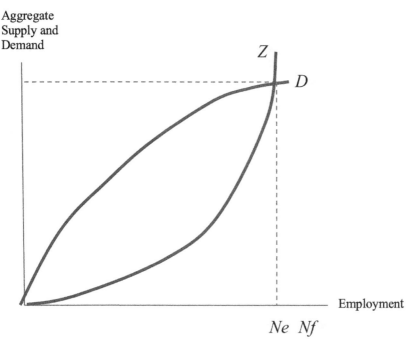

Figure 4.1   Aggregate supply and demand as described in The General
             Theory

In modern terms, *Y* replaces *Z*, and *D*1 and *D*2 are replaced by *C* and *I*,
where *Y* is national income, *C* is total consumption and *I* is total private investment. We therefore write: $Y = C + I$. It is the level of aggregate demand that is
the major determinant of employment. Whatever might be the capabilities of
the economy, the limitations imposed on it by the level of demand constrain
both the level of production and the number of employees required. If there
were insufficient demand, the economy would reach equilibrium at some level
of production, irrespective of how many actual jobseekers were unemployed.
Every macroeconomic model comes to this conclusion, whether described as
'Keynesian' or not.

AGGREGATE DEMAND

The telling phrase to indicate whether some theory is a line of descent from *The
General Theory* is 'aggregate demand'. It is pervasive, even though in many
instances it replaces what would be better described as 'aggregate production'.
An insufficient level of employment might be attributed to there being too little

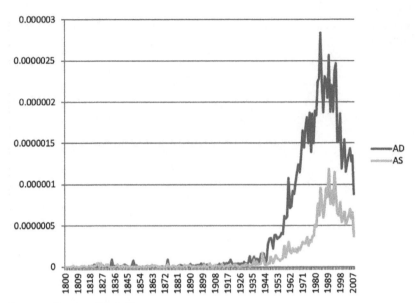

Source: Based on Google Ngram.

Figure 4.2　　Aggregate demand and aggregate supply frequency of use 1800–2007

production. To argue that it is insufficient demand is to put the explanation into the very definition of the problem. It assumes the answer to the question, why is unemployment high? Even before one begins to think through an answer, it presupposes that the cause is insufficient demand.

It was not always thus. As Figure 4.2, based on Google Ngram for the terms 'aggregate demand' (AD) and 'aggregate supply' (AS) plainly shows, the terms virtually have no existence until the 1930s, after which their use explodes. It is, of course, the publication of *The General Theory* that led to this immediate explosion. A contraction of production and a fall in aggregate demand are, for all practical purposes, one and the same in the approach that economists now take to the business cycle.

That virtually no one practising economics today appreciates the difference that the Keynesian revolution made to economic theory is in itself an aston-ishing state of affairs. Since the history of economics is now almost totally abandoned amongst economists, there are few ways that economists would come across something that should be a basic element of the framework in which they work. It makes it difficult for economists even to begin to understand what those who argue the dangers of Keynesian theory mean, since there is no association of Keynes with the single most commonly used phrase in the whole of macroeconomics.

The term 'Keynesian' to most economists no longer has much more than a vague associated conception. The history of economic thought being so infrequently taught, economists have only the most rudimentary notion of the development of economics (see Kates, 2013) and, other than a few fairy tales, know virtually nothing about economic theory prior to 1936. It is safe to say that virtually no economist could explain the theory of the business cycle as understood prior to the publication of *The General Theory*. In contrast, even the term 'Keynesian' has lost any precision as a specific description of any kind of economic theory. The following discussion highlights how little is delimited by a Keynesian model:

> These features of the Keynesian approach form the basis for the major criticism that can be made against it: Keynesian models are so vague and so flexible that they are almost impossible to refute. Like Ptolemaic astronomers with their epicycles to explain every new observation, Keynesian macroeconomics can modify their theories and postulate unobserved shocks to fit the data in almost any situation.
>
> It is easy to find examples of the flexibility of Keynesian analysis, involving issues ranging from the basic assumptions of the models to the specifics of individual episodes. ...
>
> The same flexibility characterises not just Keynesian models, but Keynesian accounts of specific episodes. The models allow for disturbances in essentially every sector of the economy – money supply, money demand, fiscal policy, consumption, investment, price-setting, wage-setting, and international trade – and thus are consistent with almost any combination of movements of different variables. ...
>
> Of course, it is possible that the economy is complicated, that there are many types of shocks, and that the modifications of Keynesian models reflect gradual progress of our understanding of the economy. But a theory that is so flexible that it cannot be contradicted by any set of observations is devoid of content. (Romer, 1996, pp. 301–2)

What connects every Keynesian model is its reliance on variations in aggregate demand to explain recessions and unemployment, which leads to 'Keynesian' policies that are designed to raise aggregate demand to lower unemployment and hasten growth. These are rightly named 'Keynesian' models as their origins are found in Keynes's *General Theory*.

SAY'S LAW

It is not as if economists had not thought about the relationship between aggregate demand and employment. The decades-long general glut debate that followed the publication of T.R. Malthus's *Principles of Political Economy* in 1820, was about exactly that. After a generation-long debate among the economists of the time, it was thereafter universally agreed within the mainstream that demand deficiency was never a cause of recession. We identify that conclusion as Say's Law. Although there is much more to discuss about Say's Law, we must first turn to a further aspect of Keynes's explanation of his purpose in writing *The General Theory*.

Keynes had argued that the classical theory of unemployment revolved around a disequilibrium in the labour market, with aggregate demand irrelevant to the outcome. If it were merely no more than market adjustment, Keynes argues, the economy would always be at full employment, so there must be something else. If it were merely about an economy moving towards equilibrium, 'the aggregate demand price' (the total revenue generated from selling) would always be equal to 'the aggregate supply price' (the total cost of production). This Keynes refers to as 'Say's Law' and states that if it were true, full employment would always be guaranteed. Since it is not true, he wrote, not only do we have unemployment, but there is an area of economic theory that needs to be examined, which the rest of *The General Theory* sets out to do. This following is the exact quote from the text with bold type added to emphasize Keynes's crucial issue:

> [According to classical economic theory] effective demand ... is an infinite range of values all equally admissible; and the amount of employment is indeterminate except in so far as the marginal disutility of labour sets an upper limit.
>
> If this were true, competition between entrepreneurs would always lead to an expansion of employment up to the point at which the supply of output as a whole ceases to be elastic, i.e. where a further increase in the value of the effective demand will no longer be accompanied by any increase in output.
>
> Evidently this amounts to the same thing as full employment. ... namely a situation, in which aggregate employment is inelastic in response to an increase in the effective demand for its output.
>
> **Thus Say's law, that the aggregate demand price of output as a whole is equal to its aggregate supply price for all volumes of output, is equivalent to the proposition that there is no obstacle to full employment.**
>
> If, however, this is not the true law relating the aggregate demand and supply functions, **there is a vitally important chapter of economic theory which remains to be written** and without which all discussions concerning the volume of aggregate employment are futile. (Keynes, *Collected Writings* [1936] 1981, VII, p. 26; bold emphasis added; please also note that this passage was originally published as a single paragraph but has been separated into its individual sentences)

Yet, the meaning of Say's Law as defined by Keynes is found earlier in the text and is unusually found separate from his term of choice. As Keynes begins his history of the meaning of Say's Law within classical economics, he writes:

> From the time of Say and Ricardo the classical economists have taught that **supply creates its own demand**; meaning by this in some significant, but not clearly

defined, sense that the whole of the costs of production must necessarily be spent in the aggregate, directly or indirectly, on purchasing the product. (Ibid., p. 18; bold emphasis added)

Keynes discusses the same assumption, that classical economists had argued that total outlays would be equal to total costs, but in this case uses the phrase that has remained the standard definition within economic theory. Say's Law, that total revenue must cover total costs, is defined by the statement, 'supply creates its own demand'.

It is their acceptance of Say's Law that, according to Keynes, is the crucial element in classical theory that had prevented economists from understanding why large-scale unemployment occurred and recessions were so common. There is no understanding Keynes's intent, nor modern macroeconomics, without an understanding of the consequences that have followed from Keynes's rejection of what he described as Say's Law.

SAY'S LAW VERSUS SAY'S *LOI*

There is a crucial distinction that needs to be made that has sowed confusion since the publication of *The General Theory*. The following two propositions are related but are not the same. The actual name of each is highlighted in bold.

First is Say's **loi des débouchés**, which Say first discussed in 1803 using that term, stating that goods and services are purchased using money earned by selling other goods and services. It focused on the mechanism of exchange and was developed by Say specifically to deny that goods and services fail to sell because there is not enough of the medium of exchange available to allow all desired transactions to occur. This was never described as 'Say's Law' at any time during the period up until the publication of *The General Theory*.

There is then **Say's Law**, which is something quite different. The term 'Say's Law', as discussed above, was introduced into economics in the 1920s by an American economist, Fred Taylor, who with absolute certainty, first invented this term, as he makes clear himself. What 'Say's Law' referred to was a deficiency of demand, or using the phrase more commonly applied at the time, the 'overproduction' of output in total relative to the level of demand. It was impossible for an economy to produce more output than a community would be willing to buy. The concept went back to the early days of classical economic theory, but until Taylor provided the name, no technical term had been applied to the rejection of the possibility of overproduction or demand deficiency as a cause of recession. Taylor is discussed in more detail below (see pp. 72ff.).

Say's Law, in Taylor's sense, was a principle that had been developed initially by James Mill in replying to William Spence in 1808. Spence had argued that economies would always be at full employment as long as there was enough demand, which could be ensured if a sufficiently high level of spending could be induced. Until Taylor provided the name in the twentieth century, it was universally accepted by the mainstream of the economics community in English-speaking countries that recessions and high unemployment are never caused by a deficiency of aggregate demand and that therefore, recession and high levels of unemployment cannot be cured by an increase in the aggregate level of spending.

This confusion of terms has made understanding the Keynesian revolution almost impossible, since, on the one hand, Keynes had referred to Say's Law, by which he appeared to mean some principle that had been devised by J.-B. Say – which Keynes almost certainly thought was the case – whereas *The General Theory* was written to argue in favour of demand deficiency as the principal cause of recession, which was the usage that had come from Taylor. Keynes was thus denying Taylor's version of Say's Law not Say's. And as confusing as this may appear, there is little doubt whatsoever that this is what occurred.

And what has made this an almost certainly everlasting confusion, which can only be picked through and understood by approaching this question with great care, is that when demand deficiency became a central issue among economists in 1820 following the publication of Malthus's *Principles*, Say agreed completely with Malthus's critics and denied the possibility of demand deficiency. It was probably for this reason that Taylor named the proposition after Say, which would not be a problem except that with two separate meanings of 'Say's Law' in existence it has become almost impossible for others to sort these questions out. If one is to overcome this confusion, one must first distinguish between: (1) demand is constituted by supply, which is true but non-controversial; and (2) recessions are *never* caused by a deficiency of demand – or in its classical form, 'there is no such thing as a general glut' – which was accepted universally by classical economists but which has been universally rejected by mainstream macroeconomics since 1936.

Let me also introduce Table 4.1 to help emphasize the different meanings of this same term.

Beyond these distinctions, it is equally essential to appreciate that the definition of 'Say's Law', 'supply creates its own demand', comes from the 1930s and was first stated by another American economist, Harlan Linneus McCracken (Kent, 2005; see also Kates, 1998). All this is indubitably true. Yet, beyond all the confusion that originates from the various historical settings in which each of these terms and definitions arose, there is the additional complication that Keynes insisted that he had not sought any assistance from others, which is obviously untrue once one appreciates that Keynes with cer-

Table 4.1   *The distinction between Say's Law and Say's Loi*

Economic Term	Date First Stated in Print	Introduced into Economic Theory by	Economic meaning
Say's Loi (*loi des débouchés*)	1803	Jean-Baptiste Say	To purchase one must first receive money by selling goods, services or labour (demand is constituted by supply)
Say's Law	1921	Fred Manville Taylor	Recessions and high unemployment never occur because of a deficiency of aggregate demand (also described as overproduction), although both recessions and periods of high unemployment do frequently occur for which there are many other causes other than demand deficiency

tainty took his definition of Say's Law from McCracken after having taken the term 'Say's Law' either from Taylor or one of Taylor's contemporaries.

But what matters in trying to reconstruct classical theory is to understand that Keynes was attempting to demonstrate that demand deficiency was a legitimate possibility as a cause of recession, which economists, until he wrote, completely rejected.

MALTHUS, TAYLOR AND MCCRACKEN

Keynes's discovery of Say's Law is the single most crucial element if one is to understand the Keynesian revolution. Unfortunately, none of this can be found in the massive literature on the trek from Keynes's previous work, *A Treatise on Money* (1930), to the publication of *The General Theory* in 1936. Yet, if one is to understand *The General Theory,* one has to first understand how he came to write this particular book. Keynes's own version of events is summed up in his frequently quoted letter to Harrod, written in August 1936:

I have been much pre-occupied with the causation, so to speak, of my own progress of mind from the classical position to my present views, – with the order in which the problem developed in my mind. What some people treat as an unnecessarily controversial tone is really due to the importance in my own mind of what I used to believe, and of **the moments of transition which were for me personally moments of illumination** ...

You don't mention effective demand or, more precisely, the demand schedule for output as a whole, except in so far as it is implicit in the multiplier. To me, regarded historically, **the most extraordinary thing is the complete disappearance of the theory of the demand and supply for output as a whole,** i.e. the theory of employment, after it had been for a quarter of a century the most discussed thing in economics. One of the most important transitions for me, after my *Treatise on Money* had been published, **was suddenly realising this**. It only came after I had enunciated to myself the psychological law that, when income increases, the gap between income and consumption will increase, – a conclusion of vast importance to my own thinking but not apparently, expressed just like that, to anyone else's. Then, appreciably later, came the notion of interest as being the measure of liquidity preference, which became quite clear in my mind the moment I thought of it. And last of all, after an immense lot of muddling and many drafts, the proper definition of the marginal efficiency of capital linked up one thing with another. (Keynes, *Collected Writings* [1936] 1981, XIV, p. 85; bold emphasis added)

Everything about this description suggests that as he describes the sequence himself, Keynes had been reflecting on economic issues almost in a vacuum, with various personal 'moments of illumination' that brought clarity as his inward struggle continued. There is nowhere in any part of his discussion of how he wrote *The General Theory* any mention of any assistance from anyone else or his having consulted with any other authorities. The reality, however, is quite different from the official record (see Kates, 2010b for a more complete discussion).

Thomas Robert Malthus

To begin with, it is as certain as certain can be that Keynes would not have written a book on demand deficiency had he not come across Malthus's economic writings in 1932. Keynes had published a collection of essays in 1931, his *Essays in Persuasion*. Because of its commercial success, his publisher had asked him to put together another collection of some kind, which he began in 1932, the low point of the Great Depression. In this second collection, his *Essays in Biography*, he sought to bring together all his biographical writings, which included a piece on Thomas Robert Malthus that he had originally written prior to World War I but had been expanding ever since. In updating what was in fact a speech he had often given, he turned to his close associate, Piero Sraffa, who was then at the start of putting together the collected writings of David Ricardo. Sraffa had, in 1930, discovered Malthus's letters to Ricardo, which had been lost by that stage for more than a century, and which, because of World War II, would not be generally available until published in the 1950s.

Keynes, who had never previously been interested in Malthus's economic writings, asked for access to these letters to see what he might find to add to the biographical detail. And what he found was Say's Law.

A furious controversy had followed the publication of Malthus's *Principles* in 1820, which is now referred to as the general glut debate. Malthus had argued that the recessions and increased unemployment that had occurred at the end of the Napoleonic Wars were due to a shortage of demand that had been caused by high levels of saving. He further argued that to reduce unemployment, these unused savings needed to be absorbed by additional spending, and in the context of the early nineteenth century, the only group that might be encouraged to spend were landowners. The universal condemnation that fell upon Malthus was led by David Ricardo, the most prominent economic thinker of his time. Yet, he and Malthus were close friends, and in spite of their frequent disagreements, were as cordial as if they had been on the same side of every issue.

Their disagreements had taken place in a number of places, but among them was their correspondence over whether a general glut was possible, that is, over whether it was possible for an economy to produce more output than would be bought. It was possible to have a particular glut, an excess supply of some commodity relative to its demand. But was it possible to have a general glut, an excess supply of everything? That is, could more be produced than buyers across an economy would be willing to buy? Among the letters Malthus had written were a number in which he attempted to explain to Ricardo why he believed such an outcome was not only possible but was the actual problem that England was facing right there and then. Keynes was inflamed by Malthus's vision, which is unmistakeable if one reads his 'Essay on Malthus' in which a number of excerpts from these letters are found. But to get some idea of Keynes's excitement in finding the concept of deficient demand in the midst of the Great Depression, there are these words from the essay, published in 1933 as part of his *Essays in Biography*, that make clear what he had just discovered:

> If only Malthus, instead of Ricardo, had been the parent stem from which nineteenth-century economics proceeded, what a much wiser and richer place the world would be to-day! We have laboriously to re-discover through the obscuring envelopes of our misguided education what should never have ceased to be obvious. (Keynes, *Collected Writings* [1933] 1981, X, pp. 100–101)

From the letters, Keynes then goes on to quote from Chapter VII, Section IX of Malthus's *Principles*, along with another passage from the Introduction, where Malthus's arguments on oversaving are found. He is still enthusing about Malthus's economic insights four years later, at a memorial dinner on the

100th anniversary of Malthus's death (ibid., pp. 104–8). And then once again there is this passage from *The General Theory* that indicates in precisely what way Keynes viewed Malthus's contribution both to economic theory and to his own understanding:

> The idea that we can safely neglect the aggregate demand function is fundamental to the Ricardian economics, which underlie what we have been taught for more than a century. Malthus, indeed, had vehemently opposed Ricardo's doctrine that it was impossible for effective demand to be deficient; but vainly. For, since Malthus was unable to explain clearly (apart from an appeal to the facts of common observation) how and why effective demand could be deficient or excessive, he failed to furnish an alternative construction; and Ricardo conquered England as completely as the Holy Inquisition conquered Spain. Not only was his theory accepted by the city, by statesmen and by the academic world. But controversy ceased; the other point of view completely disappeared; it ceased to be discussed. The great puzzle of Effective Demand with which Malthus had wrestled vanished from economic literature. You will not find it mentioned even once in the whole works of Marshall, Edgeworth and Professor Pigou, from whose hands the classical theory has received its most mature embodiment. It could only live on furtively, below the surface, in the underworlds of Karl Marx, Silvio Gesell or Major Douglas. (Keynes, *Collected Writings* [1936] 1981, VII, p. 32)

What has made it difficult for economists to accept this obvious cause-and-effect relationship between Malthus and the theory that was developed in *The General Theory* were Keynes's efforts to obscure if not actually deny any such relationship. Yet, every authority who has examined the shift in Keynes's thinking from his previous modes of thought into the channels that would emerge in *The General Theory*, identifies the period in which he was reading Malthus as the moment when this transformation occurred. That he was reading Malthus at the time is virtually never mentioned, or where it is mentioned it is seen only as an incidental detail with no historical significance.

Fred Manville Taylor

The term 'Say's Law' appears in *The General Theory* as if it were a long-standing phrase to describe a particular economic proposition. Since its use by Keynes, it has become a form of words universally recognized by economists, without any particular explanation for it that would indicate why it might ever have been accepted by the large proportion of economists that Keynes had said did accept it. What is important to understand, however, is that the phrase is not classical in origin, but had been coined during the twentieth century by the American economist, Fred Manville Taylor. Moreover, Taylor's understanding of the issues, although not entirely consistent with the classical concepts he was invoking, is nevertheless a rare pre-Keynesian construction of the notions that had descended from the general glut debate.

Taylor was a professor of economics at the University of Michigan from 1892 until 1929. In 1911, he had published an introductory textbook on economic theory for use only inside the university within his own classes. His text was eventually published in 1921 as the eighth edition. The chapter where the phrase 'Say's Law' is found is specifically titled 'Say's Law' and is a discussion of the classical principle that demand and supply in aggregate are one and the same. On this, Taylor had written:

> Among the fallacious notions in popular thinking that have gained very wide currency are to be found a number which grew out of misconceptions as to the real source of the *general or total demand for goods*, and as to the methods by which that demand is increased or diminished. Several types of these fallacious notions may be cited. Thus, governmental improvements of all kinds, including even those of questionable value, are often supported by business men and others on the ground that such improvements increase the total demand for goods. (Taylor, 1925, p. 196; original emphasis)

Taylor traced the refutation of this argument back to the early classical writers, and to J.-B. Say in particular. It was for this reason, he wrote, that he had given the principle showing the identity of aggregate supply and aggregate demand the name 'Say's Law'. The first sentence of the passage, given subsequent events, is especially ironic:

> The points just brought out with respect to the relation between demand and the output of goods are so evident that some will consider it scarcely legitimate to give them the dignity derived from formal statement. On the other hand, the continued prevalence throughout the larger part of the community of the fallacious notions which these considerations are designed to correct seems to furnish ample ground for any procedure which gives these points adequate emphasis. I shall therefore put the proposition we have discussed in the form of a principle. **This principle, I have taken the liberty to designate Say's Law**; because, though recognized by many earlier writers, it was particularly well brought out in the presentation of Say (1803). (Ibid., p. 201; bold emphasis added)

Taylor had, in fact, used the phrase 'Say's Law' as far back as 1909, although its more general use dates from 1921. But the crucial point is that the phrase 'Say's Law' is twentieth century in origin and comes from the American economist, F.M. Taylor. The term Say's Law was common currency in the United States during the 1920s and 1930s. How it came to the attention of Keynes is unknown. But one way or another, a conduit was needed from Taylor to Keynes. Keynes did not come up with this term himself. Thus, an important hole in the scholarship of Keynes's shift from his *Treatise on Money* to *The*

General Theory is opened up by recognition of the significance of this aspect of Keynes's own thought.

Harlan Linneus McCracken

Here I must begin with a personal recollection. In researching Say's Law, I had read every pre-Keynesian text on the business cycle, but one stood out from the rest. This was Harlan McCracken's *Value Theory and Business Cycles* that had been published in 1933. What made it so unique was its focus on Say's Law, with an in-depth discussion of the difference between Malthus and Ricardo. In particular, McCracken had argued that Ricardo's form of analysis ruled out cyclical activity, while Malthus, in contrast, had developed a form of analysis in which business cycles were possible. The similarities with the arguments that would appear in *The General Theory* were striking. These similarities were discussed in a chapter I had written dealing with 'undocumented influences' on Keynes (Kates, 1998, pp. 153–7). In 2005, I published a paper on classical parallels with the phrase 'supply creates its own demand', for which one of the referees was a Keynes scholar, Richard Kent. In his referee's report, which was expanded into an article (Kent, 2005), he argued that the phrase 'supply creates its own demand' had originated from McCracken (1933). And although I had read the book, I had overlooked the phrase. This is the passage in which the phrase is found:

> The Automatic Production-Consumption Economists [i.e., those economists who accept Say's Law] who insisted that **supply created its own demand**, that goods exchanged against goods and that a money economy was only refined and convenient indirect barter missed the significance of the money economy entirely. (McCracken, 1933, p. 159; bold emphasis added)

Other than the phrase having originated in the past tense, these are not only the exact words, but they are the exact meaning that Keynes had wished to convey. McCracken explains that the belief that supply creates its own demand implies that we are dealing in a barter economy, and in so doing, totally ignores the role of money. This is the exact argument that was to be made by Keynes.

That Keynes had read at least a portion of this book while writing *The General Theory* had been evident since the publication of Volume XXIX of Keynes's *Collected Writings* in 1981. In 'a draft of chapter 2 from the last 1933 table of contents' (Moggridge, in Keynes, *Collected Writings* [1944–46] 1981, XXIX, p. 76), there is an extended footnote that begins:

> Cf. H.L. McCracken, *Value Theory and Business Cycles*, [New York, 1933], p. 46, where this part of Marx's theory is cited in relation to modern theory. (Ibid., p. 81n.; square brackets in the original)

Most scholars have attached little significance to this citation since neither McCracken nor Marx had appeared to have had much to contribute to our understanding of how *The General Theory* came to be written as it was. This is in spite of the fact that McCracken's *Value Theory and Business Cycles* is about the conflicting approaches to the business cycle one would be prone to take were an economist to follow Ricardo rather than Malthus. Indeed, the book is largely about the impossibility of utilizing Ricardian analysis in explaining the business cycle in contrast to the need to employ the kind of analysis pioneered by Malthus. All this is set out in McCracken's Preface. First, McCracken discusses Ricardo:

> The analysis appears to show that no embodied value theorist can logically explain a business cycle. He either involves himself in a dual theory of value, a logical inconsistency, or explains nothing but a secular trend. The presentation is quite critical, since it deals, as we believe, with the 'false trails,' based upon an erroneous theory of value, formulated by Ricardo. (McCracken, 1933, p. v)

Keynes, in arguing that because his contemporaries were following in the steps of Ricardo the notion of involuntary unemployment is a 'possibility of which the classical theory does not admit' (Keynes, *Collected Writings* [1936] 1981, VII, p. 15), or that there is a 'vitally important chapter of economic theory which remains to be written without which all discussions concerning the volume of aggregate employment are futile' (ibid., p. 26) appears to be making a claim almost identical to the characterization made by McCracken: an inability to explain or even to admit to the existence of a cyclical downturn appeared to be a consequence of adopting a Ricardian approach to the business cycle. In turning to Malthus, however, McCracken presents an argument that would be mirrored in *The General Theory*:

> **Malthus serves as a logical starting point for the consideration of business cycles**, first, because he stressed the importance of 'short run' factors, **and second, because his value approach was from the demand side**. Consistent with his theory of value, he held that business might be depressed, either by **a voluntary failure of demand on the part of those who had the power but not the will**, or by an involuntary failure of demand by those who had the will but not the power. (McCracken, 1933, pp. v–vi; bold emphasis added)

This is the point that would be made by Keynes.

KEYNES'S LETTER TO MCCRACKEN: 31 AUGUST 1933

There was, therefore, no denying that Keynes and McCracken had an overlapping understanding of the causes of the business cycle, and that they held similar views on Malthus and Ricardo. There was also no denying that Keynes had read McCracken's book, or at least he had read those sections that related to Marx. But had Keynes read the sections on Malthus? As far as the genealogy of *The General Theory* is concerned, this is the crucial issue. The answer was provided in a letter written by Keynes to McCracken, dated 31 August 1933, which I found in the McCracken archive at Louisiana State University (LSU). The letter is published in full and in colour in Kates (2019):[1]

> Dear Dr. McCracken
> Having now read your book, I must again thank you for having sent it to me. For I have found it of much interest, particularly perhaps the passages relating to Karl Marx, with which I have never been so familiar as I ought to have been.
>
> In the matter of Malthus, you will perhaps have seen from my account of him in my lately published 'Essays in Biography', which appeared before your book was out, but after I think you had written it, that I wholly agree with you in regarding him as a much under-estimated pioneer in the line of thought which to-day seems to me by far the most likely to lead to progress in the analysis of the business cycle. Your contrast between Ricardo and Malthus contains, I am convinced, the essence of the matter.
> Yours very truly,
> J.M. Keynes

A number of important conclusions follow from this letter:

1. As the opening lines of the letter state – 'having now read your book' – Keynes had read the entire book, not just the sections on Marx.
2. McCracken had sent the book to Keynes, which is why it was in Keynes's hands in the first place.
3. There is a letter, now missing, in which Keynes had previously written to McCracken to thank him for sending him the book since Keynes specifically states, 'I must again thank you for having sent it to me'.
4. Neither this letter nor the previous letter referred to by Keynes are to found in the Keynes Archive at King's College, Cambridge.
5. Keynes focuses on the passages from Marx, which he indicates that he had learned much from.
6. Keynes reveals that his interest in Malthusian economic theory was early on in the period when he was writing *The General Theory*. Malthus and his relationship to Say's Law was not a late discovery.
7. In many ways the crux of the letter, Keynes wishes to make clear that he had already discovered Malthus before he had received the copy of *Value Theory and Business Cycles*. Because Keynes had himself already turned to examine Malthus, he very clearly seems to have wanted to establish that he had come to these conclusions even before he had read McCracken's book. His 'Essays', Keynes emphasizes, had been published prior to *Value*

Theory and Business Cycles, so it could not be said that McCracken had influenced Keynes in turning to examine Malthus's writings. As this is a personal note, it seems to have been meant to warn McCracken away from suggesting that he had had any such influence on Keynes.

8. Of most importance, Keynes writes that Malthus had been 'a much under-estimated pioneer in the line of thought which to-day seems to me by far the most likely to lead to progress in the analysis of the business cycle'. One might argue that this is no more than Keynes acknowledges in including Malthus among his 'brave army of heretics' (Keynes, *Collected Writings* [1936] 1981, VII, p. 371). His acknowledgement of Malthus is found in the last section of *The General Theory*, which he titled, 'Short Notes Suggested by the General Theory'. In contrast, his letter to McCracken was not written when he is looking back after the book had been completed, and discovering others who had had similar ideas before he had. It was written at a very early stage in the writing of *The General Theory*, well before the book had taken its final shape. At the time, Keynes was trying to think through how Malthus's conclusion that demand deficiency is the cause of recession and unemployment can be shaped into a theoretical framework that could be applied to the circumstances of his own time.

There is no question that Keynes came upon Malthus on his own. He was sent and read McCracken after he had reached his own preliminary conclusions, based on his having read Malthus's letters to Ricardo. But, it is as certain as anything can be that Keynes wrote *The General Theory* to explain the importance of demand deficiency because, and only because, he had read Malthus attempting to argue exactly the same point. Keynes had never written a single sentence on demand deficiency prior to his coming across Malthus at the end of 1932. It was his reading of Malthus that gave Keynes his organizing principle. A proper understanding of *The General Theory* must travel back through Malthus to the general glut debate and the debates of the 1820s on whether too much saving could cause recessions. That had been Malthus's conclusion, which became the central argument of *The General Theory* and which has, as a direct result, become the single most important element of macroeconomic theory and policy to this day.

The classical literature on most occasions discussed this conclusion as a denial of 'overproduction' as a possible cause of recession. It denied that it was possible to produce more output than a community would be willing to purchase. This is formally equivalent to stating that there was not enough demand relative to the flow of output. As a reminder of the actual nature of the original debate, it is therefore useful to recall Ricardo's reply to Malthus as part of their personal correspondence just after Malthus's *Principles* had been published. In a letter dated 9 October 1820, Ricardo wrote to Malthus to express his disagreement, where he stated:

> Men err in their productions, there is no deficiency of demand. (Ricardo, [1819–21] 1973, VIII, p. 277)

To translate: recessions are due to some derangement on the supply side of the economy, not because aggregate demand is too low. It is this issue that continues to remain at the heart of whether modern macroeconomic theory, based as it is on deficient aggregate demand, explains why downturns in the business cycle occur, accompanied as they are by high levels of mass unemployment.

THE SIGNIFICANCE OF THE MONEY ECONOMY

Let us return to the quote from McCracken previously discussed but highlighting a different set of words:

> The Automatic Production-Consumption Economists [i.e., those economists who accept Say's Law] who insisted that supply created its own demand, that goods exchanged against goods and that a money economy was only refined and convenient indirect barter **missed the significance of the money economy entirely**. (McCracken, 1933, p. 159; bold emphasis added)

This same sentiment was then echoed in *The General Theory*:

> The conviction, which runs, for example, through almost all Professor Pigou's work, that money makes no real difference except frictionally and that the theory of production and employment can be worked out (like Mill's) as being based on 'real' exchanges **with money introduced perfunctorily in a later chapter**, is the modern version of the classical tradition. (Keynes, *Collected Writings* [1936] 1981, VII, p. 20; bold emphasis added)

In this instance, it cannot be said with any kind of certainty that Keynes drew this conclusion because he had read McCracken. Nevertheless, it can be said that the entire classical tradition based its understanding of the economy on an understanding of the interplay between the real elements beneath the surface, bringing in the monetary side only afterwards. But in no sense whatsoever were the effects of money on the real economy seen as being 'introduced perfunctorily'. In virtually every form of the classical theory of the cycle, the problems created by monetary disturbances were either the most important element leading to recession or were a major contributing factor. It is a plain falsehood to argue that classical theory ignored the disturbing contributions of monetary disarray.

Haberler, in his comprehensive analysis of the contemporary theory of the business cycle, undertaken for the League of Nations and published in 1937, explicitly states:

> Money and credit occupy such a central position in our economic system that it is almost certain that they play an important rôle in bringing about the business cycle, either as an impelling force or as a conditioning factor. ... The analysis of a theory which puts the monetary factor at the centre of its scheme of causation will almost certainly reveal features of the business cycle which no adequate synthesis can afford to neglect. (Haberler, 1937, p. 13)

To emphasize the role of money and credit as an integral part of the classical theory of the cycle, one should examine Walter Bagehot's 1873 *Lombard Street*, whose Chapter VI is a discussion of the business cycle. Its relevance in this instance for what is a standard depiction of the cycle is found in the book's subtitle, *A Description of the Money Market*. In the passage below, let me note, I have changed the words from 'a good state of credit' to a 'bad state', then adjusted the remainder of the passage to conform to the point being made, shown in square brackets. But the role of a disturbance in credit markets is clear:

> Credit – the disposition of one man to trust another – is singularly varying. In England, after a great calamity, everybody is suspicious of everybody. ... In a [bad] state of credit, goods lie on hand a much [longer] time than when credit is [good]; sales are [slower]; intermediate dealers borrow [with difficulty] to augment their trade, and so [fewer and fewer] goods are more [slowly] and [less] easily transmitted from the producer to the consumer. (Bagehot, 1873, Chapter VI, n.p.)

In fact, if there is a reluctance to examine the role of money and credit in understanding the nature of the cycle, it has followed the publication of *The General Theory*, which turned the attention of economists away from the money market and the credit creation process to focus on aggregate demand and money saving instead.

The problem is actually deeper than this. It is not just the role of credit, but the sequencing in the logic of the underlying economic analysis. A classical economist first examined the relationships between the interacting elements – the role of specific items of capital in the hands of particular individual workers overseen by actual entrepreneurs and the management within a business. These were the actual components that were conceptualized, which is why classical theory dwelt on 'the factors of production' – land, labour and capital. These were not throwaway notions, disposed of in a single paragraph as is now largely the case. These were the tens and hundreds of millions of individuals or the numerous individual items of productive capital, that in combination constitute the elements that made up an economy that had to be understood on their own in an explanation of how an economy operated. It was these that were looked at as the 'real' economy. These elements were the economy's structure of production.

In modern theory, even the real economy is little more than a homogenized monetary construct. Everything is considered in relation to the number of units of the local currency, which is then deflated by some price index. There is no association with the actual units of production. The total level of investment is no more than a number of units of currency, rather than as so many steel mills, roadways and restaurants. The difficulties involved in making an economy responsive to shifts in demand or supply prices therefore end up obscured almost to the point where such considerations disappear into the mist.

RECESSIONS IN CLASSICAL TIMES

Among the many false statements made by Keynes in discussing 'classical economics' was that classical economists always assumed the economy was at full employment. Although utterly false, it remains astonishing that this belief permeates modern economic thought even though the evidence that Keynes was wrong is overwhelming. That this is largely unknown is an oddity, but is nevertheless the reality across almost the entire sweep of economic theory.

The following example is from John Stuart Mill's *Principles* and is as straightforward a description of recession and unemployment as one is likely to find, which could be repeated from any number of economic texts of the time and, of course, later. Some understanding of the terms used may be helpful, but although the language is nineteenth century, the meaning is clear. 'Overtrading' occurs when too much of particular products are produced so that they cannot earn a profitable return in the market. A 'commercial revulsion' is a recession. 'Rash speculation' needs no interpretation. The following passage is a description of an economic downturn in which 'hands are discharged', that is, people lose their jobs. Mill describes such downturns as 'conspicuous', which, of course, is what they were. Mill is explaining why profits do not fall too low to maintain industry over the long term. It would never have occurred to him that it would ever be suggested that he and his contemporaries always assumed an economy was at full employment:

> First among [the reasons that profits do not continuously fall], we may notice one which is so simple and so conspicuous, that some political economists, especially M. de Sismondi and Dr. Chalmers [both supporters of Malthus during the general glut debate], have attended to it almost to the exclusion of all others. This is, the waste of capital in periods of over-trading and rash speculation, and in the commercial revulsions by which such times are always followed.
>
> It is true that a great part of what is lost at such periods is not destroyed, but merely transferred, like a gambler's losses, to more successful speculators. But even of

these mere transfers, a large portion is always to foreigners, by the hasty purchase of unusual quantities of foreign goods at advanced prices.

And much also is absolutely wasted. Mines are opened, railways or bridges made, and many other works of uncertain profit commenced, and in these enterprises much capital is sunk which yields either no return, or none adequate to the outlay. Factories are built and machinery erected beyond what the market requires, or can keep in employment. Even if they are kept in employment, the capital is no less sunk; it has been converted from circulating into fixed capital, and has ceased to have any influence on wages or profits.

Besides this, there is a great unproductive consumption of capital, during the stagnation which follows a period of general over-trading. **Establishments are shut up, or kept working without any profit, hands are discharged, and numbers of persons in all ranks, being deprived of their income, and thrown for support on their savings, find themselves, after the crisis has passed away, in a condition of more or less impoverishment**. (Mill, *Principles* [1871] 1921, Book IV, Chapter IV, §5; bold emphasis added; note further that this was originally published as a single paragraph, the last half of which has been omitted)

This is the description of a downturn that has been the result of forces other than wages out of alignment with the productivity of the workforce. Moreover, the description of the effect on workers – many of whom being left 'in a condition of more or less impoverishment' – is as involuntarily a form of unemployment as could be imagined. The absence of long descriptions of these events within classical texts was not because they were ignored, but because they were so common. No one needed to be reminded of the employment effects of recessions.

THE POLEMICAL FORCE OF KEYNESIAN PROSE

In understanding Keynes's success, his brilliance as a polemicist cannot be underestimated. The economics of *The General Theory* was notoriously difficult to understand. This was entirely different when it came to the attacks on classical economics as a body of knowledge. This was treated as an enemy whose integrity must be completely destroyed, and he had the rhetorical tools to do it. This is the whole of Chapter 1:[2]

I have called this book the *General Theory of Employment, Interest and Money*, placing the emphasis on the prefix *general*. The object of such a title is to contrast the character of my arguments and conclusions with those of the *classical* theory of the subject, upon which I was brought up and which dominates the economic thought, both practical and theoretical, of the governing and academic classes of this generation, as it has for a hundred years past. I shall argue that the postulates of the classical theory are applicable to a special case only and not to the general case, the situation which it assumes being a limiting point of the possible positions of equilibrium. Moreover, the characteristics of the special case assumed by the classical theory happen not to be those of the economic society which we actually live, with the result that its teaching is misleading and disastrous if we attempt to apply it to the facts of experience. (Keynes, *Collected Writings* [1936] 1981, VII, p. 3; original emphasis)

The title itself was adopted from Einstein's 'general theory of relativity'. Keynes was virtually stating that his economics was to be distinguished from the classical economics of his predecessors in the way that Einstein's physics was to be distinguished from classical physics. This was a call to arms to overturn the economics that had seemed to fail during the Great Depression and to replace what had patiently been built over the years with a radical new departure.

Keynes continued his polemical assault, arguing that 'classical theory is only applicable to the case of full employment' and therefore, 'it is fallacious to apply it to the problems of involuntary unemployment'. From which he concluded:

> The classical theorists resemble Euclidean geometers in a non-Euclidean world who, discovering that in experience straight lines apparently parallel often meet, rebuke the lines for not keeping straight as the only remedy for the unfortunate collisions which are occurring. Yet, in truth, there is no remedy except to throw over the axiom of parallels and to work out a non-Euclidean geometry. Something similar is required today in economics. We need to throw over the second postulate of the classical doctrine and to work out the behaviour of a system in which involuntary unemployment in the strict sense is possible. (Ibid., pp. 16–17)

There was no denying that there had been a classical theory of the cycle, and a theory of unemployment. Keynes accepts that classical economists had investigated the causes of large-scale unemployment, but were hopelessly wrong in what they had done, and had not even understood that involuntary unemployment was even 'possible' however one might define the meaning of 'in the strict sense':

> To say that it has not been examined at all would, of course, be absurd. For every discussion concerning fluctuations employment, of which of there have been many, has been concerned with it. I mean, not that the topic has been overlooked, but that the fundamental theory underlying it has been deemed so simple and obvious that it has received, at the most, a bare mention. (Ibid., pp. 4–5)

Indeed, by the time he completes the last of the opening chapters, Keynes is in full polemical swing. This was meat and bone to those who sought a different approach to dealing with our economic problems:

> The completeness of the Ricardian victory is something of a curiosity and a mystery. It must have been due to a complex of suitabilities in the doctrine to the environment into which it was projected. That it reached conclusions quite different from what

the ordinary uninstructed person would expect, added, I suppose, to its intellectual prestige. That its teaching, translated into practice, was austere and often unpalatable, lent it virtue. That it was adapted to carry a vast and consistent logical superstructure, gave it beauty. That it could explain much social injustice and apparent cruelty as an inevitable incident in the scheme of progress, and the attempt to change such things as likely on the whole to do more harm than good, commanded it to authority. That it afforded a measure of justification to the free activities of the individual capitalist, attracted to it the support of the dominant social force behind authority.

But although the doctrine itself has remained unquestioned by orthodox economists up to a late date, its signal failure for purposes of scientific prediction has greatly impaired, in the course of time, the prestige of its practitioners. For professional economists, after Malthus, were apparently unmoved by the lack of correspondence between the results of their theory and the facts of observation; – a discrepancy which the ordinary man has not failed to observe, with the result of his growing unwillingness to accord to economists that measure of respect which he gives to other groups of scientists whose theoretical results are confirmed by observation when they are applied to the facts.

The celebrated optimism of traditional economic theory, which has led to economists being looked upon as Candides, who, having left this world for the cultivation of their gardens, teach that all is for the best in the best of all possible worlds provided we will let well alone, is also to be traced, I think, to their having neglected to take account of the drag on prosperity which can be exercised by an insufficiency of effective demand. For there would obviously be a natural tendency towards the optimum employment of resources in a Society which was functioning after the manner of the classical postulates. It may well be that the classical theory represents the way in which we should like our Economy to behave. But to assume that it actually does so is to assume our difficulties away. (Ibid., pp. 32–4)

Keynes knew how to use words for powerful political effect. From the moment he shot to fame with his *Economic Consequences of the Peace* (Keynes, *Collected Writings* [1919] 1981, II), his reputation was built on his ability to write scathing criticisms of the views of others. Whether this was a force for good has been the argument of those who have defended Keynes. But there is no denying how important Keynes's ability to criticize in words the views of others has been in achieving the ends he sought.

NOTES

1. Reprinted with kind permission from the Harlan Linneus McCracken Papers, Mss. 2569, Louisiana and Lower Mississippi Valley Collections, LSU Libraries, Baton Rouge, LA. As stated a full-colour reprint is found in Kates (2019).

2. With the following footnote at the end of this single-paragraph chapter:

   The classical economists' was a name invented by Marx to cover Ricardo and James Mill and their *predecessors*, that is to say for the founders of the theory which culminated in the Ricardian economics. I have become accustomed, perhaps perpetrating a solecism, to include in 'the classical school' the *followers* of Ricardo, those, that is to say, who adopted and perfected the theory of the Ricardian economics, including (for example) J.S. Mill, Marshall, Edgeworth and Prof. Pigou. (Keynes, *Collected Writings* [1936] 1981, VII, p. 3n.; original emphasis)

5. Understanding classical presuppositions, terminology and concepts

The fact of the matter is, virtually no one any longer knows what classical economists taught. What passes for such knowledge is the caricature crafted by Keynes and then immediately reinforced by the works of Joan Robinson (1937a, 1937b) and J.R. Hicks (1937). Historians of economics provide insight into pre-Keynesian economic theories only in a piecemeal kind of way and almost invariably from a Keynesian perspective, and very seldom from anyone trying to defend the classical position. There are studies on 'classical economics' that examine different aspects of the economic theories of the past, but with Keynes describing the range of economists he had classified under that banner as encompassing Ricardo through to A.C. Pigou (Keynes, *Collected Writings* [1936] 1981, VII, p. 3), to define just who these 'classical' economists were, or what they believed about any particular issue, becomes next to impossible. Certainly no economist without an expert background in the history of economic thought would have much relevant knowledge about the economic beliefs of the past. There would therefore be almost no standard from which Keynes's deviations would make much sense.

Keynes specifically accused contemporary economics of remaining chained to the Ricardian theories of 1817. But he also saw A.C. Pigou's 1933 *Theory of Unemployment* as part of the same stable of ideas. Since the differences between Ricardo and Pigou were enormous, he could do this, partly because of his concentration on the labour market and his own concentration on Say's Law, but also partly because it was difficult for Keynes's contemporaries to identify exactly what Keynes was trying to argue. How many economists, then or now, would have the breadth of historical knowledge required to rebut the various accusations he made? It would have required a more focused and comprehensive understanding of the many presuppositions that had fallen into the background among the mainstream, not to mention the actual theories of the time, along with seeing how they worked together in a coordinated whole.

Here we will deal with a number of elements that were part of the conceptual framework of classical economic theory that are profoundly different from modern macroeconomic theory. These are: the surrounding presuppositions, the wider sociological and political context, the division between micro-economics and macroeconomics, the classical meaning of Say's Law, the difference between stock variables and flow variables, the nature of saving and investment, the meaning of capital, the nature of value, the significance of value added, the difference between productive and unproductive consumption, and the different role of real variables and money in economic analysis, market and natural rates of interest, the classical meaning of the term 'inflation', and the role of the entrepreneur. Even this remains a partial list, but these were the various elements that have separated Keynesian and modern macroeconomics from the economics of the classical school.

PRESUPPOSITIONS

Let it first be emphasized that nothing may be more important than to appreciate the presuppositions that inhabit everyone's minds that make some things utterly invisible because they are so common. They are not discussed because they remain unnoticed. They are not just background but actually foreground. Their existence is not incorporated into a discussion since it would wear a reader down to be reminded of the obvious. No nineteenth-century writer would ever discuss the dependence on horses for inner-city transport and haulage. The replacement of horsepower with the internal combustion engine might have been worth mentioning at the turn of the century, but not since. Similarly, with the conceptual grounding in any discussion. The presuppositions that personal responsibility is the basis for economic decision making, that the government would never be expected to bail out a failing enterprise and that a budget deficit was economic incompetence of the highest order was just assumed, utterly never discussed because the contrary would never be considered. Every era and every society have presuppositions of their own. Recognizing and spelling out such presuppositions are essential if one is to make sense of the economics texts of a different time.

The world in which Adam Smith had written was at the very dawn of the Industrial Revolution. The enormous growth in productive power was still to come but could be seen in rough outline. During the first half of the nineteenth century, what was evident was the phenomenal growth in the ability to produce large volumes of output as well as generate new forms of goods and services, both for final consumption and as part of the productive infrastructure. The coming of steam power, railways and the factory system were major evolutionary steps in creating a level of wealth that was unprecedented both in its width and depth. The economic writings of the classical economists attempted to capture the underlying dynamic.

The questions they sought to answer were, how did this wealth suddenly come into existence? What were the social and political conditions that were needed to transform the agricultural societies of the previous 5000 years into these engines of growth and technology? What allowed the Industrial Revolution to take place? Adam Smith wrote about pin factories and the division of labour. The surrounding reality was the sudden emergence of a steam-driven economic colossus that brought with it living standards that had not only never before existed, but which no one had ever imagined were even possible. Economic theory attempted to make sense of what they saw before their eyes.

Modern economic theory, almost since the turn of the twentieth century, has taken all this for granted. We have become so used to growth, innovation and rising living standards that their existence has become almost assumed as just the way things are. There is no longer any effort made even by economists to point out how extraordinary by historical standards all this is. There is therefore no longer an effort made to explain that the necessary groundwork for prosperity is based on the political freedoms and government restraints that are essential to allow economies to grow.

The problem with presuppositions is that whatever we presuppose are, by definition, invisible. No one notices their existence since they are found everywhere, just part of the furniture. Whether it is ideological, cultural or technological, no one thinks twice about these features of the world one is living in. Ebenezer Scrooge may have been a figure of derision, but the existence of the careful managers of productive assets, who nurture growth and productivity, would have been evident at every turn. A government and bureaucratic structure that protected and promoted productive activity would have been at the centre of the political debate. There would have been many who were aghast at the transformation of England from 'a green and pleasant land' into a landscape populated by 'dark satanic mills', but the fantastic improvements in economic conditions, and particularly the economic conditions of the poor, would have restrained many a hand in trying to slow this process.

Yet, in the midst of the transformation were other forces that attempted to lessen the impact and soften the effects of the process of industrialization. Everywhere these new forms of industry took root, there were efforts made to ease the burdens on working families and their dependants. Side by side with the growth of industry was the growth of social legislation that attempted to ease the burdens on those who worked.

No one knew, moreover, how long this transformation would go on. Although it is odd today to read about the expectation that the Industrial Revolution would devolve into a steady-state economy, where the last innovation had been made and the entire economy could just go on reproducing for itself the same kinds of goods and services forever, although in more abundance, this was the expectation held by John Stuart Mill. Karl Marx had to have had the same notion at the back of his mind, since a world of continuous

change, driven by entrepreneurial innovation, is inconsistent with the world
he had anticipated when he wrote *The Communist Manifesto* (published, as it
happens, in 1848, the same year Mill published his *Principles*).

Modern economic theory is nevertheless clearly different from the classical
theory, based as it is on the assumption of ongoing and automatic growth and
innovation. There is therefore little in a modern text that outlines the process
by which output is produced and distributed. The words 'land', 'labour' and
'capital' barely find their way into a modern text, along with the occasional
reference to the entrepreneur, but are not introduced as key elements in the
dynamic, continually evolving economic structures in which we live. They are
presupposed into a nether world since there they are, virtually unmentioned
as an integral element in economics. The classical economists were instead
conscious of these requirements and featured all of these in their descriptions
of the economic mechanisms required to create an unstoppable economic
momentum that has continued into the present.

THE WIDER SOCIOLOGICAL AND POLITICAL CONTEXT

It has been said that the Industrial Revolution occurred in a fit of absent
mindedness on the part of the British governing class, who through inattention
allowed entrepreneurial activity to move forward before they had had a chance
to bring it to a halt. But, for whatever reason, there was enough leeway given
to producers and innovators to set the various mechanisms for growth in place
that turned out to be essential.

The winds of change blew through the philosophical world of the eighteenth and early nineteenth centuries, bringing with them an ethic of personal
freedom and human rights. The American Constitution, penned the same year
as the publication of Smith's *The Wealth of Nations* (1776), is an expression of
the ethos of its time, in which everyone had a right to pursue their own destiny
in the way they thought best. The various strands of thought that went into
freeing up of individuals to follow their own destiny are too many and diverse
to list and discuss. What is plain, however, was the final breakdown of the
feudal order and the birth of a desire for personal liberty that was reflected in
both the American and French Revolutions.

The economic theory of the early classical world reflected these philosophical and sociological beliefs. Economic theory was in many ways the development of those with an interest in philosophical issues, such as Adam Smith
and John Stuart Mill, or were engaged in business themselves, such as David
Ricardo and Jean-Baptiste Say. Whatever else it might have been, discussion
of economic issues was undertaken in words and argument. Modern economics, in contrast, has become an abstract 'science', in which resolution is sought

in mathematical formulations and statistical analysis. What was once known as 'political' economy has almost entirely dropped the political side, with almost the full attention of economists on resolving economic questions almost without any reference to the surrounding political and sociological conditions. These could not be more irrelevant to the economics found in both economic texts and economic journals.

Yet, the irony is that economics developed during the nineteenth century side by side with the expansion of the franchise, which was expanded to include women in the early twentieth century. Political pressures from workers and others outside the previous governing classes therefore came to be a direct influence on political decisions via the ballot box. This was recognized as placing an important burden on political judgements by those who lived through these changes. It is not by chance that 200 pages of Mill's *Principles*, one-fifth of the entire text, was devoted to the role of government, not merely because he had the aim of using the powers of government to improve the lives of the entire population, but also because there needed to be some criteria available to decide what governments should do, but also what they should not do.

Yet, economic theory as it has now become almost entirely ignores the existence of the political world, virtually ignoring the ways in which political pressures affect economic decisions.

THE POLITICAL PHILOSOPHY OF JOHN STUART MILL

Much of the economic discussion of classical economic theory is taken from John Stuart Mill's *Principles of Political Economy*, first published in 1848, but here focusing on the seventh edition published in 1871. Aside from the exemplary economics presented, whose language may be archaic but its reasoning remaining as sound as any text written with the presuppositions of the time embedded as they are, it is also useful to focus on Mill since he was arguably the principal political philosopher of his time. His *On Liberty*, published in 1859, laid down the principles of a free society that were the presuppositions that underlay his writings on the economy. The following is a brief summary of the political philosophy that underlay his economic writings:

> This last chapter [of *On Liberty*] applies the principles laid out in the previous sections. He begins by summarizing these principles:
>
> > The maxims are, first, that the individual is not accountable to society for his actions, in as far as these concern the interests of no person but himself. Advice, instruction, persuasion, and avoidance by other people if thought necessary by them for their own good, are the only measures by which society can justifiably

express its dislike or disapprobation of his conduct. Secondly, that for such actions as are prejudicial to the interests of others, the individual is accountable, and may be subjected either to social or to legal punishment, if society is of opinion that the one or the other is requisite for its protection.

Economy
Mill first applies these principles to the economy. He concludes that free markets are preferable to those controlled by governments. While it may seem, because 'trade is a social act,' that the government ought to intervene in the economy, Mill argues that economies function best when left to their own devices. Therefore, government intervention, though theoretically permissible, would be counterproductive. Later, he attacks government-run economies as 'despotic.' He believes that if the government ran the economy, then all people would aspire to be part of a bureaucracy that had no incentive to further the interests of any but itself. (Wikipedia, 2019e)

These are principles that would have been shared by the vast majority of his contemporaries at the time he wrote. It is these views that informed the policy decisions at the time. It need hardly be emphasized how different contemporary views are at the time this is being written. Many of the views on the economy expressed in the passage above would no longer be widely accepted as part of mainstream opinion today, possibly, although not necessarily, including, 'that free markets are preferable to those controlled by governments'.

MACRO/MICRO

Economic theory is now divided into its two major theoretical halves, micro-economics and macroeconomics, with a very clear division between the two. The micro side is centred on individual decision making, while the macro half is related to discussion of the operation of the economy as a whole. It is now sometimes said that macroeconomics, with its examination of the economy as a whole, travels beyond the classical approach, which it is said was almost entirely micro. This is, in fact, largely untrue. Economics, as it developed over the first hundred years following the publication of *The Wealth of Nations*, was almost completely oriented towards an analysis of the nature of the economy in its operations overall.

It was not that classical economists ignored questions of price determination or supply and demand generally. It was that these were not the core issues that concerned them but were supplementary to making sense of the operation of the economy in its entirety. The questions that mattered were how to raise living standards while working out how to promote national prosperity. Various microeconomic issues cropped up along the way, but almost none of them were central concerns.

Indeed, it remains a problem in trying to understand classical theory that the analysis often wound down to discussing how individual capitalists might respond to particular situations. But, for the most part, this was an attempt to explain the overall workings of the economic system by some kind of analogy with individual activities. The tables of contents of any classical text are issues that would naturally fit into a macroeconomic syllabus. The refinement in relation to the allocation of scarce resources among competing ends is perhaps what one might say they had in mind, but it was never expressed in that way.

Microeconomics arises with the marginal revolution. The shift in focus is towards individual decision making, with marginal utility becoming the central concern. Alfred Marshall's famous definition of economics, 'the study of mankind in the ordinary business of life' (Marshall, [1890] 2013, p. 1), is a major revision. Only four years before, Simon Newcomb had stated that the purpose of studying economics was to understand 'the causes which influence the public well-being' (Newcomb, 1886, p. iii). Marshall deals with questions that would today be almost entirely confined to a text on microeconomics. Economic theory would then become a study of the componentry of economies. The economy overall was basically seen as the sum of its parts.

SAY'S LAW

Because the term 'Say's Law' only entered the discourse among economists in the 1920s the 'classical' meaning is difficult to isolate. The law of markets, as far as J.-B. Say was concerned writing in 1803, pointed out that money was merely the transaction medium between selling one's own productions and buying someone else's so that a lack of sales was not due to a lack of money. Malthus in 1820 had argued that recessions could be caused by too much saving, leading to a lower level of total demand in an economy relative to the level of production. The conclusion at the end of the general glut debate, which followed upon the publication of Malthus's *Principles*, was that no economy ever suffered from a general glut caused by too much saving. A recession was never caused by demand deficiency. It is this conclusion that Keynes correctly attributed to classical economic theory.

However, while demand deficiency was ruled out, recessions and mass unemployment were not. It is one thing to say that recessions with their associated high unemployment cannot be caused by too little demand, but it is quite another to suggest that Say's Law implied that full employment was guaranteed. No classical economist had ever said any such thing, nor was it even remotely implied by any economist from Adam Smith to A.C. Pigou. Given how frequently recessions occurred, the very idea is ridiculous. The very cause of the general glut debate was what had led to the high unemployment that had followed the Napoleonic Wars.

The challenge for any modern economist who wishes to understand classical theory is to explain how Say's Law could be valid while there could simultaneously be deep recessions and large-scale involuntary unemployment. That is what a classical economist believed, and that was what was found in the classical theory of the business cycle. This was the universally held belief accepted universally across the mainstream of the profession from the 1820s, if not earlier, through to 1936, and accepted by some of the greatest minds economic theory has produced.

STOCKS AND FLOWS

Among the changes that have followed from the Keynesian revolution that make following the classics so difficult, has been the shift in focus from thinking in terms of the economy as an evolving series of structural relationships, rather than, as now, thinking only in terms of the increments in the final amount of final goods and services produced each year. According to Keynes, the level of employment varies directly with the level of aggregate demand. It is the demand for what is produced in the present that is the determinant of employment levels. The greater the level of demand, the higher will be the number of jobs. Any other conclusion among economists today is almost literally unthinkable. Yet, classical economists were very clear that no such relationship existed. Demand was constituted by supply and had no independent existence of its own. The level of unemployment was caused by factors aside from the level of demand.

The effect of Keynesian thinking has been to place the actual structure of the economy into the deepest background. Although living standards depend on the entire existing stock of capital, the size and capabilities of the workforce that is actually present, the resource base that business owners have access to, the regulatory environment created by governments, as well as the entrepreneurial abilities of its business community – virtually all of which are a bequest from the past – little of this is considered in looking at an economy and its ability to produce and employ.

SAVING AND INVESTMENT

Saving in a classical model referred to that proportion of existing capital assets as well as other available factors of production that were directed towards future production, rather than satisfying the needs and wants of the present moment. Most emphatically, it was a stock variable, a stock of specific items used in production. It was composed of actual machinery, labour time and physical resources. There may have been a money value associated with this stock of productive items but saving in relation to a national economy was not conceived in terms of money left unspent, but in terms of the use made of such productive resources.

In contrast, saving in a Keynesian model is the flow of money out of current income during some period of time that has not been used to buy consumer goods and services. Saving is entirely conceived in terms of money, with little connection made to the actual underlying economy.

Thinking in terms of stocks of real resources and not flows of money income, saving was necessarily equal to investment. The totality of the resource base directed towards future production – investment – was equal to the totality of the resource base that was not being used to produce consumer goods – saving. The following excerpt, from Henry Clay's 1916 *Economics: An Introduction for the General Reader*, will provide an understanding of the classical approach to saving. The book was extensively used until the publication of the second edition in 1942. There was nothing, therefore, that had superseded any of this at the time *The General Theory* was published:

> Individuals and society have at every moment to decide how much of their *income*, **how much of the productive capacity at their command**, shall be devoted to aiding future production. That part of income that is devoted to future income is said to be saved. That does not mean it is not spent or consumed; it means that it spent or consumed to aid further production. If put in a bank and the bank lends it to business men who use it to aid their work of production; or it is invested; that is, the owner puts it into a business which uses it to buy buildings plant, materials, etc. We may put the case concretely by saying that 'savings' **constitute a demand for buildings, machines, materials, and stock-in-trade**, while the rest of income is a demand for food, clothing, shelter, and other goods and services for immediate consumption; both are spent, but the object of spending is different in the two cases. (Clay, 1916, p. 235; italics and bold emphasis added)

Both saving and investment were understood in real terms. Nor were the resources used for productive purposes seen as a constant, since anything could be shifted from its use as a consumption item into a different use as part of the productive part of the economy. Whether some item was used productively was determined by its owner. A house that was lived in was a consumer item. That same house rented out was now part of national saving.

The resources used to increase the productiveness of the economy were investment. Investment is equal to saving because they are the same. The available resources were also finite so that it was an important aspect of economic policy to ensure such resources were channelled into forms of production that increased an economy's ability to produce.

The shift in the underlying concept from the economy's real resource base into thinking of saving in terms of money was part of the reason that the Keynesian framework lost its ability to illuminate what was taking place when decisions to save were being made. For those holding money in any of its forms, or for the financial system thought of as a whole, the process was viewed exclusively in terms of the flow of money. In doing so, almost everything of importance in relation to the saving-investment process disappeared from view.

Moreover, by conceiving both saving and investment as flow items, restricted only to newly produced capital items, the entire structure of the economy that lay behind current output was ignored. Even if it made sense to think of what was going on in money terms, it could not make sense in relation to the productiveness of an economy to look only at what had been newly produced. Leaving out the whole of the economy meant leaving out everything of significance in relation to the ability of the economy to produce particular volumes of output.

Then, to compound the problem, with investment and saving being thought of entirely in relation to money amounts, the structure of production that had allowed the flow of output to occur was entirely ignored. The focus was vastly narrowed. The nature of recession was conceived in terms of money expenditure, with money saving out of current income the prime obstacle to output and employment.

Saving as the productive resources made available for production was, to a classical economist, the engine of growth. Saving following Keynes has been the community's refusal to spend as much as it could, and therefore, in the absence of sufficient money investment, the cause of unemployed resources. A classical economist worried that savings were too low and insufficient to allow the economy to grow. Savings to a Keynesian economist was a potential impediment to growth.

DEFINING CAPITAL

A classical economist thought of the entire economy as one vast store of wealth that could be used to produce for present enjoyment, while what was left could be used to generate further wealth. A classical economist was continuously aware of an economy's legacy from the past. Nothing bought in the present was the instant result of some immediate decision to buy, but was, instead, the final result of some massive process that went back in time, encompassing the entire array of labour and inputs that had been essential so that the particular good or service could become available to purchase.

A freshly baked loaf of bread may have come into existence that morning. But its coming into existence at that particular moment was the result of a combination of the work of the baker that morning; the milling of the grain, possibly months before, that has produced the flour; the farmers who had grown and harvested the grain possibly a year earlier; the various transport networks that had brought the inputs together to a particular place where they could be combined; the electricity-generating capacity of long standing that had been needed to mix the ingredients; and on and on. This vast capital structure, as well as the skilled labour that had conceived, designed and built the capital, who were then capable of using it productively, all these were essential so that those final touches could be added at the bakery that particular morning.

Since the publication of *The General Theory*, almost none of this is brought into consideration in examining the way an economy works. Since job numbers are, according to Keynesian theory, related to an atemporal level of demand, the interest is in the latest set of activities and not the density of the infrastructure that lies behind. The nature of the economy taken as a whole is virtually ignored. An economy with 10 per cent growth is seen as 'doing better' than an economy with 2 per cent growth since the larger the economy's rate of growth rate, the faster the growth in employment is expected to be. The base from which the growth rate is measured is left in the background.

To help explain the classical position, the most primitive of all diagrams, the production possibility curve (PPC), is used to contrast classical and modern economics. A PPC is usually presented at an early stage of an economics course. Typically, it picks two products and shows some kind of trade-off between them, such as the guns and butter example used by Samuelson ([1948] 1998, pp. 17–21). The more you produce of one of these products, the less you can produce of the other. The diagram is, however, more profound than it is usually taken to be since it allows one to understand more completely the point that classical economists had been trying to make.

The diagram having become a staple in modern theory (cf. Mankiw, 2007, pp. 24–7) therefore has a presence that is unassailable even though it is by nature vague and imprecise. Importantly, what has to be appreciated is that the two axes of a properly designed diagram must represent two kinds of products whose production between them must exhaust the entire economy's ability to produce. Examples might include goods on the one hand and services on the other. Or it might show privately produced products and government-produced products on each of its two axes.

In Figure 5.1, the vertical axis shows forms of output that draw down on the resource base, with no attempt made to replace what has been drawn down. These are described as forms of 'consumption'. Their production uses up resources, but what is produced is not intended to contribute to production at some future date. Resources are drawn down, products are either consumed or services rendered, but the economy is now even less capable of producing for the future since the resources have been used up, while nothing has been created to replace what has been used up.

The horizontal axis represents all forms of drawing down on the economy's resource base, which are directed towards producing forms of output that will add to the economy's productive base for the future. These are referred to as 'investment'. These are products (or services such as education) that are

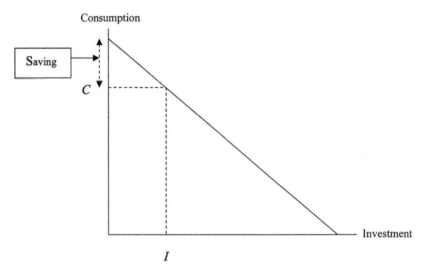

Figure 5.1   Production possibility curve – consumption and investment

intended to leave the economy able to produce an even greater flow of output at some stage in the future.

In the PPC shown, consumption and investment spending together totally exhaust the economy's ability to produce. Either because of institutional limitations, or because the economy cannot produce more than its potential, it is not possible to produce more than some combination on the curve itself.

To a classical economist, the issue was how to increase 'the wealth of nations', that is, how to increase living standards. The answer would be that it was necessary to increase the area under the PPC by moving it up and to the right. The more investment there was, the more it might move, but even under the best of circumstances, it would move outward only very slowly.

The diagram also shows the conception related to saving and investment. Inside the PPC is everything within an economy that can be used to satisfy a human need, either directly, as with consumption goods such as a loaf of bread, or indirectly, such as with a tonne of iron ore.

Some of what is found within an economy is used to produce consumer goods (flour and ovens to bake bread) or already are consumer goods (such as actual loaves of bread). And some of those existing resources are being used to produce capital goods that will eventually be used in the production process either to produce more capital or consumer goods.

The wages fund was built on a sound concept in the same way as the PPC. It is not supposed to represent anything that can be estimated exactly. It is intended to provide a conceptual tool for understanding the nature of the economy, and the source of funding for economic activity. It was described as the wages fund because it raised an issue that is no longer even considered worthy of mention among economists: what are workers paid with before the production cycle is complete?

Our economies are now so filled with products of an endless variety, and each of us in the more prosperous parts of the world have large stocks of consumer goods (such as cars and computers), that this question seems almost impossible to envisage today. In the agricultural societies in which economics originally developed, everyone understood that the farm workers tilling the fields were consuming the crops that had been grown the year before. Now there is such abundance that the sequence between production and consumption has become invisible, although by no means irrelevant.

Yet, understanding the role of saving as the building up of real productive assets, as well as the consumer goods that workers will buy and use, is a necessity if economies are to function. A town in a war zone, or caught short because of some natural disaster, soon discovers how important the stock of provisions is.

Please also note that the PPC figure captures the meaning of saving and investment in classical times. An economy's infrastructure, which is an inheritance from the past, can either be used for immediate consumption or as inputs into future productive activities.

Saving, when understood as a proportion of the productive apparatus of the economy, is then exactly equal to the level of investment. That part of the entire productive parts of the economy that is not aimed toward improving the future productivity of the economy is used to provide consumer products in the present. Both, however, draw down on the productivity of the economy.

THEORY OF VALUE

The classical theory of value was summed up in Book III, Chapter VI of Mill's *Principles*. While it was pilloried from stem to stern by the marginalists who thought of classical theory as fundamentally wrong, they fought a different battle, against the labour theory of value (LTV), which might have applied to Adam Smith and David Ricardo but which had almost entirely disappeared by the time Mill wrote. The LTV was by then the province of Marxists and socialists generally, who had depended on it to explain the surplus theory of value. Marginal utility was used to counter the LTV, which almost instantaneously replaced the classical theory of value.

The disappearance of classical value theory has had massive repercussions on the study of economics ever since, not least of which being the shift of orientation from the supply side of the economy to the demand side, with marginal analysis focused on utility rather than production costs.

Given how significant the theory of value is, the discussion of the classical theory of value will be focused on in the next chapter where the analysis will concentrate on the presentation by Mill in his *Principles*, which has been ridiculed by the marginalists and most others since. The following is a typical example, taken from the History of Economic Thought website:

> John Stuart Mill's greater economic performance was his magnificent 1848 *Principles of Political Economy*, a two-volume extended restatement of the Classical Ricardian theory. He believed Ricardo's labor theory of value to be so conclusive that, in the beginning of a discussion on the theory of value, Mill confidently notes that:
>
>> Happily, there is nothing in the laws of Value which remains for the present or any future writer to clear up; the theory of the subject is complete: the only difficulty to be overcome is that of so stating it as to solve by anticipation the chief perplexities which occur in applying it. (J.S. Mill, *Principles*, 1848: Book III, Ch. 1 [Ashley edition [1871] 1921, p. 436])
>
> Thus putting a stone on the matter, and burying supply-and-demand theory for another quarter-century. When Jevons's [sic] later grumbled at the 'noxious influence of authority' preventing the development of economics, there is little doubt he was referring to J.S. Mill. (History of Economic Thought, 2019a)

This observation by Jevons has remained a fixed point even among historians of economics since the 1870s. Yet, here are the first two of the 17 elements from Mill's 'theory of value', which is found in Book III, Chapter VI:

> I. Value is a relative term. The value of a thing means the quantity of some other thing, or of things in general, which it exchanges for. The values of all things can never, therefore, rise or fall simultaneously. There is no such thing as a general rise or a general fall of values. Every rise of value supposes a fall, and every fall a rise.
> II. The temporary or Market Value of a thing, depends on the demand and supply; rising as the demand rises, and falling as the supply rises. The demand, however, varies with the value, being generally greater when the thing is cheap than when it is dear; and the value always adjusts itself in such a manner, that the demand is equal to the supply. (Mill, *Principles* [1871] 1921, p. 478)

The first point to note is that Mill emphasizes that 'value is a relative term'. The question he, and classical economists generally were asking was, what determined the relative price of say, a pair of shoes as against the price of a cotton shirt? Modern supply and demand analysis might provide an answer to what might determine the price of each, and therefore by inference their relative value, but nothing provides a general explanation of what might determine the relative price of each one with the other, never mind the relative value of a boatload of tuna as say against the exchange value of a field of unharvested potatoes.

The second point Mill deals with is the 'temporary or Market Value' of various goods and services, and this is precisely and exactly the modern textbook answer, stated in only two sentences, rather than in a chapter-length discussion with a series of diagrams about how equilibrium is achieved, accompanied by a further discussion on elasticity along with price ceilings and price floors. To repeat:

> The ... **Market Value of a thing, depends on the demand and supply**; rising as the demand rises, and falling as the supply rises. The demand, however, varies with the value, being generally greater when the thing is cheap than when it is dear; and the value always adjusts itself in such a manner, that the demand is equal to the supply. (Ibid.; bold emphasis added)

There are then all of the additional complications discussed in Points III to XVII, which will be discussed in the following chapter. Nor did Mill believe he had exhausted the entire subject of the theory of value, writing a quote from Montesquieu in the original French at the end of the chapter (ibid., p. 482; the following is my translation):

> You do not always have to exhaust a subject so much that you leave nothing to the reader. It is not a matter of reading, but thinking.

Exactly so.

VALUE ADDED

At the very core of a Keynesian model is aggregate demand as the motor of economic activity. It was all very well to have the productive apparatus in place that would allow more to be produced, but without the willingness of others to part with their money to buy goods and services the economy would not live up to its potential. This was emphasized in no uncertain terms:

> The absurd, though almost universal, idea that an act of individual saving is just as good for effective demand as an act of individual consumption, has been fostered by the fallacy, much more specious than the conclusion derived from it, that an increased desire to hold wealth, being much the same thing as an increased desire to hold investments, must, by increasing the demand for investments, provide a stimulus to their production; so that current investment is promoted by individual saving to the same extent as present consumption is diminished. (Keynes, *Collected Writings* [1936] 1981, VII, p. 211)

The answer in a Keynesian model is to increase the level of spending. The very core proposition in any such model is the relationship between an increase in aggregate demand and a subsequent increase in the level of employment. It makes no difference whether the initial expenditure is value adding or not. The 'multiplier' effects will ensure that the spending is ultimately productive. Some have passed the following passage off as a joke, but joke or not, it has been the template for stimulus spending ever since. Although the word 'wasteful' is placed in quote marks, there is nothing ironic about the meaning of the term. Keynes literally meant that the individual project undertaken need not itself create a return greater than its cost:

> For a man who has been long unemployed some measure of labour, instead of involving disutility, may have a positive utility. If this is accepted, the above reasoning shows how 'wasteful' loan expenditure may nevertheless enrich the community on balance. Pyramid-building, earthquakes, even wars may serve to increase wealth, if the education of our statesmen on the principles of the classical economics stands in the way of anything better.
>
> It is curious how common sense, wriggling for an escape from absurd conclusions, has been apt to reach a preference for *wholly* 'wasteful' forms of loan expenditure rather than for *partly* wasteful forms, which, because they are not wholly wasteful, tend to be judged on strict 'business' principles. For example, unemployment relief financed by loans is more readily accepted than the financing of improvements at a charge below the current rate of interest; whilst the form of digging holes in the ground known as gold-mining, which not only adds nothing whatever to the real wealth of the world but involves the disutility of labour, is the most acceptable of all solutions. (Ibid., pp. 128–9; original emphasis)

The following paragraph follows directly from the paragraph above. It is a model public works example that has been followed ever since. Spend money on anything at all is the advice, and the economy will resume growth and unemployment will fall. The 'repercussions' noted are the multiplier effects:

> If the Treasury were to fill old bottles with banknotes, bury them at suitable depths in disused coalmines which are then filled up to the surface with town rubbish, and leave it to private enterprise on well-tried principles of *laissez-faire* to dig the notes up again (the right to do so being obtained, of course, by tendering for leases of the note-bearing territory), there need be no more unemployment and, with the help of the repercussions, the real income of the community, and its capital wealth also, would probably become a good deal greater than it actually is. It would, indeed, be more sensible to build houses and the like; but if there are political and practical difficulties in the way of this, the above would be better than nothing. (Ibid., p. 129)

A classical economist would have recognized that such an approach could not possibly work. One of the definitions of Say's Law in classical times was that demand is constituted by supply, but the underlying assumption that the demand needed to be value adding never had to be stated prior to the publication of *The General Theory*. That is, it was understood that 'supply' was constituted by goods that had been produced and sold on the market at prices that covered costs. And even where the public sector was undertaking some form of work-creation project, there was still an aim to ensure that whatever was being produced had a value greater than its cost of production, such as new homes or a municipal swimming pool.

What was never within the conception of any classical economist was that forms of demand that were constituted by merely spending money on goods and services, whose production costs could not be met in sales revenue, or were not intended even to be notionally value adding, could create jobs over the longer term. The drawing down of an economy's resource base, without thought to how the resource base could be rebuilt, was seen by those classical economists who commented on Keynes as utterly absurd.

VALUE IN USE VERSUS VALUE IN EXCHANGE

The distinction between value in use in contrast with value in exchange was a distinction that added a good deal of clarity to the discussion of value and its meaning within classical economics. Its presence within economic theory disappeared with the marginal revolution. Once marginal utility came into vogue, the phrase 'value in use' became superfluous, as Menger discussed in his *Principles*:

> Like Adam Smith [that is, following the usage initiated by Adam Smith], David Ricardo, Thomas Robert Malthus and John Stuart Mill [also] employ 'value in use' as synonymous with 'utility'. (Menger, [1871] 1976, p. 307)

'Value' is thus recognized to have two meanings that need to be kept separate – the value some good or service has to those who already own or wish to purchase that good or service, in comparison with the exchange value some good or service may have on the market. The final utility of some good, with everyone's homes stocked with many already purchased items, is different from the amount of money that might be received were such items to be put up for sale.

PRODUCTIVE VERSUS UNPRODUCTIVE

The disappearance of the classical distinction between productive and unproductive use of resources has left economic theory much less capable of making important distinctions in how resources are employed. With Keynesian theory shifting the elements driving the economy forward and upward to the demand side, the distinctions between C, I and G (total consumption, total private investment and total government expenditure) in relation to aggregate demand concerning their ability to create higher levels of future production has all but disappeared. A 'productive' use of resources in classical times was related to their being used to create a higher future level of economic activity and thus a higher level of prosperity. The 'unproductive' use of resources was not in any way a judgement on their utility or the benefits provided to those who incurred the expense in putting those resources to use. The phrase was meant to state that from the use of resources in that particular way, in an 'unproductive' way, there would be no future increase in the capabilities of the economy as a result. This was stated by John Stuart Mill in his essay, 'Of the Influence of Consumption on Production':

> It was triumphantly established by political economists, that consumption never needs encouragement. All which is produced is already consumed, either for the purpose of reproduction or of enjoyment. The person who saves his income is no less a consumer than he who spends it: he consumes it in a different way; it supplies food and clothing to be consumed, tools and materials to be used, by productive labourers. Consumption, therefore, already takes place to the greatest extent which the amount of production admits of; **but, of the two kinds of consumption, reproductive and unproductive, the former alone adds to the national wealth, the latter impairs it**. What is consumed for mere enjoyment, is gone; **what is consumed for reproduction, leaves commodities of equal value, commonly with the addition of a profit**. The usual effect of the attempts of government to encourage consumption, is merely to prevent saving; that is, to promote unproductive consumption at the expense of reproductive, and diminish the national wealth by the very means which were intended to increase it. (Mill, [1844] 1998, p. 48; bold emphasis added)

This loss of clarity with the disappearance of the distinction between 'productive' and 'unproductive' means that there is no longer a focus on whether some expenditure will add to the future productiveness of the economy or whether it will draw down on the resource base but leave nothing in its place. This is not a value judgement, to use 'value' in yet another sense, but a technical point about the future ability of an economy to produce more than it already does, and thus be able to raise future living standards, or at a minimum maintain those that exist already. That economists no longer routinely make this judgement makes clear the reason for their inability to distinguish growth-producing forms of activity from those that merely eat up the resource base with no future return on the outlays made.

CONSUMPTION

Another important distinction between the economics of the classical economists and modern economic theory is also seen in the above quote from Mill.

It is in the different usage of the term 'consumption'. In the passage above, consumption means to use up resources in some kind of economic activity.

Here is Kenneth Boulding discussing, in 1945, 'The Consumption Concept in Economic Theory':

> One would suppose that with so long a history the meaning of the term would be moderately clear. Unfortunately, this is not so. It is only a slight exaggeration to say that the classical economists, up to and including Marshall, had a fairly clear concept of consumption but no adequate theory of how consumption fitted into the whole economic process. In spite of Adam Smith, Say, and Malthus, in whose writings there is at least the germ of a theory of consumption, the influence of Ricardo switched the line of development of economic thought for over a century towards production, distribution and exchange. Marshall, for instance, having defined consumption fairly accurately, immediately leaves the subject and devotes the rest of his Book III to a discussion of the related, but by no means identical, topic of demand. It was not until the development of the Keynesian system that a consumption concept took its place in the theory of the whole economic process. Unfortunately, however, while the Keynesians had a fairly good theory of consumption, they worked with a very inadequate and confused concept, and to this fact must be attributed many of the quite unnecessary difficulties and confusions of Keynesian economics. (Boulding, 1945, p. 1)

Here Keynes is seen to have rescued the concept from the understanding of the term by the classical economists right through to Alfred Marshall. Boulding explains the meaning of consumption as understood by classical economists:

> Up to the time of Marshall the meaning of the word 'consumption' was fairly clear. It meant, what it literally means, the destruction of commodities – i.e., of valuable things – in the way in which they were intended to be destroyed. ... As above defined, there is, of course, no particular virtue in consumption. It is, unfortunately, a necessary incident in the business of living. We cannot eat without destroying food; we cannot walk without destroying shoes; we cannot drive without destroying gasoline, tires, and cars; and so on. Were we possessed of unbreakable china, widow's cruses, waters of life, undying fires, immortal garments and inexhaustible energy we would presumably be better off, economically, though what we would do with all these riches is, of course, another question. Any discovery which renders consumption less necessary to the pursuit of living is as much an economic gain as a discovery which improves our skills of production. Production – by which we mean the exact opposite of consumption, namely, the creation of valuable things – is only necessary in order to replace the stock pile into which consumption continually gnaws. (Ibid., pp. 1–2)

While Boulding sees the Keynesian appropriation of the term 'consumption' as a step forward, it is actually a loss in clarity in understanding the operation of an economy. It is a transformation that emphasizes the loss in understanding of the processes of an economy by turning aside from the supply side of the economy to focus only on demand.

MONEY VERSUS THE REAL ECONOMY

A classical model was conceived in real terms, with money only brought in at the end. An economist was trained to watch the flow of goods and services as actual forms of output. The wages fund was made up of the actual food, clothing and other products and services that wage earners would buy with their incomes, and not, of course, literally stored by the individual entrepreneur to be parcelled out as payment for labour. The focus was on the actually available products that had to exist if wage earners were to transform their hours of labour into items they could purchase.

The capital stock was, in the same way, understood as actual and specific forms of human-produced productive items, from a paper clip to an ocean liner. If it were an item that did not occur in nature but had gone through the production process, and was used as part of a production process rather than as a consumption item, it was a capital item. Here is John Stuart Mill discussing the meaning of capital, which he wishes to be understood as distinct from money:

> Capital, by persons wholly unused to reflect on the subject, is supposed to be synonymous with money. ... Money is no more synonymous with capital than it is with wealth. Money cannot in itself perform any part of the office of capital, since it can afford no assistance to production. To do this, it must be exchanged for other things; and anything, which is susceptible of being exchanged for other things, is capable of contributing to production in the same degree. What capital does for production, is to afford the shelter, protection, tools and materials which the work requires, and to feed and otherwise maintain the labourers during the process. These are the services which present labour requires from past, and from the produce of past, labour. Whatever *things* are destined for this use – destined to supply productive labour with these various prerequisites – are Capital. (Mill, *Principles* [1871] 1921, p. 54; italics emphasis added)

However inelegant the word may be, capital is 'things'. Money may allow you to buy capital, but capital consists of items that are used productively. By thinking in terms of the tens of millions of items that are used in the production process, and not reducing these to a sum of money left unspent on consumer goods, a classical economist would not come to the conclusion that a fall in interest rates would increase the flow of capital across an economy, and indeed, would appreciate that a fall in rates, because it would lower the price paid, would lead to the availability of even less capital than would otherwise have been provided.

MARKET AND NATURAL RATES OF INTEREST

The market rate of interest is the payment for borrowed money or credit. Goods or services are delivered at one date and the payment occurs at a later date. The difference between what would have been the payment at the time of purchase versus the payment at the later date is the amount of interest paid. This is an entirely visible payment and the rate is easily calculated.

The natural rate of interest, on the other hand, is entirely notional. It is the rate of interest that will equalize the flow of capital goods that will be made available for productive investment with the demand for those capital goods. It is the supply and demand for 'things'. It is a concept that was developed towards the end of the nineteenth century, but which was almost entirely dismantled with the publication of *The General Theory*. Curiously, Keynes had made use of the natural rate of interest in his previous book, *A Treatise on Money* (1930), but then denies its significance in *The General Theory*:

> I am now no longer of the opinion that the concept of a 'natural' rate of interest, which previously seemed to me a most promising idea, has anything very useful or significant to contribute to our analysis. It is merely the rate of interest which will preserve the *status quo*; and, in general, we have no predominant interest in the *status quo* as such. (Keynes, *Collected Writings* [1936] 1981, VII, p. 243)

Given Keynes's authority, the natural rate has disappeared almost entirely from macroeconomic theory. Its disappearance has been a major loss to our understanding of the operation of an economy.

In classical theory, however, if the market rate of interest is above the natural rate, that is, if money rates of interest are pushed up, there is a shortfall in the demand for capital goods and a consequent fall in investment. If, on the other hand, the money rate of interest is lower than the equilibrium natural rate, the supply of capital goods is lower than the demand. There is a shortage of capital items.

In equilibrium, as shown in Figure 5.2, the supply and demand for money and credit are equal at the same rate of interest at which the supply and demand for capital goods are also equal (that is, where $i = r$). It is difficult to ensure whether the two rates are in equilibrium but the natural forces of the economy, if left to themselves, will tend to bring them together.

The most significant issue for modern economic management is the use of artificially low rates of interest to stimulate investment, and thus raise demand and presumably employment, in relation to the diagram. Yet, the inclusion of the natural rate side by side with the market rate demonstrates the folly of any such approach. In the diagram, the market rate of interest is lowered through an increase in the money supply, which pushes the supply of money and credit

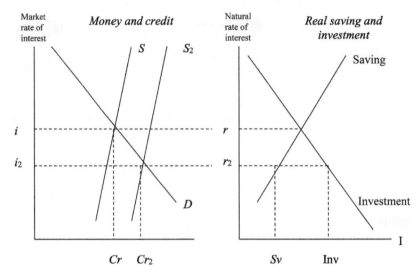

Figure 5.2   Market and natural rates of interest

from S to S_2. The market rate, accordingly, falls from i to i_2. But while the supply of money and credit in an economy can be increased, the same cannot be said about the stock of capital. It is more or less fixed at some particular level.

The fall in the equilibrium level of market rate of interest does not change the equilibrium for the natural rate. That remains at r where the supply and demand for capital goods are equal. The fall in money rates, however, creates an excess demand for capital goods at the lower natural rate, r_2, which is equal to the money rate, from which a series of consequences follow.

The first is that the fall in rates leads to lower investment. Unless the supply of saving were perfectly inelastic, the lower rate of interest diminishes the supply of saving, that is, reduces the flow of productive resources made availa-ble to the market, and thus lowers the amount of investment that can physically occur. The diminished investment leads to lower rates of economic growth as the economy's capital base deteriorates.

Second, the excess demand for savings means that there are more savings sought than there are savings available. The result is that shortages occur within the economy that are translated into higher costs of capital goods and a misdirection of the capital that does exist into less productive forms of investment. Over time, the quantum of capital diminishes, as both new forms of capital do not come into existence, while existing capital is allowed to run down without repair and replacement. This, too, will tend to lower the rate of growth over the medium to longer term.

Third, the increase in the supply of money and money rates of interest allows public spending to increase at a more rapid rate. An increase in the proportion of total spending by governments and less by the private sector contributes to the slower rates of growth that occur.

Fourth, there is upwards prices pressure. There is an increase in the level of demand across the economy with a diminished level of supply to meet that demand. Where prices are particularly vulnerable is in relation to asset prices, such as stocks and house prices. The fear of a rise in prices, in conjunction with the easier flow of money within the economy, causes a shift in purchases away from productive assets and into various forms of wealth holding in which real value is expected to be maintained.

Fifth, the fall in real growth rates leads to slower employment growth simultaneously with either a diminished growth in real incomes or an actual fall. The economy has shifted away from its most productive forms of production and is creating jobs that are either low productivity or even entirely non-value adding.

INFLATION AS SOMETHING THAT WAS DONE VERSUS INFLATION AS THE CONSEQUENT MOVEMENT OF PRICES

The word 'inflation' has experienced such a transformation since the 1930s that it is now impossible to read pre-Keynesian discussions of the cycle without careful preparation. Inflation prior to the publication of *The General Theory* was something a government did, not a rise in the price level. The reason for the shift in meaning was almost certainly because Keynesian demand management was literally a policy of inflation in the earlier sense of the word.

Inflation today means a rise in the price level. In earlier times, a rise in prices was a possible consequence of inflation, but inflation referred to an expansion in the amount of money circulating within an economy and was normally understood to be the result of an increase in public spending unfinanced by tax revenue. It is interesting to see Keynes in *The General Theory* note this difference, since his book is itself the transition document between the older meaning and the one that is now universally used:

> The view that *any* increase in the quantity of money is inflationary (**unless we mean by *inflationary* merely that prices are rising**) is bound up with the underlying assumption of the classical theory that we are *always* in a condition where a reduction in the real rewards of the factors of production will lead to a curtailment in their

supply. (Keynes, *Collected Writings* [1936] 1981, VII, p. 304; original italics; bold emphasis added)

Since then, of course, by inflation we do indeed mean 'merely that prices are rising' and nothing else. Inflation has therefore lost its previous meaning as increased government spending beyond revenue. The effect has been to suppress any immediate concern when public spending rises and the government deficit grows. There is therefore no warning thrown up by the spending data themselves. A deficit is no longer seen as an immediate cause for concern.

In addition, since a rise in public spending does not necessarily lead to a rise in the measured price level, a sense of complacency with public spending results. A number of reasons may lead to the official measure of inflation not rising, which may be due to the effect of public spending creating a slowdown in consumer demand or the increase in prices being diverted into asset prices that are not included in the official measure.

There are also various means in which price inflation can be suppressed, with the most important being through the deterioration in the economy's capital stock rather than through rising business prices. This shift disguises a much worse outcome for an economy since the effects of the money demand inflation are experienced in falling living standards.

EMPLOYMENT CREATION

In a Keynesian model, the level of employment is determined by the level of aggregate demand. Other considerations, and in particular the real wage, are excluded. It is aggregate demand that matters. The policy that almost automatically follows from the utilization of a Keynesian model is based around undertaking measures that will raise demand; most notably increases in the level of public spending. It is this that is considered the essence of a 'Keynesian' policy.

Recessions are identified by the abnormally high levels of unemployment. There was nothing unusual in Keynes's association of recessions with unemployment. What was highly unusual was his argument that classical economists had no theory to explain the high rates of unemployment that accompanied recessions. This absence of a theory of unemployment he attributed to their acceptance of Ricardian economic theory, a conception he perhaps took from McCracken (see Kates, 2010b).

There were, of course, many theories of recession and unemployment. But what there was as well was a theory that denied that recessions and unemployment were caused by too much saving and a deficiency of aggregate demand, for which the classic statement is John Stuart Mill's Fourth Proposition on Capital, 'demand for commodities is not demand for labour' (Mill, *Principles*

[1871] 1921, p. 79; see Kates, 2015a for a more complete discussion). This is the direct refutation of 'Keynesian' theory written almost a century before *The General Theory* was published.

First, if saving consists of actual capital goods directed into productive uses, there is no meaning to the notion of oversaving. It is not money that would have to be withheld but actual productive resources that could earn their owners an income. The notion that someone would choose not to use the capital assets they owned to earn an income makes no sense if economic conditions are reasonably stable. It is why Adam Smith could write, 'a man must be perfectly crazy who, where there is tolerable security, does not employ all the stock which he commands, whether it be his own or borrowed of other people' (Smith, *Wealth of Nations* [1776] 1976, p. 310). Intolerable insecurity may make many reluctant to put capital to work. It may also require a major change in relative prices to put unemployed capital back to work after a downturn. But oversaving in the sense of keeping capital assets unemployed when there are viable alternatives makes no sense.

Keynes, on the other hand, and therefore modern economic theory to the extent that it follows Keynes, thinks of saving in relation to money. Money left unspent is now described as saving, and it is this unspent money that is identified as the reason an economy struggles to recover and increase employment. Unspent money is not, however, unused resources. The process of recovery occurs where such assets are repriced in the market so that they can be bought or rented as part of the production process. The confusion of national saving with the mechanism of personal saving is a major debilitating flaw in modern economic theory.

Second, all production decisions are forward looking. The past is an indication of what might happen in the future, but is only one part of the full spectrum of circumstances that will determine the level of production and therefore the level of employment. Public spending does not raise the level of aggregate demand, but raises the demand for particular goods and services, in this case chosen by governments. Unless producers of the specific goods and services purchased expect a continuation into the future, there is no reason to expect that the particular firms that have had their sales increase will translate these purchases into an expectation of higher sales in the period ahead.

Third, output must be value adding to increase the total amount that is purchased across an economy. Spending that does not have a counterpart in an income that was earned in producing purchasable product ultimately falls short. That demand is constituted by supply is the classical definition associated with Say's Law. Demand can only be sustained by expenditures that are part of an actual exchange, however abstract and distant that exchange is from being visible to those who buy and sell. Demand that is manufactured out of deficit finance through printing money is no more sustainable than activity that is the result of the printing of counterfeit money. There are sales of actual goods and services, but somewhere in the economy there is a shortfall. Those who receive the money spent find they cannot buy as much as they expected they would with the funds they have received.

Fourth, the point that Mill was trying to make, although he does not put it this way, is that employment varies directly with the productivity of the economy and inversely with the real wage. This may be the core proposition of classical macroeconomics. The more capital there is – that is, the more productive assets there are – the higher the number of workers who can be employed at any given real wage. The more on average each worker absorbs out of available saving, the fewer workers that can and will be employed.

Indeed, the problem is worse, since the spending that has gone into projects of the government's choosing are notoriously non-value adding. They use up resources but do not replace what has been used up with output of equal or higher value. The economy ends up being able to produce even less at the going real wage, so that either the real wage or employment growth fall back, or both occur at the same time. It is like eating one's seed corn. To have transferred the underlying dynamic of an economy from the supply side to the demand side may be the most devastating consequence *The General Theory* may have produced.

The classical literature never tired of pointing out this fallacy, but did so under the phrase that there could never be overproduction. More produced than people will buy is formally identical to people will not buy everything that has been produced. There is too much output relative to the demand for that output, and not because of some difficulty in the adjustment process, but because they chose not to buy. Every generation since the Industrial Revolution has lived in more abundant times than their parents, and there have always been arguments that by having become so wealthy, there is no longer the willingness or the ability for the population to absorb everything produced. It is an absurd belief that has never been established at any time.

Every recession eventually ends and the willingness to purchase everything produced returns. The belief that unemployment is caused by an absence of aggregate demand that will persist through time unless steps are taken to raise demand levels ought to be seen in a world of scarcity as impossible from the word go. That such a view has since 1936 become the basis of macroeconomic theory and policy would defy belief were it not so unmistakeably the case.

THE ROLE OF THE ENTREPRENEUR

In a classical model, the role of the entrepreneur, often referred to using the less precise terminology of nineteenth-century English economic writing as the capitalist, was recognized as the driving force behind the direction an economy took. Whatever the particular question that might be asked of theory, it was always understood and explained that there was a guiding intelligence that was making the various decisions that were made inside a business. Economies were not automatically self-sustaining, and adjustment did not magically take place out of thin air. All changes that took place within an economy were seen to have been the result of human decision making based on the circumstances that then existed and the range of possibilities that were seen to be available. The ultimate decision maker within a business was the entrepreneur.

As with so much of modern economics, Keynesian theory, and therefore modern macroeconomics, dispenses with the entrepreneur in attempting to make sense of economic events. While there is discussion of uncertainty and expectations, these are not actually an intrinsic part of the analysis, since with everything looked at through an aggregated lens, individual decision making is almost entirely washed out of the system.

Instead, it is an aggregated level of demand that is said to affect an aggregated level of employment. There are no individual decision makers adjusting either production or their offers of employment based on new circumstances. Wage earners are trapped in some kind of 'sticky wage' environment, so that they, too, are unable to adjust to new circumstances. The framework emphasizes its rigidity.

A Keynesian framework is the polar opposite of the nature of recession within classical theory, being based, as it was, around entrepreneurial error. There was an actual human agency, with their scattered and multifaceted reactions to the circumstances of the world. In a Keynesian model, motivations are reduced to their minimum. Short-run sales revenue is the prime concern, and as far as policy is concerned, there is not much more to it than that.

Almost entirely eliminated are the calculating, planning, thinking individuals running their own firms, making decisions based on the world as they see it. Since it is largely entrepreneurial decision making that is the major cause of dislocation between the past and the future, the absence of an entrepreneurial force, both in understanding the downturn or the subsequent upturn, not to mention innovation, empties such models of virtually any real-world dynamic.

The notorious absence of microfoundations for Keynesian macro is frequently noted. It is a reflection of the absence of any genuine linkage between the macroeconomic sphere and the underlying activities of those who are trying to better themselves economically. There is no motivation seen to underpin macroeconomic activity.

Even worse, there are no individuals reacting to relative prices, or themselves adjusting the prices of the goods and services they sell to allow their unsold stocks to clear. And because there are no actual individual products, other than 'consumption' or 'investment', the relative adjustment of prices and production is ignored.

Thus, the one agent most capable of allowing an economy in recession to find its way back to prosperous times, the entrepreneur, is locked out of the analysis. It is instead a series of rigid forces, entirely made up of variables capable of being measured in some way, that take the place of entrepreneurial activity in such models.

Often the major role for the entrepreneur in modern theory is as an innovator, the person who introduces new technologies or new products into the market. And while this is an important role for the entrepreneur, it bypasses what is the most important role an entrepreneur has, which is the day-to-day operation of the business in keeping it afloat and seeking a profitable outcome while avoiding loss and keeping costs to a necessary minimum.

6. The classical theory of value and the marginal revolution

The first major radical shift away from classical economic theory occurred in the 1870s with the marginal revolution, which was largely founded on its challenge to the classical theory of value. As discussed briefly in the previous chapter, the ridicule that has been extended ever since by economists has never let up, with the following from the History of Economic Thought website being typical, repeated from the previous chapter:

> John Stuart Mill's greater economic performance was his magnificent 1848 *Principles of Political Economy*, a two-volume extended restatement of the Classical Ricardian theory. He believed Ricardo's labor theory of value to be so conclusive that, in the beginning of a discussion on the theory of value, Mill confidently notes that:
>
>> Happily, there is nothing in the laws of Value which remains for the present or any future writer to clear up; the theory of the subject is complete: the only difficulty to be overcome is that of so stating it as to solve by anticipation the chief perplexities which occur in applying it. (J.S. Mill, *Principles*, 1848: Book III, Ch. 1 [Ashley edition [1871] 1921, p. 436]).
>
> Thus putting a stone on the matter, and burying supply-and-demand theory for another quarter-century. When Jevons's [sic] later grumbled at the 'noxious influence of authority' preventing the development of economics, there is little doubt he was referring to J.S. Mill. (History of Economic Thought, 2019a).

It is undoubtedly making oneself hostage to fortune to argue about any theoretical statement that there is 'nothing … which remains for the present or any future writer to clear up' (cf. Newton on gravity). Nevertheless, it will be argued here that while there was much about the classical theory as outlined by Mill that required expansion and more detail, Mill's discussion more than holds its own against modern theory of value.

Two points might be noted before going into more detail. First, the theory presented by Mill was not based on the labour theory of value, although the cost of labour did matter. The same, of course, might be said about modern theory. That the cost of labour was the end all and be all of relative costs was the case with Adam Smith and David Ricardo, although not even entirely with them, and aside from within socialist literature, had all but disappeared by the 1840s. The labour theory of value was made the focus by the Austrian marginalists – Menger, Weber and Böhm-Bawerk in particular – because they were attempting to refute Marxist economics with its theory of surplus value that was utterly dependent, for what little coherence it had, on the labour theory of value (LTV). It may even have been integral to continental economic theory, but it was not the basis of the classical economics of J.S. Mill, nor of his mainstream contemporaries nor anyone thereafter among economists in the English-speaking world. It is a straw-man caricature not based on fact.

Second, of crucial importance is the notion of 'natural value', which Mill refers to as its 'permanent' value. It might even be thought of as the prices found in a Walrasian equilibrium. The actual prices, the 'temporary' prices found in the market, oscillate around a product's 'natural value', which is the relative price that would emerge if all of the vagaries of the market were finally to come to a halt and equilibrium should occur. It is the steady-state outcome, which was a possibility that Mill and many in his time thought would eventually occur at some point in the very long run. It is an eventuality that no one any longer thinks of as even remotely possible. Given the constant change in technology and the flood of innovation, it is a price that will never emerge in practice, although in Mill's time it did seem a realistic future possibility in perhaps a century or two.

With these considerations in mind, here are Mill's 17 elements in his theory of value as published in his *Principles*:

I.   Value is a relative term. The value of a thing means the quantity of some other thing, or of things in general, which it exchanges for. The values of all things can never, therefore, rise or fall simultaneously. There is no such thing as a general rise or a general fall of values. Every rise of value supposes a fall, and every fall a rise.

II.   The temporary or Market Value of a thing, depends on the demand and supply; rising as the demand rises, and falling as the supply rises. The demand, however, varies with the value, being generally greater when the thing is cheap than when it is dear; and the value always adjusts itself in such a manner, that the demand is equal to the supply.

III.   Besides their temporary value, things have also a permanent, or as it may be called, a Natural Value, to which the market value, after every variation, always tends to return; and the oscillations compensate for one another, so that, on the average, commodities exchange at about their natural value.

IV.   The natural value of some things is a scarcity value; but most things naturally exchange for one another in the ratio of their cost of production, or at what may be termed their Cost Value.

V.   The things which are naturally and permanently at a scarcity value are those of which the supply cannot be increased at all, or not sufficiently to satisfy the whole of the demand which would exist for them at their cost value.

VI.   A monopoly value means a scarcity value. Monopoly cannot give a value to anything except through a limitation of the supply.

VII.   Every commodity of which the supply can be indefinitely increased by labour and capital, exchanges for other things proportionally to the cost necessary for producing and bringing to market the most costly portion of the supply required. The natural value is synonymous with the Cost Value and the cost value of a thing, means the cost value of the most costly portion of it.

VIII.   Cost of Production consists of several elements, some of which are constant and universal, others occasional. The universal elements of cost of production are, the wages of the labour, and the profits of the capital. The occasional elements are taxes, and any extra cost occasioned by a scarcity value of some of the requisites.

IX.   Rent is not an element in the cost of production of the commodity which yields it; except in the cases (rather conceivable than actually existing) in which it results from, and represents, a scarcity value. But when land capable of yielding rent in agriculture is applied to some other purpose, the rent which it would have yielded is an element in the cost of production of the commodity which it is employed to produce.

X.   Omitting the occasional elements; things which admit of indefinite increase, naturally and permanently exchange for each other according to the comparative amount of wages which must be paid for producing them, and the comparative amount of profits which must be obtained by the capitalists who pay those wages.

XI.   The comparative amount of wages does not depend on what wages are in themselves. High wages do not make high values, nor low wages low values. The comparative amount of wages depends partly on the comparative quantities of labour required, and partly on the comparative rates of its remuneration.

XII.   So, the comparative rate of profits does not depend on what profits are in themselves; nor do high or low profits make high or low values. It depends partly on the comparative lengths of time during which the capital is employed, and partly on the comparative rate of profits in different employments.

XIII.   If two things are made by the same quantity of labour, and that labour paid at the same rate, and if the wages of the labourer have to be advanced for the same space of time, and the nature of the employment does not require that there be a permanent difference in their rate of profit; then, whether wages and profits be high or low, and whether the quantity of labour expended be much or little, these two things will, on the average, exchange for one another.

XIV.   If one of two things commands, on the average, a greater value than the other, the cause must be that it requires for its production either a greater quantity of labour, or a kind of labour permanently paid at a higher rate; or that the capital, or part of the capital, which supports that labour, must be advanced for a longer period; or lastly, that the production is attended with some circumstance which requires to be compensated by a permanently higher rate of profit.

XV.   Of these elements, the quantity of labour required for the production is the most important: the effect of the others is smaller, though none of them are insignificant.

XVI.   The lower profits are, the less important become the minor elements of cost

of production, and the less do commodities deviate from a value propor-
tioned to the quantity and quality of the labour required for their production.

XVII.   But every fall of profits lowers, in some degree, the cost value of things
made with much or durable machinery, and raises that of things made by
hand; and every rise of profits does the reverse. (Mill, *Principles* [1871]
1921, pp. 478–80)

Overall, the point is that the exchange value of goods and services, that is, their
relative price in relation to each other, is based on their relative production
costs tempered by how scarce each happens to be relative to the general desir-
ability of each of the products put on the market. It is supply and demand writ
large, but with the added complications on the supply side dependent on how
scarce a product can be made by restrictions of supply. Also affecting the relative price of any product is whether it is still being produced (think of antiques
or Old Masters) or whether there are particular difficulties on the supply side
that limit the potential volume of production relative to the demand.

A SIMPLIFIED LIST OF MILL'S THEORY OF VALUE

Here is Mill's list simplified, so that the 17 elements can be more easily read
and digested by a modern reader. All of it is perfectly acceptable to modern
theory. No additional words have been added, while some have been removed
to provide clarity to the points Mill had been attempting to make:

I.   Value is a relative term.
II.   The market value of a thing depends on demand and supply.
III.   Things have a natural value to which the market value, after every variation, always tends to return. On the average, commodities exchange at
about their natural value.
IV.   The natural value of some things is a scarcity value; but most things naturally exchange for one another in the ratio of their cost of production.
V.   The things which are naturally and permanently at a scarcity value are
those of which the supply cannot be increased at all, or not sufficiently
to satisfy the whole of the demand.
VI.   A monopoly value means a scarcity value. Monopoly cannot give
a value to anything except through a limitation of the supply.
VII.   Every commodity of which the supply can be indefinitely increased,
exchanges for other things proportionally to the cost necessary for
producing and bringing to market the most costly portion of the supply
required.
VIII.   The universal elements of cost of production are, the wages of the labour,
and the profits of the capital. The occasional elements are taxes, and any
extra cost occasioned by a scarcity value of some of the requisites.

IX.   When land capable of yielding rent in agriculture is applied to some other purpose, the rent which it would have yielded is an element in the cost of production of the commodity which it is employed to produce.

X.   Things which admit of indefinite increase, exchange for each other according to the comparative amount of wages which must be paid for producing them, and the comparative amount of profits which must be obtained by the capitalists who pay those wages.

XI.   High wages do not make high values, nor low wages low values. The comparative amount of wages depends partly on the comparative quantities of labour required, and partly on the comparative rates of its remuneration.

XII.   The comparative rate of profits depends partly on the comparative lengths of time during which the capital is employed, and partly on the comparative rate of profits in different employments.

XIII. If two things are made by the same quantity of labour, and that labour paid at the same rate, and if the wages of the labourer have to be advanced for the same space of time, and the nature of the employment does not require that there be a permanent difference in their rate of profit, these two things will, on the average, exchange for one another.

XIV.   If one of two things commands, on the average, a greater value than the other, the cause must be that it requires for its production either a greater quantity of labour, or a kind of labour permanently paid at a higher rate; or that the capital, or part of the capital, which supports that labour, must be advanced for a longer period; or lastly, that the production is attended with some circumstance which requires to be compensated by a permanently higher rate of profit.

XV.   The quantity of labour required for production is the most important: the effect of the others is smaller, though none of them are insignificant.

XVI.   The lower profits are, the less important become the minor elements of cost of production.

XVII. Every fall of profits lowers, in some degree, the cost value of things made with much or durable machinery, and raises that of things made by hand. Every rise of profits does the reverse.

What becomes clear is that the market is a massive entity in which prices are in constant motion in relation to each other. It makes the notion of a market price a much more significant matter in relation to the adjustment process. Indeed, Mill makes the adjustment process one of the core issues in understanding how a market economy functions. The one element that may not be immediately understood is the seventh:

> Every commodity of which the supply can be indefinitely increased, exchanges for other things proportionally to the cost necessary for producing and bringing to market the most costly portion of the supply required.

This is no more than pointing out that in supply and demand analysis, the equilibrium price is the price charged by the most expensive supplier of the good or service. This is seldom pointed out, although it is of interest since those suppliers who are able to provide these goods and services at a much lower production cost are earning large amounts of profit, since they would have supplied at lower prices, often much lower prices given the way upward sloping supply curves are typically drawn.

A FURTHER WORD ON NATURAL VALUE

That Mill's conceptions in regard to value retained their hold within economic theory even after the marginal revolution may be seen by an examination of Henry Clay's *Economics: An Introduction for the General Reader* that was published in 1916, an introductory text extensively discussed in Kates (2016a). Published though it was at the start of the twentieth century, Clay's *Economics* is a restatement of the economics of John Stuart Mill. It is now commonly assumed that Mill's influence had virtually disappeared by the end of the nineteenth century and it was the economics of Marshall, Jevons and the marginalists that had replaced Mill. Yet, not only does Mill have a live presence in the text, Clay explicitly embraces the area of Mill's economics that most economists today would have thought had by then been long transcended – his theory of value. The following passage is from Clay's 1942 second edition as an indication of Mill's enduring influence, which mirrors Clay's original 1916 text:

> There have been three theories of value of historical importance – the Labour Theory, the Cost of Production Theory, and the Marginal Utility Theory. The three theories have a common starting-point; they agree, to quote Mill, that 'the temporary or market value of a thing depends on the demand and supply; rising as the demand rises and falling as the supply rises.' But Mill goes on, 'besides their temporary value, things have also a permanent value, or, as it may be called, a Natural Value, to which the market value, after every variation, always tends to return; and the oscillations compensate for one another, so that, on the average, commodities exchange at about their natural value.' It is about this permanent, normal, or natural value that the theories differ. (Clay, 1942, p. 275)

Clay then provides a prolonged historical discussion of the three theories to show that both the demand side and the cost side are involved in the determination of value through the forces of supply and demand. But in reaching the end of this discussion some 33 pages later, Clay's summation is in terms of Mill's natural or normal price:

> The Long Term adjustment is the most important aspect of the so-called Law of Supply and Demand. So far as any price can be described as the Normal Price, it is the price which over a period of time brings into balance output and consumption and covers Total Cost – all the expenses of producing that amount. If society wants this amount, it must in the long run pay this price; if industry wants to sell this amount, it must produce at this price. (Clay, 1942, p. 308)

This is the concept of supply and demand embedded in a dynamic framework in which buyers and sellers continuously adjust what they do to accommodate each other. Clay, as with the classics generally, did not think of these prices as just so many units of currency for any single good or service looked at in isolation, as we tend to do in modern theory, but related the price of an individual product to the entire structure of supply for all goods and services, from which buyers decided which among those offered for sale they would choose to purchase.

A CRITIQUE OF THE MODERN THEORY OF PRICE DETERMINATION AND THE ACCOMPANYING DIAGRAMS

The first point to notice is that, unlike within modern microeconomic theory, the principal aim among classical economists was to determine the relative prices of goods and services, not the price of a single product in isolation. This was thought of as a relatively trivial issue since it was more or less stated by Mill in a throwaway opening sentence. A single price was determined according to the forces of supply and demand, whose outcome would be affected by all the usual issues, from scarcity, production costs through to the intensity of demand relative to supply. It was the circumstances prevailing in the market that mattered. One might therefore conclude that in principle there is little different between modern theory and its classical ancestor.

Modern theory has become somewhat static, formalized within its present array of diagrams purporting to show how prices are derived from within the Procrustean bed into which price theory has been placed. In many ways, the formalization within the framework of supply and demand curves for individual products has made theory less useful in analysing the way in which markets adjust. Price adjustments are not embedded within macroeconomic discussions and are seldom incorporated in understanding the processes of adjustment that allow an economy first to avoid recession and then, when in a recession, to allow recovery to occur.

Even in terms of microeconomic adjustment, the classical model focused on the elements that were the most important in shaping prices. In modern discussions, one begins with supply and demand curves that are presented as a concrete version of these underlying forces. One might ask what the effect of a shift of the demand curve to the left would be, as one might ask what would be the effect of a snowfall on the movement of traffic. To classical economists, the elements within these curves were elements creating pressures on the business in determining its price, but in no sense was there any suggestion that an entrepreneur had any genuine idea of where these curves were, whether or not they had moved or what price was the equilibrium price in the market or which was the optimal price it should sell the product at. All was trial and error, as businesses and individuals across the economy found their way forward.

Supply and demand analysis, and even more so the use of the conceptual tools surrounding marginal cost and marginal revenue, are examined and looked at as if there is enough information available for some sort of reasonably accurate estimate to be made of the real-world outcome when the economy is in motion. In reality, no one ever knows the shape or position of the demand curves they face for the products they sell. The information needed to calculate marginal revenue is therefore never available. The conceptual issue, that everyone attempts to work out what is best for themselves going forward and that is all that can be done, is what the classical analysis was designed to explain. The approach taken by modern theory presumes too much knowledge and precision.

The same kind of knowledge and precision is embodied in the notion of utility. It was, of course, assumed by classical economists that consumers bought what they bought because ownership of the products they had purchased would provide them with utility of some sort, and that the more they bought of particular items, the more they preferred the items they did buy to the ones they did not, and also in preference to the retention of the money they had spent. To have added the kinds of pseudo-mathematical precision to what were really abstract and extremely vague notions added nothing to the analysis. Indeed, such an analysis may instead have taken away something of value, an appreciation that all actions of both consumers and producers were attempts undertaken in the dark about the consequences for the future of the various decisions taken before the outcomes would be known.

Indeed, the introduction of mathematics into the presentation of economic theory, along with the introduction of various static diagrams, may have provided a false sense of precision to what really were intended to be no more than broad indications of how a market economy would unfold. What may have been especially unfortunate was the omission of the always-present possibility of errors in the decisions that were made. The very nature of classical theory was to underscore the possibility of error. The processes incorporated into the creation of value were intended to be seen as imprecise. The notion that a point of profit maximization could be identified on a diagram, and that this would provide any genuine insight into the operation of a dynamic economy, is a complete nonsense. It undermined the recognition of the uncertainty at the heart of economic decision making that ought instead to be at its very forefront. It may still be there technically but is never emphasized and often ignored entirely.

VALUE AND MONEY

Following the discussion on value, which is mostly a description of how prices are determined in the market, in the chapters that come next, Mill goes on to 'consider in what manner the principles of the mutual interchange of commodities are affected by the use of what is termed a Medium of Exchange' (Mill, *Principles* [1871] 1921, p. 483). The logical order among classical economists, so that the underlying issues could be properly understood, was to begin with the real issues before investigating how the existence of money complicates economic processes. Keynes reversed this, to such an extent that the real economy is almost entirely ignored in discussing macro issues, money being brought in right from the start. This is Keynes:

> The conviction, which runs, for example, through almost all Professor Pigou's work, that money makes no real difference except frictionally and that the theory of production and employment can be worked out (like Mill's) as being based on 'real' exchanges with money introduced perfunctorily in a later chapter, is the modern version of the classical tradition. … They have not drawn sufficiently far-reaching consequences; and have not revised their fundamental theory. In the first instance, these conclusions may have been applied to the kind of economy in which we actually live by false analogy from some kind of non-exchange Robinson Crusoe economy, in which the income which individuals consume or retain as a result of their productive activity is, actually and exclusively, the output *in specie* of that activity. (Keynes, *Collected Works* [1936] 1981, VII, p. 19)

Whether this was the lead that others then followed, the fact is that virtually the whole of macroeconomic theory commences from a discussion of money aggregates. Certainly, all the major diagrams in macro have adjustments occurring in relation to sums of money. In particular, when saving is discussed, the savings are conceived in terms of sums of money either spent or left unspent. The notion of saving as capital is almost never disaggregated into various physical items that can be applied to the production process. It is perhaps on occasion implied, but almost never stated as such. When saving is said to be equal to investment, it is money totals that are always meant, not the proportion of the economy's existing stock of capital assets that are used to produce new capital assets.

Mill, well before Mises, had entered into the socialist calculation debate, explains the role of money in allowing businesses to calculate production costs:

> In order to understand the manifold functions of a Circulating Medium, there is no better way than to consider what are the principal inconveniences which we should experience if we had not such a medium. The first and most obvious would be the want of a common measure for values of different sorts. ... As it is much easier to compare different lengths by expressing them in a common language of feet and inches, so it is much easier to compare values by means of a common language of pounds, shillings, and pence. In no other way can values be arranged one above another in a scale; in no other can a person conveniently calculate the sum of his possessions; and it is easier to ascertain and remember the relations of many things to one thing, than their innumerable cross relations with one another. This advantage of having a common language in which values may be expressed, is, even by itself, so important, that some such mode of expressing and computing them would probably be used even if a pound or a shilling did not express any real thing, but a mere unit of calculation. (Mill, *Principles* [1871] 1921, pp. 483–4)

Moving beyond this, Mill's discussion on the role of money in an economy is far more sophisticated than anything found in a modern text. This is from Mill's *Principles*, where he perfectly describes the operation of the quantity theory of money:

> If we assume the quantity of goods on sale, and the number of times those goods are resold, to be fixed quantities, the value of money will depend upon its quantity, together with the average number of times that each piece changes hands in the process. The whole of the goods sold (counting each resale of the same goods as so much added to the goods) have been exchanged for the whole of the money, multiplied by the number of purchases made on the average by each piece. Consequently, the amount of goods and of transactions being the same, the value of money is inversely as its quantity multiplied by what is called the rapidity of circulation. And the quantity of money in circulation [M] is equal to the money value of all the goods sold [PT], divided by the number which expresses the rapidity of circulation [V]. (Ibid., p. 494; letters in square brackets added)

Note that the money value of all goods sold is PT, with the T standing for transactions. This is the accurate rendering of the concept since the same item might be sold many times over. A sack of flour might find itself sold first to a distributor, and then to a retailer and then finally to a consumer. It is the number of transactions that matter, not the total level of output. The transactions also incorporate all the sales between input producers that occur well before, perhaps years before, some item is sold as a final good to a consumer.

Thereafter, we come to the quantity equation that is actually a quantity identity since it is true by definition. It is true only because it could not be anything else:

$$M \equiv PT/V$$

Or, in its more typical formulation:

$$MV \equiv PT$$

The number of times a unit of money is exchanged is equal to the total money value of all sales that take place inside an economy. Since there is no means to calculate T or the average price of all the items that are turned over in the market, PT is a number that can never be calculated.

Following that paragraph from *Principles* are a large number of additional considerations that help make sense of the point and also make it more comprehensible in relation to the operation of an economy. Moreover, whatever else Mill is or is not trying to do, what he is not trying to do is provide some means to regulate an economy by trying to adjust any of the four elements within the identity.

MONEY, CREDIT AND THE BUSINESS CYCLE

The truly phenomenal ignorance of modern economists of the classical theory of the cycle, and the mythology surrounding the Keynesian revolution that it was not until 1936 that a theory of recession and mass unemployment had even been brought into existence, ought to be seen as a scandal. A chemist will have a vivid concept not just of the modern theory of chemical reactions but also some sense of how chemistry had developed from the experimentations of the alchemists, through Lavoisier and Mendeleev and into modern times. An economist knows none of this, believing that, as far as the cycle goes, the theory began with Keynes, and as far as micro, it all started with the marginalists. There is perhaps a smattering of knowledge of Adam Smith and the 'invisible hand'. Beyond that, nothing.

With this in mind, let us turn to John Stuart Mill's theory of the cycle, which is embodied in his theory of money and credit found in Book III, Chapter XII of his *Principles*: 'Influence of Credit on Prices'. We start with the reasons for upwards and downwards shifts in the price level, and the argument will be carried forward with direct quotes from Mill, followed by a summary of each of Mill's statements.

This is how Mill begins his discussion on the relationship between money, credit and the business cycle:

> It is not with ultimate or average, but with immediate and temporary prices, that we are now concerned. These, as we have seen, may deviate very widely from the standard of cost of production. Among other causes of fluctuation, one we have found to be the quantity of money in circulation. (Mill, *Principles* [1871] 1921, p. 523)

There are other causes for changes in the price level, but Mill emphasizes that changes in the volume of money is one amongst these.

He then goes on to discuss other factors that affect prices. Gold was the basis for exchange when Mill wrote, so he treated bank notes as a separate category that in no way affected the argument:

> We have now found that there are other things, such as bank notes, bills of exchange, and cheques, which circulate as money, and perform all the functions of it: and the question arises, Do these various substitutes operate on prices in the same manner as money itself? (Ibid.)

Mill does not believe these affect prices. This is what he does believe, that it is the flow of credit that causes prices to fluctuate:

> I apprehend that bank notes, bills, or cheques, as such, do not act on prices at all. What does act on prices is Credit, in whatever shape given, and whether it gives rise to any transferable instruments capable of passing into circulation or not. (Ibid., p. 524)

Mill now discusses how the amount of money in circulation might be affected by what Keynes would later describe as the 'precautionary motive' or perhaps even the 'speculative motive'. In any case, he without question describes how individuals might hoard cash:

> Money acts upon prices in no other way than by being tendered in exchange for commodities. The demand which influences the prices of commodities consists of the money offered for them. But the money offered is not the same thing with the money possessed. It is sometimes less, sometimes very much more. In the long run indeed, the money which people lay out will be neither more nor less than the money which they have to lay out: but this is far from being the case at any given time. **Sometimes they keep money by them for fear of an emergency, or in expectation of a more advantageous opportunity for expending it**. In that case the money is said not to be in circulation: in plainer language, it is not offered, nor about to be offered, for commodities. Money not in circulation has no effect on prices. (Ibid., p. 524; bold emphasis added)

But what may happen instead, rather than there being a quiescent process whereby money in the form or currency backed by gold represents the totality of purchasing power, this is replaced by credit creation backed by nothing at all:

> In the case however of payment by cheques, the purchases are at any rate made, though not with money in the buyer's possession, yet with money to which he has a right. But he may make purchases with money which he only expects to have, or even only pretends to expect. He may obtain goods in return for his acceptances payable at a future time; or on his note of hand; or on a simple book credit, that is, on a mere promise to pay. All these purchases have exactly the same effect on price, as if they were made with ready money. (Ibid., p. 525)

There is therefore a much larger amount of purchasing power within the economy than the amount limited by the actual amount of money available. It is not always spent, but if the right sort of circumstances arise, it will be spent indeed, and often in a great flood. This flood of money demand has occurred without a single additional unit of currency having gone into circulation:

> Suppose that, in the expectation that some commodity will rise in price, he determines, not only to invest in it all his ready money, but to take up on credit, from the producers or importers, as much of it as their opinion of his resources will enable him to obtain. Every one must see that by thus acting he produces a greater effect on price, than if he limited his purchases to the money he has actually in hand. He creates a demand for the article to the full amount of his money **and credit taken together**, and raises the price proportionally to both. And this effect is produced, though none of the written instruments called substitutes for currency may be called into existence; though the transaction may give rise to no bill of exchange, **nor to the issue of a single bank note**. (Ibid., p. 525; bold emphasis added)

The increase in credit, combined with a speculative frenzy, drives others into the market to buy up in advance of the expectation of a future rise in demand:

> When people go into the market and purchase with money which they hope to receive hereafter, **they are drawing upon an unlimited, not a limited fund**. Speculation, thus supported, may be going on in any number of commodities, **without disturbing the regular course of business in others**. It might even be going on in all commodities at once. We could imagine that in **an epidemic fit of the passion of gambling**, all dealers, instead of giving only their accustomed orders to the manufacturers or growers of their commodity, commenced buying up all of it which they could procure, as far as their capital and credit would go. All prices would rise enormously, even if there were no increase of money, and no paper credit, but a mere extension of purchases on book credits. (Ibid., p. 527; bold emphasis added)

All this must come to a bad end.

COMMERCIAL CRISES

It is from these premises that Mill explains the coming of a commercial crisis. And while these events occurred well after Mill had been writing, he has described the events that led up to the Great Depression in 1929 and the Global Financial Crisis in 2007–08. Although the following was published as a single paragraph, to improve its clarity, the text is separated into its individual sentences:

This is the ideal extreme case of what is called a commercial crisis.
There is said to be a commercial crisis, when a great number of merchants and traders at once, either have, or apprehend that they shall have, a difficulty in meeting their engagements.
The most usual cause of this general embarrassment, is the recoil of prices after they have been raised by a spirit of speculation, intense in degree, and extending to many commodities.
Some accident which excites expectations of rising prices, such as the opening of a new foreign market, or simultaneous indications of a short supply of several great articles of commerce, sets speculation at work in several leading departments at once.
The prices rise, and the holders realize, or appear to have the power of realizing, great gains.
In certain states of the public mind, such examples of rapid increase of fortune call forth numerous imitators, and speculation not only goes much beyond what is justified by the original grounds for expecting rise of price, but extends itself to articles in which there never was any such ground: these, however, rise like the rest as soon as speculation sets in.
At periods of this kind a great extension of credit takes place.
Not only do all whom the contagion reaches employ their credit much more freely than usual; but they really have more credit, because they seem to be making unusual gains, and because a generally reckless and adventurous feeling prevails, which disposes people to give as well as take credit more largely than at other times, and give it to persons not entitled to it.
In this manner, in the celebrated speculative year 1825, and at various other periods during the present century, the prices of many of the principal articles of commerce rose greatly, without any fall in others, so that general prices might, without incorrectness, be said to have risen.
When, after such a rise, the reaction comes, and prices begin to fall, though at first perhaps only through the desire of the holders to realize, speculative purchases cease: but were this all, prices would only fall to the level from which they rose, or to that which is justified by the state of the consumption and of the supply.
They fall, however, much lower; for as, when prices were rising, and everybody apparently making a fortune, it was easy to obtain almost any amount of credit, so now, when everybody seems to be losing, and many fail entirely, it is with difficulty that firms of known solidity can obtain even the credit to which they are accustomed, and which it is the greatest inconvenience to them to be without; because all dealers have engagements to fulfil, and nobody feeling sure that the

portion of his means which he has entrusted to others will be available in time, no one likes to part with ready money, or to postpone his claim to it.
To these rational considerations there is superadded, in extreme cases, a panic as unreasoning as the previous overconfidence; money is borrowed for short periods at almost any rate of interest, and sales of goods for immediate payment are made at almost any sacrifice.

Thus general prices, during a commercial revulsion [recession], fall as much below the usual level as during the previous period of speculation they have risen above it: the fall, as well as the rise, originating not in anything affecting money, but in the state of credit; an unusually extended employment of credit during the earlier period, followed by a great diminution, never amounting, however, to an entire cessation of it, in the later. (Mill, *Principles* [1871] 1921, pp. 527–8; bold emphasis added)

These were, moreover, not just theoretical conclusions but were observations based on the contours of various recessions and depressions that had occurred during the nineteenth century. In the pages that followed the above depiction (ibid., pp. 528–9), Mill describes the causes of other actual recessions that had occurred in his own time that had been due to failures within the credit creation system. What ought to be clear is that Mill traverses through the nature of the real economy, then introduces money, then the credit creation system, and from these explains the causes of economic downturns that we have experienced ever since, and with almost the identical effects as occurred in both the Great Depression and the Global Financial Crisis.

NO SUCH THING AS A GENERAL GLUT

Mill goes even beyond that by specifically denying that demand deficiency can be the cause of an economic downturn. He, along with the entire classical school, thought overproduction as a cause of recession was absurd, and with Mill we are talking about the world of 1848. To believe in 1848, or in 1936, or at any time since, that an economy had reached the stage where it was able to produce so much that the population did not wish to purchase everything that could be produced, is as utterly absurd as it is unimaginable. No recession that has ever occurred can be attributed to such a cause. Here Mill disposes of the possibility, again with the text taken from his *Principles*:

Few persons would hesitate to say, that there would be great difficulty in finding remunerative employment every year for so much new capital and most would conclude that there would be what used to be termed a general glut; that commodities would be produced, and remain unsold, or be sold only at a loss. But the full examination which we have already given to this question,* has shown that this is not the mode in which the inconvenience would be experienced. The difficulty would not consist in any want of a market. If the new capital were duly shared among many varieties of employment, it would raise up a demand for its own produce, and there

> would be no cause why any part of that produce should remain longer on hand than formerly. (Mill, *Principles* [1871] 1921, p. 732; asterisk in the original)

This is Keynes's interpretation of Say's Law, that it forbade a general glut. And classical economists did indeed deny the possibility of a general glut but did not in any way whatsoever deny the possibility of recessions. They only denied that when such recessions occurred, it was not because the economy had produced so much that there was too little demand for what the economy could produce. The asterisk in the passage refers the reader to Book III, Chapter XIV, which is the chapter titled 'Of Supply', in which Mill refutes even the remotest possibility that an economy could go into recession because of a lack of demand, but in no way whatsoever denies the possibility of recession. Mill does, however, further discuss the nature of recessions and how they are misinterpreted as the result of a refusal to use available savings, therefore plunging an economy into recession. Mill acknowledges that such recessions are conceivable in theory, but virtually impossible as an actual outcome because of the nature of the commercial world, since there are always forces that will ensure that there are always potential investments that will absorb available savings. What are these forces that prevent demand deficiency from occurring? Mill again:

> What, then, are these counteracting circumstances, which, in the existing state of things, maintain a tolerably equal struggle against the downward tendency of profits, and prevent the great annual savings which take place in this country from depressing the rate of profit much nearer to that lowest point to which it is always tending, and which, left to itself, it would so promptly attain? The resisting agencies are of several kinds. (Ibid., p. 733)

The first of these is a discussion of the arguments of those who had argued that economies were in danger of falling into periods of insufficient demand. Sismondi and Chalmers had been the leading advocates of demand deficiency, along with Malthus, in Mill's time:

> First among them, we may notice one which is so simple and so conspicuous, that some political economists, especially M. de Sismondi and Dr. Chalmers, have attended to it almost to the exclusion of all others. This is, **the waste of capital** in periods of **over-trading** and rash speculation, and in the **commercial revulsions** by which such times are always followed. It is true that a great part of what is lost at such periods is not destroyed, but merely transferred, like a gambler's losses, to more successful speculators. ... Mines are opened, railways or bridges made, and many other works of uncertain profit commenced, and in these enterprises much capital is sunk which yields either no return, or none adequate to the outlay. Factories are built and machinery erected beyond what the market requires, or can keep in employment. Even if they are kept in employment, the capital is no less sunk; it has been converted from circulating into fixed capital, and has ceased to

have any influence on wages or profits. Besides this, **there is a great unproductive consumption of capital, during the stagnation which follows a period of general over-trading**. (Ibid., p. 733; bold emphasis added)

There is no doubt whatsoever that Mill is describing first the very existence and then the industrial consequences of recessions. And then Mill goes on to discuss the employment consequences that should put to rest any notion that Mill's observations of the effects of a cycle on employment were any different from anyone else's since that time, and that includes Keynes:

> Establishments are shut up, or kept working without any profit, hands are discharged, and numbers of persons in all ranks, being deprived of their income, and thrown for support on their savings, find themselves, after the crisis has passed away, in a condition of more or less impoverishment. Such are the effects of a commercial revulsion. (Ibid., p. 734)

To be in a state of 'impoverishment' is as dire a situation as can be imagined, and this was pre-welfare state during the nineteenth-century Industrial Revolution. This is the very essence of 'involuntary unemployment', define it how you might. Keynesian economics, and the Keynesian revolution, were built on the most obvious fabrication in the history of economic theory.

THE STATIONARY STATE

The conception that Mill had entertained, while he had been writing his *Principles* in the 1840s, was that there would come a time when at some point in the long run, but still at some point in the conceivable future, the economy would reach a steady-state equilibrium. Rather than this being thought of in negative terms, it was an end point of expansion when everything had gone about as far as it could go – the railroad and steamship technology, along with everything else had been brought to their peak of development and no further profitable returns were possible – so that everyone could continue to improve their lives but not through adding any further to their material comforts:

> It must always have been seen, more or less distinctly, by political economists, that **the increase of wealth is not boundless**: that at the end of what they term the progressive state lies the stationary state, that all progress in wealth is but a postponement of this, and that each step in advance is an approach to it. We have now been led to recognize that this ultimate goal is at all times near enough to be fully in view; that we are always on the verge of it, and that if we have not reached it long ago, it is because the goal itself flies before us. **The richest and most prosperous countries would very soon attain the stationary state, if no further improvements were made in the productive arts**, and if there were a suspension of the overflow of capital from those countries into the uncultivated or ill-cultivated regions of the earth. (Mill, *Principles* [1871] 1921, p. 746; bold emphasis added)

In this kind of world, but no other, there might be a curtailment of the demand for additional capital (i.e., savings) and labour. But while it was conceivable, it was a long way off in 1848, just as it is a long way off today, and will be applicable as far into the future as the eye can presently see. No matter when you read these words, it will be as true for you as it is for me. Whatever else, it was just as true when Keynes wrote as when Mill had written. This is the next reason Mill discusses in his explanation why demand deficiency cannot occur this side of the steady-state economy. I have removed all the exceptions to his straightforward comments while also leaving out the possible contrary tendencies that might occur where he explains how productivity-improving innovations will stand in the way of the emergence of a steady-state economy:

> This brings us to the second of the counter-agencies, namely, improvements in production. These evidently have the effect of extending ... the field of employment, that is, they enable a greater amount of capital to be accumulated and employed without depressing the rate of profit. ... All inventions which cheapen any of the things consumed by the labourers ... in time lower money wages: and by doing so, enable a greater capital to be accumulated and employed. (Ibid., p. 736)

The fantastic explosion of innovation and capital accumulation that have occurred since 1848 were unimaginable in Mill's time. The notion that an economic downturn due to a period of demand deficiency or secular stagnation has ever occurred since Mill's time, or at any time in history, is nonsensical. Every downturn has had a proximate cause that was the actual cause of the events of the time. Recessions do seem tragically long when an economy is in the midst of a period of high unemployment and slower than usual growth. But even the Great Depression lasted only four years and the Global Financial Crisis – at least the crisis phase – lasted a year at most. The reality is that no economy has ever found itself in a position where the bulk of its stock of capital assets could find no productive uses. It is always the case that some forms of capital become redundant because innovation, or overcapitalization of particular industries, have left these without commercial value – any antique shop is filled with such items from past eras. No period in history has found itself in a situation where there would have been no further capital accumulation that would not have had others willing to absorb whatever additional goods and services this additional capital would have been capable of producing.

7. Keynesian theory overruns the classics

The phenomenal and rapid success of the Keynesian revolution is unprecedented within economics, and probably across the whole of the social sciences. *The General Theory* was published in 1936 and within a decade and a half had conquered virtually the whole of economic theory. By the start of the 1950s, to be an economist meant one was a Keynesian. The example set by Haberler's *Prosperity and Depression* makes the entire transformation completely plain.

Haberler had published the first edition in 1937, which attempted, in the first half of the book, to outline all theories of the business cycle that were then in existence, and in the second half to provide a synthesis of his own. Yet, within two years, he was forced to publish a revised edition with an entirely new Chapter 8 that covered 'new theories of the cycle', which was entirely about the innovations in economic theory that had been introduced by Keynes. And then, just two years after that, in 1941, a third edition was published that had an entirely new third section of the book appended to the previous two sections, 113 pages in length, and this, too, was entirely devoted to a further discussion of the changes wrought by *The General Theory*. No one was any longer interested in the classical theory of the cycle to the extent they even knew what it was. The only interest, especially among those just entering the profession, was in the arguments that had been developed by Keynes.

It is, by now, impossible to appreciate how rapidly the change occurred, nor is it entirely possible to capture the reasons for the transformation. Yet, there are a number of particular publications by others that helped accelerate the change in direction. This note from the History of Economic Thought website provides some sense of the divide that occurred at the time, especially between younger economists and the older generation, as well as noting the powerful influence that Keynes's own students had on the debate:

> The response to the publication of John Maynard Keynes's *General Theory of Employment, Interest and Money* (1936) was immediate and controversial – and a cleavage between young economists and their older counterparts was immediately carved.
>
> From Cambridge, Keynes's students rushed to publication to further explain his ideas: Joan Robinson (1937) and James E. Meade (1936, 1937), two of the members of Keynes's 'Circus', produced particularly able 'restatements' of the General Theory. The exposition of a third member of the Circus, Austin Robinson (1936,

The Economist), reached a wider audience. Two of Keynes's tutorial students also rushed to publish reviews: W.B. Reddaway (1936, *Economic Record*) and D.G. Champernowne (1936, RES), with the latter being slightly more critical.

However, among the Cambridge professors, the consequences were grievously divisive (for an account, see Kahn, 1984; Skidelsky, 1992). J.M. Keynes almost completely ruptured his relationships with his old Cantabrigian colleagues – Arthur C. Pigou, Hubert D. Henderson, Dennis H. Robertson and Ralph G. Hawtrey. Although the strife was confined largely to personal exchanges within the Cambridge halls, some anger found its way into the printing presses. A.C. Pigou (1936, *Economica*), portrayed as the 'villain' by the General Theory, tried to go immediately on the counterattack but his counterblast was feeble. H.D. Henderson (1936, *Spectator*) fired off an even more personally vindictive fusillade. In contrast, Dennis Robertson's (1936, *QJE*) reply had a bit more of substance and engendered a short journal debate with Keynes.

The generational differences in reception were also evident outside of Cambridge. Elsewhere in Britain, the youthful Abba Lerner (1936, *Int Lab Rev*), John Hicks (1936, *EJ*) and Roy Harrod (1937, *Econometrica*) produced quite sympathetic reviews.

Surprisingly, neither of Keynes's old rivals at the London School of Economics, Friedrich A. von Hayek and Lionel Robbins, reviewed or even responded to Keynes's new book. But the damage was permanent: the enthusiasm for the *General Theory* by their most promising students – particularly Lerner, Hicks and, eventually, Kaldor – was the beginning of the end of the L.S.E.'s attempt to steal the crown of English economics from Cambridge.

From America, the initial response was cold: the main reviews by Jacob Viner (1936, *QJE*), Alvin Hansen (1936, *JPE*), Joseph Schumpeter (1936, *JASA*), Frank Taussig (1936, *QJE*), Wassily Leontief (1936, *QJE*), C.O. Hardy (1936, *AER*) and Frank Knight (1937, *Canadian JE*) were almost uniformly negative. Of all his reviewers, Keynes only deigned to respond to Viner's in his now-famous article, 'The General Theory of Employment' (Keynes, 1937, *QJE*).

With the unfortunate exception of Nazi Germany (where a translation was published 'on paper rather better than usual and the price not much higher than usual', as Keynes put it), Keynes's *General Theory* was largely ignored on the European continent. The few reviews that emerged from there, particularly those by Gustav Cassel (1937, *Int Lab Rev*) from Sweden and Gottfried Haberler (1936, *ZfN*) from Austria, were quite hostile. In France, the professional (and personal) hostility of influential conservative economists such as Jacques Rueff guaranteed that the book would not even be translated until 1948. (History of Economic Thought, 2019b; citations not referenced in the Bibliography)

Let us then look more closely at a few of the staging posts along the road to the establishment of Keynesian theory within the economics community. The period covered will begin with the publication of the first of the summary statements made of *The General Theory* published in 1937 and end at the start of the 1950s with Alvin Hansen's *Guide to Keynes* and T.W. Hutchison's *A Review of Economic Doctrines 1870-1929*, which were both published in 1953. By this latter date there is virtually nothing published critical of Keynesian theory and whatever there might have been had no impact on the economics profession.

J.R. HICKS: 'MR KEYNES AND THE "CLASSICS"' (1937)

Among the most important publications instrumental in establishing Keynesian theory was J.R. Hicks's, 'Mr. Keynes and the "Classics": A Suggested Interpretation' (1937). Its opening paragraphs help explain much of what took place on the publication of *The General Theory*. Some passages have been emphasized with bold type, whose significance will be discussed below:

> It will be admitted by the least charitable reader that the entertainment value of Mr. Keynes' *General Theory of Employment* is considerably enhanced by its satiric aspect. But it is also clear that many readers have been left very bewildered by this Dunciad. Even if they are convinced by Mr. Keynes' arguments and humbly acknowledge themselves to have been 'classical economists' in the past, **they find it hard to remember that they believed in their unregenerate days the things Mr. Keynes says they believed**. And there are no doubt others who find their historic doubts a stumbling block, which prevents them from getting as much illumination from the positive theory as they might otherwise have got.
>
> One of the main reasons for this situation is undoubtedly to be found in the fact that Mr. Keynes takes as typical of 'Classical economics' the later writings of Professor Pigou, particularly *The Theory of Unemployment*. Now *The Theory of Unemployment* is a fairly new book, and an exceedingly difficult book; so that it is safe to say that it has not yet made much impression on the ordinary teaching of economics. To most people its doctrines seem quite as strange and novel as the doctrines of Mr. Keynes himself; so that to be told that he has believed these things himself leaves the ordinary economist quite bewildered.
>
> For example, **Professor Pigou's theory runs, to a quite amazing extent, in real terms**. Not only is his theory a theory of real wages and unemployment; but numbers of problems which anyone else would have preferred to investigate in money terms are investigated by Professor Pigou in terms of 'wage-goods.' The ordinary classical economist has no part in this tour de force.
>
> But if, **on behalf of the ordinary classical economist, we declare that he would have preferred to investigate many of those problems in money terms**, Mr. Keynes will reply that there is no classical theory of money wages and employment. **It is quite true that such a theory cannot easily be found in the textbooks**: But this is only because most of the textbooks were written at a time when general changes in money wages in a closed system did not present an important problem. There can be little doubt that **most economists have thought that they had a pretty fair idea of what the relation between money wages and employment actually was**.
>
> In these circumstances, **it seems worth while to try to construct a typical 'classical' theory**, built on an earlier and cruder model than Professor Pigou's. If we can construct such a theory, and show that it does give results which have in fact been commonly taken for granted, but which do not agree with Mr. Keynes' conclusions, then we shall at last have a satisfactory basis of comparison. We may hope to be

able to isolate Mr. Keynes' innovations, and so to discover what are the real issues in dispute.

Since our purpose is comparison, **I shall try to set out my typical classical theory in a form similar to that in which Mr. Keynes sets out his own theory**; and I shall leave out of account all secondary complications which do not bear closely upon this special question in hand. Thus I assume that I am dealing with a short period in which the quantity of physical equipment of all kinds available can be taken as fixed. I assume homogeneous labour. I assume further that depreciation can be neglected, so that the output of investment goods corresponds to new investment. This is a dangerous simplification, but the important issues raised by Mr. Keynes in his chapter on user cost are irrelevant for our purposes. (Hicks, 1937, pp. 147–8; bold emphasis added)

The General Theory is a massive sprawl of a book. Few would have read it at the time with any deep confidence in having seen the crucial points Keynes was attempting to make. Many would have found the book impossible to fathom without assistance. Possibly of more significance was that those who did attempt to read the book found it, as Hicks stated, 'hard to remember that they believed in their unregenerate days the things Mr. Keynes says they believed'. What precisely was it that Keynes said that was different, and what was that classical economics that apparently surrounded them in everything they read? This is where Hicks's article was so pivotal. Not only would it seem to unravel what Keynes had said, but it would also lay out clearly what classical economists had supposedly said. As Hicks wrote, 'it seems worth while to try to construct a typical "classical" theory', which is what posterity has accepted he had done. That what Hicks constructed in no way overlapped with the actual theory of the cycle or the theory of employment that then existed at the time made no difference to the gratitude of those many who were at last able to understand something.

Hicks then added that, 'I shall try to set out my typical classical theory in a form similar to that in which Mr. Keynes sets out his own theory'. The theory that Hicks therefore constructed was not based on the prevailing economic theory of the time, but attempted to replicate the straw-man caricature that Keynes had constructed to knock over.

Nor could one assume that Hicks had much understanding about the nature of classical theory. Moreover, like Keynes, he dealt with a theory of employment rather than classical economics in total. He wrote:

Professor Pigou's theory [of unemployment] runs, to a quite amazing extent, in real terms. Not only is his theory a theory of real wages and unemployment; but numbers of problems which anyone else would have preferred to investigate in money terms are investigated by Professor Pigou in terms of 'wage-goods.' The ordinary classical economist has no part in this tour de force.

The classical theory of employment was constructed in real terms. Even today, the effect of wages on employment would almost invariably be constructed in real terms. There would have been nothing peculiar in Pigou having used real wages as a determinant of the level of employment either then or now. The issue of the time was framed by the falling price level that prevailed during the Great Depression that made lowering real wages without lowering money wages impossible. That Hicks framed classical theory in money terms was therefore noteworthy in two respects. First, Hicks's own first book-length publication was his *Theory of Wages*, published in 1932. Can one infer that at the time he saw it as a conceptual error to relate employment to real wages? Did this allow him to accept Keynes's point that it was an error to begin an investigation looking at the underlying real situation and then bring money in later on? Whatever the reason, Hicks took Keynes's side in this crucial issue. More to the point, Hicks did not understand the classical approach, which was the approach that had been taken by Pigou, only three years before in his text on the *Theory of Unemployment* (1932). There is no point in trying to work out why Hicks believed that an investigation in money terms without reference to the real wage would be superior, but there is no question that he did. He was therefore instrumental, perhaps inadvertently, in shifting the analytical frame of reference from the real side of the economy to the monetary.

Yet, of all the clouding of the issues between classical and Keynesian, nothing Hicks had done in creating his 'IS–LL' apparatus (see below) may have been more significant than the transfer of the focus of attention from the supply side of the economy to the demand side, and away from the factors of production in creating conditions for growth and towards an abstract analytical framework in which the entrepreneur disappears.

HICKS'S DEMAND-SIDE ANALYTICAL FRAMEWORK

The most significant effect of Hicks's article was to crystallize the meaning of both Keynesian economics and classical within a single diagram (Figure 7.1), now universally taught to economists and referred to as IS–LM curves, and often as just IS–LM. The diagram shows the presentation in Hicks's article, with IS referred to as *IS* while the LM curve is merely *LL*. What the curves show is the equilibrium point between the real economy, represented by the *IS* curve (investment/saving), and the money economy, represented by the *LL* curve (*L* for liquidity). The *i* on the vertical axis represents the rate of interest and the *I* on the horizontal axis represents income (which is now represented by the letter *Y*).

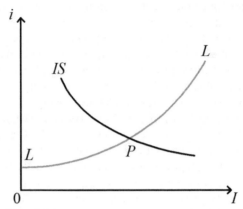

Source: Based on Hicks (1937).

Figure 7.1   *Hicks's Figure 1: The point of real and monetary equilibrium*

Hicks notes, with great accuracy, what has seldom since then been recognized:

> Income and the rate of interest are now determined together at *P*, the point of intersection of the curves *LL* and *IS*. They are determined together; just as price and output are determined together in the modern theory of demand and supply. Indeed, **Mr. Keynes' innovation is closely parallel, in this respect, to the innovation of the marginalists.** (Ibid., p. 153; bold emphasis added)

The marginalists had also shifted the focus of their analysis to the demand side via marginal utility and, as here, had assumed the supply side of the economy would conform to the wishes and expenditure patterns of those who buy without any in-depth investigation of the processes through which this might happen. And while diagrams played a large part in simplifying the arguments and helped transform economic theory away from the verbal and philosophical approach that had predominated until then, it was the mathematical treatment that was also crucial in shifting the nature of economic debate.

JOAN ROBINSON: *THEORY OF EMPLOYMENT* (1937)

Joan Robinson, as close an associate of Keynes as it is possible to find, published two books in 1937 to spread the Keynesian message: *Introduction to the Theory of Employment* (1937a) and *Essays in the Theory of Employment* (1937b). Both pursue the same message. The discussion here will follow the first of these two volumes in looking at Robinson's discussion. She sets out her intentions in the first paragraph of her Foreword:

> The purpose of this book is to provide a simplified account of the main principles of the Theory of Employment for students who find that they require some help in assimilating Mr. Keynes *General Theory of Employment, Interest and Money*, and the literature which is growing around it. (Robinson, 1937a, p. v)

And from the first sentence of the Introduction, she goes on the offensive against the received theory of her time:

> The modern economic system fails to produce employment continuously for all who desire to work. (Ibid., p. 1)

She then adds:

> This volume is intended to guide the reader towards an understanding of the problem, but not to tell him what ought to be done. (Ibid.)

Except that the very next section, still on the first page, is headed 'Deficiency of Demand' from which begins an entirely Keynesian explanation of the reason unemployment is so high. The villain is saving, not as the stock of resources available for productive investment, but as the sum of money available because income earners chose not to spend:

> The desire to save does not promote investment. … One man's expenditure is other men's income, and when one man spends less, other men earn less. As incomes fall the amount that individuals want to save is cut down, and income for the community as a whole is reduced to the level at which the actual rate of saving is no greater than the rate of investment. … If the desire of individuals to save increases, but the desire of entrepreneurs to create new capital goods does not increase, then no increase in the rate of aggregate saving can take place and the impulse to save runs to waste. (Ibid., pp. 10–11)

Following this, the argument moves in a more resolutely Keynesian direction. Chapter III deals with 'The Multiplier'. And while she begins the discussion looking at the employment multiplier, how two additional employees in the consumption goods industry will perhaps lead to an additional employee in the capital goods industry (ibid., p. 16), the remainder deals with the multiplier as it has passed down into the modern text. Her conclusion:

> However willing or reluctant the community may be to save, the rate of saving is always equal to the rate of investment. (Ibid., p. 19)

Finally, Robinson looks at monetary policy in the context of a secular stagnation in which the avenues for new investment have dried up:

> Since the increase in population is rapidly approaching its end in the western world, no fresh continents remain to be discovered, and a new age of invention comparable with the nineteenth century is scarcely to be hoped for, **it appears that in the near future powerful stimulants will have to be applied to the economic system if chronic unemployment is to be avoided**. (Ibid., p. 98; bold emphasis added)

Not right then, of course, will the economy need such stimulants but 'in the near future', since Britain had already reached full employment, even before *The General Theory* had been published in 1936, and through using classical policies. Yet, one of the lasting legacies has been the theory of demand deficiency instigated by that relatively brief period of high unemployment in the early 1930s.

GOTTFRIED VON HABERLER: *PROSPERITY AND DEPRESSION: A THEORETICAL ANALYSIS OF CYCLICAL MOVEMENTS* (1937, 1939, 1941)

The League of Nations in September 1930 'decided that an attempt should be made to co-ordinate the analytical work then being done on the problem of the recurrence of periods of economic depression' (Haberler, 1937, p. iii). It was intended to be what *The General Theory* became, the central text in business cycle research. Its structure was to summarize all then-existing theories of the cycle in Section I and then provide a synthesis of the existing theory of the cycle in Section II. The book was eventually published seven years after having been originally commissioned. Even then, its release had been postponed for a year while Haberler, the economist who had been selected to write the book, took an additional period of time to assimilate the lessons of *The General Theory*. In the first edition, Haberler had argued that Keynes had said nothing particularly new or novel. That he saw little that was original was, to an important extent, also because he actually had made some adjustments to his arguments to incorporate Keynes's views (see Kates, 1998, pp. 128–9). However, the changes he made did not prove to be enough. Although Keynes was cited 22 times, there were no extended passages in the text discussing the then single most important addition to the theory of the cycle – Keynesian theory. This was certainly changed in the editions that followed. The fact was, virtually no one any longer had much interest in the pre-Keynesian theory of the cycle.

A second edition was therefore published in 1939 that contained an entirely new Chapter 8, with the title, 'New Theories of the Cycle'. The new theories were entirely those that had been brought forth by Keynes. Even the inclusion of an entirely new chapter was insufficient, so, in 1941, a third edition was published that contained an entirely new Section III, also entirely devoted to Keynesian theory. The result was that Haberler, in a sense merely responding to the market, spread the Keynesian message across the world, not only ensuring it would be read and absorbed, but also providing Keynesian theory with the imprimatur of the League of Nations. As much as Haberler would deny in later years that there had been much of value in what Keynes had written, it was nevertheless Haberler's own publication that did much, via the League of Nations, to spread Keynesian ideas across the world.

JOAN ROBINSON (AGAIN): *AN ESSAY ON MARXIAN ECONOMICS* (1942)

An important additional consideration that allowed *The General Theory* easy passage into the mainstream was that rather than his theoretical approach being opposed by the left as just another defence of the capitalist system, Keynes actually, and almost entirely by accident, put together a critique of what was then 'modern' theory in a way that largely paralleled Marxist economics. Neither Keynes nor Robinson were Marxists, it is important to emphasize, but the structure of Keynesian theory in many ways mirrored the approach taken by Marxists, as Robinson discussed in her book.

It is also interesting that Robinson, unlike many who did follow Marx, did not think of Marx as having himself opposed Say's Law. She writes:

> The confusion between this long-run cycle, which might be found in a world subject to Say's Law, and the short-run cycle of effective demand, accounts for the ambiguity of Marx's attitude to the problems of under-consumption. Part of the time he is accepting Say's Law and part rejecting it. Push in the Say's Law stop, and effective demand is dominant – the poverty of the workers is then seen to be the last cause of all real crises. Does it follow that a crisis would be relieved by increasing the consuming power of the workers? Pull out the Say's Law stop, and the answer is no. With a given total output, increased real wages meant lower profits, and lower profits – push back the stop again – mean crisis. (Robinson, [1942] 1966, p. 86)

Where the overlap does occur is fully articulated in Chapter VIII: 'The General Theory of Employment'. This is the barrow she wishes to push:

> Mr. Keynes, in his *General Theory of Employment, Interest and Money*, challenged the view, taken completely for granted in the orthodox scheme, that saving promotes accumulation of capital. (Ibid., p. 65)

She then amplifies the point by showing an overlap with Marxian theory:

> The long-period extension of Mr. Keynes's theory brings the problem of the reserve army of labour into the foreground of the picture. The propensity to save and the rate of investment determine the level of real output, at any moment. As time goes by, the productivity of labour increases and the amount of employment corresponding to a given level of output declines. Thus the technique of production plays an important part in determining the level of employment.
>
> Finally, Mr. Keynes justifies Marx's intuition that the chronic conflict between productive and consumptive power is the root cause of crises. The maldistribution of income restricts consumption, and so increases the rate of investment required to maintain prosperity, while at the same time it narrows the field of profitable investment, by restricting the demand for the consumption goods which capital can produce. …
>
> The maldistribution of income is quite as deeply imbedded in the capitalist system as Marx believed the tendency to falling profits to be, and cannot be eliminated without drastic changes in the system. (Ibid., pp. 71–2)

To which she immediately adds this, which would have attracted a Marxist sympathizer:

> The case for revolution, as opposed to reform, might have been argued just as well on the basis of the analysis in Volume II of *Capital* as on the basis for Volume III. (Ibid., p. 72)

The following, too, would have attracted a Marxist – a summing up that was the last paragraph of the book:

> Marx, however imperfectly he worked out the details, set himself the task of discovering the law of motion of capitalism, and if there is any hope of progress in economics at all, it must be in using academic methods to solve the problems posed by Marx. (Ibid., p. 95)

Nothing written by a non-Marxist would have bridged the ideological gap between the mainstream and Marxist theory, but would have helped attract some into the mainstream who might otherwise have looked for more radical alternatives. It would also have allowed a Marxist to speak and write positively about Keynesian theory since it did seem to close the gap between the two schools of thought. This overlap will be discussed further below when we look at the views of Paul Sweezy, who was a more orthodox scholar of the Marxist left.

WILLIAM BEVERIDGE: *FULL EMPLOYMENT IN A FREE SOCIETY* (1944)

In 1942, William Beveridge had conducted a British government report into which extensions of the welfare state might be introduced. In 1944, he published his *Full Employment in a Free Society*, what might have looked like a government report given its style and layout but was published on his own account and as a private citizen. It was nevertheless influential in carrying the Keynesian message into post-war policy settings after 1945. The message was spelled out in a number of places, but the following passage is representative of the entire text:

> Employment depends on spending, which is of two kinds – for consumption and for investment; what people spend on consumption gives employment. What they save, i.e. do not spend on consumption, gives employment only if it is invested, which means not the buying of bonds or shares but expenditure in adding to capital equipment, such as factories, machinery, or ships, or in increasing stocks of raw material. There is not in an unplanned market economy anything that automatically keeps the total of spending of both kinds at the point of full employment, that is to say, high enough to employ all available labour. Adequate total demand for labour in an unplanned market economy cannot be taken for granted. (Beveridge, 1944, pp. 93–4)

This was the essence of the Keynesian message. Trite and banal if said today, but then represented the shift in analysis and policy that had captured both the economic and political establishment in the UK. He was himself an economist, a senior public servant and even briefly a Member of Parliament, and in these three roles he helped solidify Keynes's theoretical conclusions both in terms of economic theory and the policy that would emerge as a result.

PAUL SWEEZY: A TEN-YEARS-AFTER REVIEW OF *THE GENERAL THEORY* (1946)

Paul Sweezy's discussion of *The General Theory* has a special place in the literature, given his Marxist perspective. And what is notable is that he could recognize on behalf of a mainstream audience that Keynes had, almost certainly by accident, come to the same conclusion about bourgeois economics as had Marx, that recessions were frequent and their cause was a deficiency of demand. This is from the article he wrote on Keynes's death in 1946:

> Keynes' *magnum opus*, called *The General Theory of Employment, Interest, and Money* (1936) opens with an attack on what he calls orthodox economics – neo-classical economics, in the terminology of this article – and sustains it almost continuously to the end. The gist of this Keynesian criticism can be summed up

simply as a flat rejection and denial of what has come to be known as Say's Law of Markets* which, despite all assertions to the contrary by orthodox apologists, did run like a red thread through the entire body of classical and neo-classical theory. It is almost impossible to exaggerate either the hold which Say's Law exercised on professional economists or its importance as an obstacle to realistic analysis. The Keynesian attacks, though they appear to be directed against a variety of specific theories, all fall to the ground if the validity of Say's Law is assumed. (Sweezy, [1946] 1964, pp. 400–401; asterisk in the original)

The asterisk in the above passage directs the reader to the following footnote, which exactly restates Keynes's conclusion:

Say's Law in effect denies that there can ever be a shortage of demand in relation to production. Ricardo expressed it as follows: 'No man produces but with a view to consume or sell, and he never sells but with an intention to purchase some other commodity which may be useful to him, or which may contribute to future production. By producing then, he necessarily becomes either the consumer of his own goods, or the purchaser and consumer of the goods of some other person. … Productions are always bought by productions, or by services; money is only the medium by which the exchange is effected.' *Principles of Political Economy* (Gonner ed.), p. 273 and 275. (Ibid., p. 401)

And he makes no effort to hide his own Marxist approach. Referring to Keynes, he wrote:

He was apparently quite ignorant of the fact that there was a serious body of economic thought, as closely related to the classical school as the doctrines on which he himself was brought up. … In Keynes' eyes, Marx inhabited a theoretical underworld along with such dubious characters as Silvio Gesell and Major Douglas; and there is no evidence that he ever thought of any of Marx's followers as anything but propagandists and agitators. (Sweezy, [1946] 1964, p. 403)

Sweezy emphasized that Marx had 'rejected Say's Law from the outset' (ibid., p. 403). None of this is to suggest that Keynes was following Marx's lead or that he was a Marxist. The significance here is that in this one rare instance, mainstream economic theory was brought into alignment with the Marxist tradition over the issue of Say's Law and the theory of overproduction. Moreover, he further links these two previously independent traditions through a discussion of Joan Robinson's publication on Marx. Sweezy sees in *The General Theory* the possibility that there may yet be progress in changing the structure of social relations in the right direction, that is, in a Marxist direction:

Perhaps the clearest indication that this is so is to be found in Joan Robinson's little book *An Essay on Marxian Economics* published in England early in the war. Mrs. Robinson, a member of the inner Keynesian circle, is one of perhaps half a dozen top-flight British economic theorists. Marxists will not be able to agree with everything she says, but they will find in her a sympathetic critic ready and anxious to discuss problems with them in a sober and scientific spirit. Can it be pure accident that one of the most prominent followers of Keynes should be the author of the first honest work on Marxism ever to be written by a non-Marxist British economist? (Ibid., p. 405)

One cannot go much further than this. Robinson was not a Marxist nor was Keynes. The important point here was that in attacking Say's Law as he did, Keynes drew a sympathetic response from the political and economic left, which helped overcome whatever resistance there might have been among the mainstream. Sweezy's article would reach an even larger audience when it was reprinted the next year as part of Seymour Harris's, *The New Economics: Keynes's Influence on Theory and Public Policy* (1947).

One additional point might be noted that would have been more readily recognized by a scholar of nineteenth-century economic theory, which Sweezy's in-depth study of Marx would have meant he was. It allowed Sweezy to distinguish the economics of John Stuart Mill from the economics of Alfred Marshall, emphasizing how far apart they were:

Keynes himself used the term 'classical economists' to include the subjective value theorists – especially Marshall and his followers in the Cambridge group – of the late nineteenth and twentieth centuries. For reasons which should be clarified by the subsequent discussion, this practice seems to me to be misleading. It is preferable to regard John Stuart Mill as the last of the classical economists and to label the Marshallians the 'neo-classical' school. (Ibid., p. 398)

Although Marshall made immense efforts to show that his approach to economics was in a direct line of descent from Mill's, they are nevertheless very different, which Sweezy was absolutely right to argue. Mill was also not the last classical economist, but the rise of the marginalists with their demand-side microeconomic orientation limited the influence of the classical approach, which nevertheless held on within the theory of the cycle until the publication of *The General Theory*.

LORIE TARSHIS: *THE ELEMENTS OF ECONOMICS* (1947)

The first introductory economics text based on Keynesian theory was written by Lorie Tarshis, one of Keynes's students at Cambridge during the years *The General Theory* was being put together. Indeed, Tarshis's own notes are melded into Thomas Ryme's *Keynes's Lectures, 1932-35: Notes of a Representative Student* (Ryme, 1990). Before discussing the text itself, it is worth mentioning the controversy that arose in the United States on the publication of Tarshis's book. This is how it is briefly discussed in Tarshis's Wikipedia entry:

> Arthur M. Schlesinger, Jr. describes the attack on Tarshis [following the publication of his text]:
>
> > In August 1947, on the letterhead of an organization calling itself the National Economic Council, Inc., a man named Merwin K. Hart wrote to every member of the boards of trustees of colleges using *Elements of Economics*, an economic text written by Professor Lorie Tarshis of Stanford University. An enclosed review denounced the book for its exposition of the doctrines of Lord Keynes and identified Keynesianism as a form of Marxism. (Wikipedia, 2019c)

A more comprehensive discussion is found in a paper by Colander and Landreth (1997). They follow the controversy through to its most significant moment – the attack on Tarshis's text by William Buckley Jr – about which they write:

> He certainly is not a foe of capitalism, but he does openly favor significant government intervention in order to make capitalism operate effectively. Tarshis's position is not essentially different from that of prevailing 1990s ideology, but compared to the 1930s pro-market ideology that Buckley held, Tarshis's position was a violation of what economics was. (Colander and Landreth, 1997, under 'A Clash of Ideologies', last paragraph)

What is incontestable is that while Tarshis mentions Keynes by name only briefly (Tarshis, 1947, pp. 346–7), he then continues with 12 subsequent chapters outlining Keynesian theory (noted in advance, ibid., p. 346n.). There is no doubt that the attack on Tarshis's text led to its failure to gain more sales and to its disappearance. In my view it was the superiority of Samuelson's text, published in the following year, that also caused its demise. More importantly, it made Samuelson and other economic writers more cautious in how they discussed Keynesian theory. A passage such as the following would never again enter a Keynesian text, as accurate a reflection of the theory though it may actually have been:

> To put it bluntly, employment and income, in money terms, can be expended to respond equally whether the government sponsors useful public works like highway construction, or completely useless ones like digging ditches and filling them up again. In either case, because the income of the newly employed would be higher than before, they would increase their spending, so that the output of consumers' good would be expanded and the upward swing begun. Naturally we should prefer projects which directly add to our real wealth. Flood-control projects, highways, parks, school buildings, research projects, housing, and so on are better than leaf-raking and useless excavations. But the latter are better than nothing, for even though the projects are useless, carrying them out leads to an increased output of

consumers' goods. And even though the men responsible for the increased demand were idlers and good-for-nothings, their dollars, in our economy, are as powerful as any others in increasing consumption, income, and employment. (Tarshis, 1947, p. 518)

Possibly the most revealing passage in the entirety of Keynesian literature.

SEYMOUR HARRIS: *THE NEW ECONOMICS* (1947)

Seymour Harris's collection of articles, published a mere eleven years after *The General Theory*, may be taken to represent the final takeover of economic theorizing by Keynesian economics. It was written as a commemorative volume 'as a tribute to the man and the economist' (Harris, 1947, p. 3) following Keynes's death the year before. The compilation is not entirely of Keynes's disciples and followers, although virtually all were. The significance lies in the notional declaration of victory of Keynesian thought among economists even then. As Harris noted in his opening chapter:

The miracle of Keynes is that despite the vested interests of scholars in the older theory, despite the preponderant influence of press, radio, finance, and subsidized research against Keynes, his influence both in scientific circles and in the arena of public policy has been extraordinary, and much beyond what could have been expected by Keynes or others in 1936. (Ibid., p. 3)

Harris continues in a manner that was not then, nor would be considered over the top even now:

In the last fifteen years he was the outstanding figure in the world of economists. In the wide scope of his interests, in his eloquence and persuasiveness, in the virtually complete command over economic forums, both of subjects to be discussed and manner of discussing them, in the impression he made upon our quasi-capitalist system, in the influence upon economists and men of action of his day – in these jointly, and probably in each separately, Keynes had not an equal. (Ibid., pp. 3–4)

Yet, among the more than 40 articles, two were indeed critical, one by J.A. Schumpeter and the other, but only weakly, by Gottfried Haberler. It is worth having a brief look at each. Each provides an insight into the surrounding circumstances in which *The General Theory* was published. First Schumpeter, which was a reprint of the obituary notice that had been published on Keynes's death the year before in 1946. He discusses the immediate impact *The General Theory* had had:

The success of the *General Theory* was instantaneous and, as we know, sustained. Unfavorable reviews, of which there were many, only helped. A Keynesian school formed itself, not a school in that loose sense in which some historians of economics speak of a French, German, Italian school, but a genuine one which is a sociological entity, namely, a group that professes allegiance to one master and one doctrine, and has its inner circle, its propogandists, its watchwords, its esoteric and its popular doctrine. (Schumpeter, [1946] 1947, p. 97)

He then attempted to explain the attraction *The General Theory* had had for so many:

Many of the men who entered the field of teaching and research in the twenties and thirties had renounced allegiance to the bourgeois scheme of life, the bourgeois scheme of values. Many of them sneered at the profit motive and at the element of personal performance in the capitalist process. But so far as they did not embrace straight socialism, they had to pay respects to saving – under penalty of losing caste in their own eyes and ranging themselves with what Keynes so tellingly called the economists' 'underworld.' But Keynes broke their fetters: here, at last, was theoretical doctrine that not only obliterated the personal element and was, if not mechanistic itself, at least mechanizable, but also smashed the pillars into dust; a doctrine that may not actually say but can easily be made to say both that 'who tries to save destroys real capital' and that, via saving, 'the unequal distribution of income is the ultimate cause of unemployment.' *This* is what the Keynesian revolution amounts to. (Schumpeter, [1946] 1947, p. 99; original emphasis)

According to Haberler, the great divide in economics was less the permission to remain an economist in good standing while still supporting socialism, but more importantly to believe that saving is a potentially harmful activity. Saving might still be necessary to create physical capital, but oversaving was a danger, as was an unequal distribution of income. That he had endorsed oversaving as a possible economic problem meant, in all practical respects, that he had agreed with Keynes in relation to what might lead to recessions and underemployment and had abandoned the classical denial of oversaving as a potential cause of recession.

The remainder of Harris's collection underscored the immense significance for economic theory and policy that had occurred as a result of the Keynesian revolution. Schumpeter and Haberler notwithstanding, the publication of this volume helped further the Keynesian message and advance its policy prescriptions.

PAUL SAMUELSON: *ECONOMICS* (1948)

Possibly the singularly most important influence on the spreading of Keynesian macroeconomic theory throughout the world was Paul Samuelson's introductory text, *Economics: An Introductory Analysis*. It was first published in 1948 and has been reprinted continually in new editions ever since, which have included local editions across the world that have been co-authored by a local economist who has adjusted the text to incorporate local circumstances. Although Samuelson himself died in 2009, new editions continue to be published by his co-authors. His contribution to the spread of Keynesian theory was the invention and popularization of the 45-degree line and the equation representing aggregate demand: $Y = C + I + G + (X - M)$ (where Y is aggregate demand, C, consumer spending, I, private investment, G, government spending, X, exports and M, imports), along with his diagrammatic representation of the equilibrium of saving and investment. Both the diagrams and the accompanying equations have made understanding Keynesian theory clear to millions who have read Samuelson directly, along with the many millions more who have read Samuelson-clone texts. Although the diagrams have been superseded since around the 1980s by the aggregate demand–aggregate supply diagram, Samuelson's text established aggregate demand along with oversaving as the core concepts of macroeconomic theory, and did so in a way that was both easy to teach and easy to learn. However wrong the theory presented might actually be as explanations of how an economy operates, the reasons recessions occur or the kinds of policies that will lift an economy from recession, it is these that are now taught across the world.

It might be noted that part of the process by which Samuelson was able to introduce Keynesian theory so successfully into the economics curriculum in the United States was through denying that he was actually teaching the economics of Keynes. This is how he introduced his 'theory of income determination':

> Although much of this analysis is due to the economics of an English economist, John Maynard Keynes ... today its broad fundamentals are increasingly accepted by economists of all schools of thought, including, it is important to notice, many writers who do not share Keynes' particular policy viewpoints and who differ on technical details of analysis. (Samuelson, [1948] 1998, p. 253)

Samuelson's next paragraph may by 1948 have largely become non-controversial, but only because, with the dozen years since the publication of *The General Theory*, the pre-war classical theory of the cycle had for all practical purposes disappeared:

> **The income analysis here described is itself neutral**: it can be used as well to defend private enterprise as to limit it, as well as to attack as to defend government fiscal intervention. When business organizations such as the Committee for Economic Development or the National City Bank use the terminology of saving and investment, it is absurd to think that this implies that they are 'Keynesian' in the sense of **belonging to that narrow band of zealots associated with some of the policy programs that Keynes himself espoused during the great depression**. (Ibid., pp. 253–4; bold emphasis added)

He had learned from Tarshis's example. Samuelson's analysis is based on the argument that recessions are due to insufficient aggregate demand caused by excess levels of saving. This is the first statement made in the text on which all that follows depends:

> The most important single fact about saving and investment is that in our industrial society they are largely done by different people and for different reasons. ...
> Whatever the individual's motivation to save, it has practically nothing to do with investment or investment opportunities. (Ibid., p. 254)

What he then states, reverts to classical economic theory:

> We have defined 'net investment' or capital formation to be the net increase in the community's real capital (equipment, buildings, inventories, etc.). But the man on the street speaks of 'investing' when he buys a piece of land or old security, or any title to property. For economists these are clearly *transfer* items. What one man is investing, some one else is disinvesting. There is net investment only when new real capital is created. (Ibid., p. 255; original emphasis)

Utterly classical, which in classical times had been matched by the notion that saving was also conceptualized in real terms, as the economy's provision of additional capital. The sleight of hand occurs in two subtle shifts. The initial reference is made to individuals rather than to the economy as a whole, with the presentation then shifting from the real economy to the monetary. Here are the steps Samuelson takes:

1. 'Thus, we are left with our proposition that *saving and investing are done by different **individuals** and for largely different reasons*'.
2. 'Net capital formation ... takes place largely in **business enterprises**'.
3. '*The extreme variability of investment is the next important fact to be emphasized*'.
4. '[A capitalist free enterprise system] cannot guarantee that there will be just exactly the right amount of **investment** to ensure full employment'.
5. 'Nor is there any "invisible hand" guaranteeing that the good years will equal the bad, or that our scientists will discover at just the right time precisely sufficient new products and processes to keep the system on an even keel'. (Ibid., pp. 255–6; italics in the original; bold emphasis added)

This then was formalized into a diagram that was taught across the economics world for the next 30 years, educating two generations of economists on the nature of macroeconomic equilibrium, which occurs where saving equals investment, as shown in Figure 7.2. The heading for the section of the text, which is virtually repeated on the diagram, was: 'How Income is Determined at Level where Saving and Investment Schedule Intersect'.

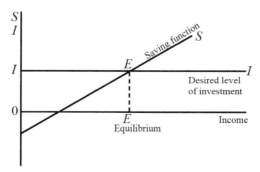

Source: Based on Samuelson (1948).

Figure 7.2   *How saving and investment determine income*

But this is where the notion of saving and investment are transmogrified from real entities into sums of money. From 'equipment, buildings, inventories, etc.', investment is turned into sums of money so that they can be compared with particular sums of money that are designated as the level of saving. This is the Keynesian sleight of hand found in *The General Theory*, now transformed into a diagram and equation.

More devastating still to the classical conception, the entire comparison is reduced into a narrow time period, into a quarter or single year. Rather than saving being identified as the entire resource base – all the equipment and buildings or even inventories that have been accumulated over time that are then in existence that can be applied to build the future productive potential of the economy – these are now reduced to the money sums that have been applied in the present period. It is, indeed, the Keynesian conception, but here it is crystallized into a simplified model that would go on to capture the economics world through to the present day, and which will undoubtedly continue to dominate our texts for many years to come.

It was, however, the aggregate demand curve and its related equation that would become the core of macroeconomic policy, as it remains to this day. On the vertical axis on Figure 7.3 are the elements of demand: personal consumption (C), business investment (I), government spending (G), and net exports (NX), which are comprised of exports less imports $(X - M)$. The level of total output (Y) is measured along the horizontal axis. Along the 45-degree line, the level of demand is equal to the level of output, which is the reason output is designated as Ye, the equilibrium level of income.

The diagram shown in Figure 7.3 was near universal from the late 1940s until it was superseded by aggregate demand–aggregate supply curves after the

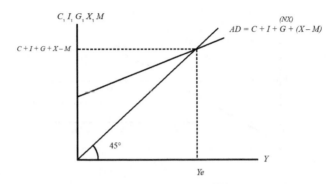

Figure 7.3   Equilibrium on the 45-degree line

Great Inflation of the 1970s. It was the basic Keynesian diagram used in virtually every text until it became necessary to mesh the Keynesian demand-side underemployment apparatus with an explanation for the rapid growth in the price level that emerged from around the late 1960s.

$C + I + G$ – aggregate demand – was then embodied within the AD curve but the conceptual demand-side framework remained intact and central. The AS curve was introduced to allow for a contraction in production to affect the equilibrium level of activity, and therefore the price level across the economy, and not just consumer prices. The level of aggregate demand nevertheless remained paramount in the determination of the level of employment. So far as policy went, shifting the AD curve – that is, raising the level of aggregate demand – remained the crucial element in maintaining full employment and economic growth.

However, while *Ye* may be the equilibrium, it does not require everyone in the economy who wishes to work to be working to produce that level of output. But since this is the equilibrium point, that is where the economy is stuck unless the community can be induced to buy more than they already are. Interestingly, none of what was to come appeared in the first edition. Ultimately, however, an upwards shift in the aggregate demand curve through an increase in public spending became the basis for fiscal policy. An increase in public spending would shift the AD curve up, which would lead to an increase in production in the economy itself, and therefore to an increase in employment. In the first edition, this was stated as merely a possibility:

> One weapon in the battle for stability is government fiscal policy: an increase in government expenditure, taken by itself, has expansionary effects on national income, much like those of private investment. (Ibid., p. 278)

Later editions were quite explicit. This is from the 1964 international edition:

> Aside from the central bank, the government has another major way of affecting current spending. As part of its *fiscal policy* it can expand its expenditures: build useful public roads and schools, hire more civil servants, increase defense expenditure, do a hundred and one useful (**or foolish**) things to expand total spending. (Samuelson, [1948] 1964, p. 331; italics in the original; bold emphasis added)

He then shows the same effect using the 45-degree diagram, as Samuelson specifically notes himself:

> Better still, we can show it as an upward shift in the G component of the $C+I+G$ schedule that was used as an alternative way to show income equilibrium. [The diagram] recapitulates the demonstration on page 243 [of Samuelson, 1964] of how an expansion of public expenditure G leads to an expansion of income. (Ibid., p. 331)

And again, as with Keynes, any old expenditure will do, whether useful or 'foolish'. It is the expenditure of itself, via the multiplier, that creates economic growth and employment. No one has done more to establish this belief than Samuelson himself. As he wrote in 1946, even before he had written his own text:

> Finally, and perhaps most important from the long-run standpoint, the Keynesian analysis has begun to filter down into the elementary textbooks; and as everybody knows once an idea gets into these, however bad it may be, it becomes practically immortal. (Samuelson, 1946, p. 189)

It is possible that more wealth has been destroyed by the publication of Samuelson's easily explained but theoretically unsound version of Keynesian economics than through any other economic principle ever stated other than perhaps the economic theories of Marx, but perhaps not even those.

DUDLEY DILLARD: *THE ECONOMICS OF J.M. KEYNES* (1948)

The Keynesian momentum was swept forward by the publication of Dudley Dillard's widely used crib that attempted to bring Keynes's message into the undergraduate classroom. This was the first sentence of the first chapter:

> Within the first dozen years following its publication, John Maynard Keynes' *The General Theory of Employment, Interest and Money* (1936) has had more influence upon the thinking of professional economists and public policy makers than any other book in the whole history of economic thought in a comparable number of years. ... Many economists who were at first highly critical of Keynes have deserted

their old position for the Keynesian camp. In book after book, leading economists acknowledge a heavy debt to the stimulating thought of Lord Keynes. (Dillard, 1948, p. 1)

The particular aspect that Dillard deals with is found in the book's subtitle, *The Theory of Monetary Policy*. The focus is on an aspect of *The General Theory* that did not age well – the argument that demand deficiency occurs because individuals hoard money if interest rates cannot fall low enough so that those with money to lend actually choose to lend rather than hold on to their cash. But that was a technical matter.

More significantly, Dillard goes on, in Chapter 2, to restate Keynes's critique of classical economic theory. Remarkably, he perfectly states with phenomenal precision Keynes's own critique of pre-Keynesian economics without getting a single element of classical theory correct. It demonstrates how within the period of not much more than a decade, the entire version of what has descended to us today was crafted to explain the supposed flaws in classical theory, by those who had actually learned their economics within the classical tradition.

Chapter 2 is titled, 'The Classical Background', in which there is an eight-page summary of what Dillard describes as 'The Content of Classical Economics' (Dillard, 1948, pp. 16–24). As far as his depiction of classical theory is concerned, it is false from end to end. He is only accurate where he discusses Keynes's contrasting view to the straw-man he has constructed. Let me begin with the first paragraph of this summary, which will be familiar to any modern student of economic theory, but in which there is not a single accurate statement made in relation to the beliefs that classical economists had actually had. Although published as a single paragraph, I will separate the sentences into single sentences, which I have numbered, and then comment below:

1. Classical economic theory rests on the assumption of full employment of labor and other resources.
2. There may be lapses from full employment, but these are regarded as abnormal and their explanation does not constitute a basic part of the subject matter of classical economics.
3. If at any time there is not actually full employment, the classical theory asserts there is always a *tendency* toward full employment.
4. The normal situation is stable equilibrium at full employment.
5. If disturbance does persist, it is attributed by the classical school to interferences by government or private monopoly with the free play of market forces.
6. As a general rule to which there are minor exceptions, the social policy which guarantees full employment is laissez-faire, the absence of government control of private enterprise.

7. In contrast with this, Keynes takes the normal condition of laissez-faire capitalism to be a fluctuating level of employment.
8. The primary purpose of Keynes' theory is to explain what determines the volume of employment at any time. (Dillard, 1948, p. 16; original emphasis)

Dillard writes as if there had never previously been a theory of the business cycle that every economist was perfectly well aware of. These had all been explained in detail in many texts and had been brought together by Haberler in his comprehensive 1937 *Prosperity and Depression*. Dillard has no excuse for suggesting (number 1 in the above list) that this entity, 'classical economic theory', assumed full employment of labour. In describing the operation of an economy, the same approach was taken as if one were describing the operation of an automobile. Mechanical failure would only be discussed when one had first learned how an automobile operates when it is running smoothly.

Lapses from full employment, far from being thought of as abnormal (2), were recognized as intrinsic to the business cycle. In the four phases of the cycle, periods of recession, the trough itself and then at least for part of the upturn, the assumption would be that employment was below its optimal 'full employment' level. Only during the final stage of a recovery and then at the peak of the cycle, would there have been full employment, and even then there would have been unemployment due to the adjustments required as some enterprises were closing while others were opening up.

Thus, the tendency was not always towards full employment (3) since during the down phase, the tendency was towards even higher rates of unemployment until stability eventually occurred when the trough of the cycle was reached. There would then be an upwards turn in the economy from which there was a 'tendency', to use Dillard's word, towards the peak level of employment at the peak of the cycle.

In an economy there was no 'normal situation' (4). A period of recession was just as 'normal' as a period of rapid growth.

But, at least Dillard recognizes that classical economists did indeed recognize unemployment might well persist, but as Haberler (1937) made clear, there were many different explanations for the coming of a crisis and a downturn in an economy. As Haberler had, however, also made clear, virtually none of the standard explanations revolved around interferences by government or private monopoly (5), although there was no reason to rule these explanations out either. A classical recession was a natural outcome of different sets of circumstance. As Haberler explained, the causes of a downturn were the result of forces set in motion during the upturn. High unemployment was an inevitable but unfortunate aspect of a market economy.

And as far as stating that 'the social policy which guarantees full employment is laissez-faire' (6), it was Keynes himself in his 'The End of *Laissez-Faire*'

([1926] 1981) who pointed out that from the time of John Stuart Mill onwards, no major economist had advocated a policy of *laissez-faire*. Mill, in his own *Principles*, had devoted a fifth of the text, 200 pages in length, to discuss the role of government and had ended up by stating that his discussion was in no sense exhaustive.

Keynes argues that the normal condition of an economy, *laissez-faire* or otherwise (7), was for there to be fluctuating levels of employment. There was nothing unique in Keynes having to provide an explanation of what determines the volume of employment (8). It was merely the mythology that Keynesians such as Dillard had included as part of their endeavour to promote the new economics that spread like wildfire following the publication of *The General Theory* in 1936.

DILLARD (STILL 1948) ON SAY'S LAW

The guilty party within classical theory was, of course, Say's Law. Again, Dillard provides a near-perfect construction of the argument that has remained in place since the publication of *The General Theory*, but because he was trained within the classical tradition, provides a much more nuanced version. Below is Dillard's text that is published in a single paragraph but is broken into different sections and numbered. Some of the statements in this paragraph are actually correct, which I have placed in bold. Comments follow.

1. Acceptance of full employment as the normal condition of an exchange economy is justified in classical economics by the assumption that supply creates its own demand.
2. This assumption or 'principle' is called Say's Law of markets, after J.B. Say, an early nineteenth-century French economist who was the first to state the 'law' in dogmatic form.
3. By supply creating its own demand is meant that every producer who brings goods to market does so only in order to exchange them for other goods.
4. Say assumed that the only reason people work and produce is in order to enjoy the satisfaction of consuming.
5. In an exchange economy, therefore, whatever is produced represents the demand for another product.
6. **Additional supply is additional demand**.
7. The analysis is carried on in terms of barter, but the fact that sales and purchases are made with money is assumed not to affect the process, except that exchange based on money is more efficient that exchange based on barter.
8. When a resource is put to work a product (output) is produced and income is paid to those who contribute to production.
9. The sales receipts or proceeds which an employer can expect to receive from the output produced is assumed to cover the cost of the output for all levels of employment in the economic system, provide the contributors of resources are willing to accept rewards commensurate with their productivity.

10. This does not mean that each additional worker need purchase exactly the same product which he himself produces. It signifies merely that the new income from his employment will create sufficient demand to take off the market an amount of output equivalent to that produce by virtue of his employment.
11. As long as production is directed into proper channels, whatever is produced can be sold.
12. Misdirected production may result in temporary over-supply of some particular items but there can be no general overproduction as long as supply creates its own demand.
13. **If errors result in excess production of some particular items of output, this will be corrected when entrepreneurs shift from the production of things they cannot sell (at a profit) to the production of things they can sell (at a profit).**
14. **In brief, Say's Law of markets is a denial of the possibility of general over-production, that is, a denial of the possibility of a deficiency of aggregate demand.**
15. Therefore the employment of more resources will always be profitable and will take place up to the point of full employment, subject to the limitation that the contributors of resources are willing to accept rewards no greater than their physical productivity justifies.
16. There can be no general unemployment, according to this view, if workers will accept what they are 'worth'. (Dillard, 1948, pp. 18–19; bold emphasis added)

Dillard quotes the phrase, 'supply creates its own demand' (1) as if it was a well-known phrase before it showed up in *The General Theory*, even though it was a phrase that was invented in the twentieth century by Harlan McCracken and first stated on page 159 in the latter's 1933 text on the business cycle. This is the definition Keynes used to define 'Say's Law' (2), which is a term first used by Fred Manville Taylor, again in the twentieth century (see Taylor, 1925, Chapter XV).

It is difficult to determine whether the exchange process of $C - M - C'$ (one set of commodities [C] sold for money [M] and then the money used to buy a different set of commodities [C'], using the notation first adopted by Marx) was seen by Dillard as incorrect or problematic in some way (3). It is difficult, however, to imagine why anyone would open a business or others work within such firms if the ultimate intent was not to spend what one earned to buy from others.

Nor was it Say alone who assumed that 'the only reason people work and produce is in order to enjoy the satisfaction of consuming' (4). There may be other psychological motives, but in relation to understanding the operation of an economy, that seems like a proper working hypothesis. What is certainly the case is that in an exchange economy, whatever is produced and sold represents the basis of demand for another product (5).

However one might look at it, additional supply is the absolute basis for additional demand (6). Only if more is produced can more be demanded.

What is, however, absolutely false is that 'the analysis is carried on in terms of barter' (7). To demonstrate how false this is, one need only return to Say's first discussion of his principle in 1803, which was an attempt to deal with those who argued that recessions were due to a shortage of money. Money was intrinsic to the process from the start.

What was never assumed by any economist, probably ever, was that once something was produced, it was certain that the product would be sold at a price that covered all of its costs of production (8–10).

The next sentence (11) is almost correct, but the error in the wording is intrinsic to Keynesian analysis: 'as long as production is directed into proper channels, *whatever is produced can* be sold' (my emphasis). To state the classical conclusion, if production is directed into producing what others wish to buy, whatever is produced will be bought, and thus will be sold and more importantly sold at a profit. Selling at a loss is always possible.

Misdirected production (12), of course, occurs for all sorts of output all the time where a profitable return turns out to be impossible. But what is important here is to appreciate that misdirected production, if it is pervasive enough, was at the heart of the classical theory of recession. So, while there was no 'over-production' there was nevertheless the potential for an economy to slow and fall into recession because of misdirected production.

The adjustment process will occur as goods that cannot be sold at a profit are no longer produced with other products produced in their stead. Resources shift from the production of one set of goods to the production of another (13).

The following is a correct statement of classical economic theory. 'Say's Law of markets is a denial of the possibility of general overproduction, that is, a denial of the possibility of a deficiency of aggregate demand' (14). When misdirected production occurs over a large enough segment of the economy, prolonged recessions can and do occur. The recessions that then occur are not the result of an absence of demand, but a mismatch between what producers are producing as against what others, both consumers and investors, wish to buy.

It is, moreover, difficult to see how anyone could ever have been thought to have believed that 'the employment of more resources will *always* be profitable' (my emphasis) when it was always perfectly well understood that resources were frequently used in unprofitable ventures (15). Without this assumption, everything Keynes said about classical theory falls to the ground.

Finally, unemployment was due to structural problems, not a misalignment of wages and productivity (16), although this, too, could be a genuine problem leading to unemployment. It was just not the typical cause of mass unemployment in the midst of a recession and was not at the core of the classical theory of recession.

To sum up, Keynes brought into the mainstream the theoretical possibility that overproduction and demand deficiency were possible. He went even further, by denying not just the possibility of other causes of recession but also their very existence. Dillard outlined the Keynesian version of why classical economists could not understand how recessions and mass unemployment occurred and explained the entire analysis in exactly the way it might be explained today. And remarkably, the classical theory of the cycle has remained outside mainstream teachings ever since. There would be virtually no modern economist who could explain the classical theory of recession in any way other than how it was explained by Dillard at the very start of the Keynesian revolution in 1948, a mere 12 years after *The General Theory* had been published.

A.C. PIGOU: *KEYNES'S 'GENERAL THEORY': A RETROSPECTIVE VIEW* (1951)

Among the first published reviews of *The General Theory* was one by A.C. Pigou. Pigou was from 1908 to 1943 Marshall's successor as Professor of Political Economy at Cambridge. He began the review with a criticism that captured the direction the review would take. This is Pigou's second paragraph:

> The group of persons whom, on this occasion, he parades as a foil, are the 'classical economists,' with, as particular examples, 'Ricardo, Marshall, Edgeworth and Professor Pigou.' The device of lumping all these persons together is an ingenious one; for it enables the shortcomings of one to be attributed to all. For example, Professor Pigou, in a book on Unemployment, which is 'the only detailed account of the classical theory of employment which exists,' (p. 7) has committed a variety of sins. Professor Pigou is a classical economist; therefore the classical economists have committed these sins! Moreover, when one of the arraigned persons has palpably not made a particular mistake, the method of lumping enables Mr. Keynes to say that he ought to have made it, and that, in not making it, he has been false to the 'logic' of his own school – has allowed his 'good common sense to overbear his bad theory,' (p. 277). Finally, this device has, for anyone adopting it, the great advantage that it renders any complete reply impossible. When a man goes on a sniping expedition in a large village, nobody will have the patience to track down the course of his every bullet. The best that can be done is to illustrate his methods by selected examples and to enquire in a broad way into his total accomplishment. (Pigou, 1936, pp. 115–16)

Pigou was in many ways the exemplar of bad classical economics for large parts of *The General Theory*. Pigou had, in turn, written a scathing review. In 1949, some 13 years later and by which time Keynesian theory had been firmly embedded as the mainstream, Pigou asked and was given permission to provide his own retrospective view on Keynesian theory. His presentation has been generally seen as a surrender to the Keynesian perspective that he had not quite been able to appreciate at the time. This entry from Wikipedia captures how history has looked at Pigou's presentation:

> In a couple of lectures delivered in 1949 he made a more favourable, though still critical evaluation of Keynes' work: 'I should say … that in setting out and developing his fundamental conception, Keynes made a very important, original and valuable addition to the armoury of economic analysis'. He later said that he had come with the passage of time to feel that he had failed earlier to appreciate some of the important things that Keynes was trying to say. (Wikipedia, 2020a)

Although by the time of this presentation, there was no turning back, Pigou's lectures were seen as the final surrender by the classical school to the emerging Keynesian consensus. The reality was, however, quite different. While Pigou was generous in recognizing that *The General Theory* had struck out in a new direction that others could learn from and perhaps extend, his last chapter before the conclusion was titled, 'Limitations and Achievements of Keynes's Analysis', where the emphasis was on the limitations. Here is his own summation:

> In my original review article on the *General Theory* I failed to grasp its significance and did not assign to Keynes the credit due for it. Nobody before him, so far as I know, had brought all the relevant factors, real and monetary at once, together in a single formal scheme, through which their interplay could be coherently investigated. His doing this does *not*, to my mind, constitute a revolution. Only if we accepted the myth – as I regard it – that earlier economists ignored the part played by money, and, even when discussing fluctuations in employment, tacitly assumed that there weren't any, would that word be appropriate. (Pigou, 1951, p. 65; original emphasis)

There is more in the text itself in defence of classical thought and critical of Keynes. Pigou was not as conciliatory as he has been made out to be. But other than from W.H. Hutt (1960, 1963, 1974, 1979), there was no further published comment on Keynesian economic and *The General Theory* from the mainstream classical economists that entered the discourse within the profession.

ALVIN HANSEN: *A GUIDE TO KEYNES* (1953)

Alvin Hansen, even more than Dillard, did much to spread Keynesian theory through his *Guide to Keynes*, which, like Dillard's, found its way into classrooms across the world. His Wikipedia reference states in its opening paragraph:

> Often referred to as 'the American Keynes' ... More effectively than anyone else, he explicated, extended, domesticated, and popularized the ideas embodied in Keynes' *The General Theory*. In 1967, Paul McCracken, chairman of the President's Council of Economic Advisers, saluted Hansen: 'It is certainly a statement of fact that you have influenced the nation's thinking about economic policy more profoundly than any other economist in this century'. (Wikipedia, 2020b)

What makes Hansen's views especially noteworthy is that he had a deep understanding of the classical theory of the cycle well before he first came to read *The General Theory*. Wikipedia notes this as well:

> Hansen's doctoral dissertation, titled 'Cycles of Prosperity and Depression,' was published in 1921. He published a further text on the same issues, *Business Cycle Theory*, in 1927. He co-authored an introductory text, *Principles of Economics*, published in 1928. Finally, still prior to the publication of *The General Theory*, his own *Economic Stabilization in an Unbalanced World* was published in 1932. Thus, by the time he read *The General Theory*, of which he wrote a 20-page review for the *Journal of Political Economy* (Hansen, 1936), Hansen had the kind of background that was rare among economists who supported the change in economic direction the Keynesian revolution led to.' (Ibid.)

Wikipedia adds this:

> His most outstanding contribution to economic theory was the joint development, with John Hicks, of the so-called IS–LM model, also known as the 'Hicks–Hansen synthesis.' The IS–LM diagram claims to show the relationship between the investment-saving (IS) curve and the liquidity preference-money supply (LM) curve. It is used in mainstream economics literature and textbooks to illustrate how monetary and fiscal policy can influence GDP. ...
>
> Hansen's 1941 book, *Fiscal Policy and Business Cycles*, was the first major work in the United States to entirely support Keynes's analysis of the causes of the Great Depression. Hansen used that analysis to argue for Keynesian deficit spending. (Ibid.)

Yet, it may have been his *Guide to Keynes* that was his most significant contribution to the spread of Keynesian economics. Published in 1953, it provided a chapter by chapter examination of the arguments of *The General Theory*. But what may have been of most significance were his criticisms of classical economic theory, of which not only was he an expert, but was also drenched in the classical theory of the cycle, which he had touched on at the end of his review of *The General Theory*:

> In conclusion, a word should be said about Keynes's view of the trade cycle. Let it be noted that *The General Theory of Employment, Interest and Money* is only incidentally concerned with the trade cycle. Cyclical fluctuations may occur in either a full-employment equilibrium system or in an underemployment equilibrium system. **The theory of the trade cycle is, therefore, something substantially apart from the theory of long-run under-employment or full-employment equilibrium.** ...
> A complete explanation of the cycle must, moreover, involve an analysis of the crisis – the sudden and violent turning point from boom to depression. (Hansen, 1936, p. 684; bold emphasis added)

It was his own belief that the major economic problem was secular stagnation that allowed Hansen to adopt and adapt Keynesian economics to provide a comprehensive crib that for many students was the closest they ever came to reading *The General Theory* itself. Important here in a discussion of the transition from classical theory to modern macroeconomics was its opening chapter on classical economics and Say's Law. Looking into the years before 1936, Hansen wrote:

> As part of the widespread dissatisfaction with the state of economic theory, Say's Law in particular was subjected to serious question. But despite numerous attempts, no one succeeded in making a strong theoretical case against the basic premise that the price system tended automatically to produce full employment. (Hansen, 1953, p. 6)

He discusses the many who, in his view, came close but could never quite do the job. Yet, he notes that Say's Law was not the issue in relation to the cycle:

> It has often been said [by Keynes, for example] that the widespread theoretical pre-occupation with business-cycle problems in the period referred to is adequate proof that few, if any, economists any longer adhered to the doctrine of Say's Law. I do not believe, however, that an examination of the literature will support this view. (Ibid., p. 12)

Yet, while Hansen focuses correctly on the more important aspects of the theory, including a long discussion of J.S. Mill (ibid., pp. 12–13), in the end, he equates Say's Law with a belief in an automatic and rapid return to full employment following a downturn in the cycle. Still, it is a start, in that Hansen recognizes and asserts that acceptance of Say's Law did not rule out recessions or high unemployment, nor did it outlaw the existence of the business cycle. What Hansen nevertheless does, is explain how the acceptance of Say's Law was consistent with recessions and mass unemployment.

And while on the one hand this was inconsistent with the specific conclusion Keynes had reached, on the other it opened a means to adopt Keynesian type policies, since, in Hansen's mind, the problem was secular stagnation, which still meant investment would not reach a level sufficient to employ all those who wished to work. Therefore, as far as the remainder of the book was concerned, it provided an entirely straightforward discussion of the operation of an economy, in which insufficient aggregate demand was a perennial problem. And by following *The General Theory* chapter by chapter, using Keynes's terminology and definitions, Hansen's *Guide* eased the way forward, not only for the adoption of Keynesian economic theory throughout higher education, and thereafter by policy makers across the world, but also for the Keynesian terminology and technical definitions that have blockaded comprehension of classical theory ever since.

T.W. HUTCHISON: *A REVIEW OF ECONOMIC DOCTRINES: 1870-1929* (1953)

T.W. Hutchison was a great scholar of classical economic theory, who later in life became sceptical about Keynesian theory, but 1953 was in the very midst of the years of high Keynesian economics. No one's reputation would have survived any attempt to take Keynes on, especially a young scholar, as Hutchison then was. It is not being suggested that Hutchison wrote anything other than what he personally believed. It *is* suggested, however, that surrounded as he was at the time by wall-to-wall Keynesian thought, he was a Keynesian by osmosis given the virtually universal acceptance of Keynesian theory and Keynes's near-universally accepted critique of classical economic thought. The interest in Hutchison is in his direct criticisms of Mill in relation to Say's Law, which represents an enormous ability to understand the classical position. Unlike almost all others writing at the time, he completely understood Mill's argument even while disagreeing fundamentally with Mill's conclusions.

Whether or not Say's Law is properly understood as the propositions that recessions are never caused by a deficiency of demand and that recessions can neither be brought to an end or employment levels improved by an increase in aggregate demand, no one could have said so in the early 1950s while still maintaining their standing within the economics community. Although completely siding with Keynes, Hutchison (1953) thoroughly discusses these issues, in an, unusual for the time, accurate and fair-minded way. The propositions are examined through the writings of John Stuart Mill's *Principles* (1848). The passage below is entirely as written by Hutchison. He is explaining how Say's Law was absolutely accepted by Mill and his contemporaries at the time he wrote. He begins by citing Mill and Mill's amazement that his own predecessors as recently as the turn of the nineteenth century had believed that demand deficiency could have been identified as a cause of recession. This is Hutchison quoting Mill:

> The idea [wrote Mill] 'that produce in general may, by increasing faster than the demand for it, reduce all producers to distress, ... strange to say, was almost a received doctrine as lately as thirty years ago; and the merit of those who have exploded it is much greater than might be inferred from the extreme obviousness of its absurdity when it is stated in its native simplicity'. ...
>
> Mill again agrees that in fact in commercial crises 'there really is an excess of all commodities', which is a regular though transient phenomenon; but on the other hand, 'it is a great error to suppose with Sismondi that a commercial crisis is the effect of a general excess of production'. He [that is, Mill] goes on to denounce the latter notion (but not of course the former) as being (all in one paragraph) 'a chimerical supposition', 'a confused idea', 'essentially self-contradictory', 'a fatal misconception', 'a fatal error', and 'a veil not suffering any one ray of light to penetrate'. Finally, he makes a pronouncement (later faithfully quoted by Fawcett) affecting the whole shape and task of political economy:
>
>> The point is fundamental; any difference of opinion on it involves radically different conceptions of political economy, especially in its practical aspect. On the one view, we have only to consider how a sufficient production may be combined with the best possible distribution; but on the other hand there is a third thing to be considered – how a market can be created for produce, or how production can be limited to the capabilities of the market.
>
> And this *third thing* (or the problem of equilibrium of aggregate effective demand and supply) was a chimerical supposition. (Hutchison, 1953, pp. 349–52; original emphasis)

That was Hutchison in 1953. He was part of the tide of intellectual thought that helped drive Keynesian economics forward while eliminating classical theory entirely from within the mainstream of economic thought. This was a broadside that no one at the time would have disagreed with. To challenge Hutchison would have required a phenomenal level of scholarship, and even then, would have required a standing well beyond the level possessed by any anti-Keynesian economist at the time, should there even have been one willing to take on this task at the time, or that had recognized its significance.

Hutchison was able to dismiss Mill in favour of Keynes's conclusions and in no uncertain terms. This was, however, a set of convictions that was not to last through the upheavals that Keynesian policies created during the 1960s and 1970s. As Hutchison noted, 'in the seventies, serious problems of profound disequilibrium came back again in the form of chronic inflation accompanied by severe shocks from the supply side' (Hutchison, [1979] 1981, p. 254). In 1979, he published an article on 'The Limitations of General Theories in Macroeconomics', in which Keynes's *General Theory* was the centre of attention and in which these suddenly apparent deficiencies in Keynesian theory were discussed. By then he was able to quote the following passage with complete approval:

> The typical Keynesian model is an exercise in institutional ad hocery. Its performance depends crucially on some piece of specific irrationality (such as wage rigidity or money illusion) for which no theoretical justification is given. (Hutchison, [1979] 1981, p. 247)

And while this disillusionment with Keynesian theory did occur following the catastrophes of the Great Inflation of the 1970s, in tandem with a small minority of others who had discovered how fallacious Keynesian economic theory actually is, they were unable to convince the majority of their colleagues. The theory of aggregate demand has therefore maintained its place as the dominant economic theory of the cycle, with a public sector stimulus remaining as the core policy tool to implement should a recession occur.

AN UNEXPECTED CRITIC: KEYNES ON THE 'CLASSICAL MEDICINE' (1946)

Last, from Keynes himself. He has notoriously been quoted as saying, 'I am not a Keynesian'. This may in fact be true, as his last, posthumous, article from *The Economic Journal* may make clear. Keynes, by 1946, may have been the last of the classical economists. By the time this was published, Keynes had died, which may be why it is not found in the 30-volume *Collected Writings of John Maynard Keynes*. He is discussing the forces at work that help bring economies towards an international equilibrium that will occur by leaving things to the market:

> I find myself moved, not for the first time, to remind contemporary economists that the classical teaching embodied some permanent truths of great significance, which we are liable to-day to over-look because we associate them with other doctrines which we cannot now accept without much qualification. There are in these matters deep undercurrents at work, natural forces, one can call them, or even the invisible hand, which are operating towards equilibrium. If it were not so, we could not have got on even so well as we have for many decades past. ...
>
> We have here sincere and thoroughgoing proposals, advanced on behalf of the United States, expressly directed towards creating a system which allows the classical medicine to do its work. It shows how much modernist stuff, gone wrong and turned sour and silly, is circulating in our system, also incongruously mixed, it seems, with age-old poisons, that we should have given so doubtful a welcome to this magnificent, objective approach which a few years ago we should have regarded as offering incredible promise of a better scheme of things.
>
> I must not be misunderstood. I do not suppose that the classical medicine will work by itself or that we can depend on it. We need quicker and less painful aids

of which exchange variation and overall import control are the most important. But in the long run these expedients will work better and we shall need them less, if the classical medicine is also at work. And if we reject the medicine from our systems altogether, we may just drift on from expedient to expedient and never get really fit again. The great virtue of the Bretton Woods and Washington proposals, taken in conjunction, is that they marry the use of the necessary expedients to the wholesome long-run doctrine. It is for this reason that, speaking in the House of Lords, I claimed that 'Here is an attempt to use what we have learnt from modern experience and modern analysis, not to defeat, but to implement the wisdom of Adam Smith'. (Keynes, 1946, pp. 185–6)

One cannot walk away from a text such as this without wondering what Keynes's own judgement may have been on what 'Keynesians' had done with his arguments:

It shows how much **modernist stuff, gone wrong and turned sour and silly**, is circulating in our system, also incongruously mixed, it seems, with **age-old poisons**. (Ibid.; bold emphasis added)

Nor what he meant when he wrote:

I must not be misunderstood. I do not suppose that **the classical medicine** will work by itself or that we can depend on it. We need quicker and less painful aids of which exchange variation and overall import control are the most important. But in the long run these expedients will work better and we shall need them less, **if the classical medicine is also at work**. And if we reject the medicine from our systems altogether, we may just drift on from expedient to expedient and never get really fit again. (Ibid.; bold emphasis added)

This is no idle speculation, given how badly the modern prescriptions of that Keynesian medicine have left our economies. Economies never get really fit again, using Keynes's words, until the 'Keynesian' prescriptions are reversed. Keynes seems to have recognized just how badly those who had supposedly carried his message forward had mangled the policy mix. Unfortunately, in the immediate post-war period, he was no longer there to explain just what those errors were. T.W. Hutchison, however, was there, and had seen the Great Inflation of the 1960s and 1970s accompanied by very high levels of unemployment. He had seen the way in which Keynes's message had been mangled by his disciples, though having been one himself. He therefore wrote a booklet intended to remind economists of what Keynes had actually meant, *Keynes v. the 'Keynesians': An Essay in the Thinking of J.M. Keynes and the*

Accuracy of Its Interpretation by His Followers (Hutchison, 1977). There he made himself very clear:

> Let us begin with some articles written in 1937, one year after *The General Theory* (but not yet made available in his *Collected Writings*). 1937 was a peak year, and unemployment was back around 12 per cent. These articles are probably Keynes's only, or much his most significant, contribution regarding current policies for dealing with the upper turning-point of the cycle, as contrasted with the depths of the depression. Moreover, they were his last pronouncements on current domestic policy-problems under peace-time assumptions and it is very remarkable that they have not received more attention. The first of them was entitled 'How to Avoid a Slump'.

> *Policy proposals to avoid another slump: 'a rightly distributed demand'*
> Keynes begins by remarking that we have 'climbed out of the slump'. There was not 'a precarious boom'. There was 'nothing wrong', but the time had come to level off activity and above all to take precautions against a descent into another slump. Keynes maintained:

>> We are in more need today of a rightly distributed demand than of greater aggregate demand.

> He insisted that economists were

>> faced with a scientific problem which we have never tried to solve before.

> He claimed – emphasizing broad agreement on policy questions, as contrasted with the pressing of extreme disagreements in *The General Theory* – that

>> we have entirely freed ourselves – *this applies to every party and every quarter* – from the philosophy of the *laissez-faire* state.

> He added somewhat modestly and tentatively: 'Perhaps we know more'.
>   Keynes went on:

>> Three years ago it was important to use public policy to increase investment. *It may soon be equally important to retard certain types of investment, so as to keep our most easily available ammunition in hand for when it is more required.* … Just as it was advisable for the Government to incur debt during the slump, so for the same reasons it is now advisable that they should incline to the opposite policy. … Just as it was advisable for local authorities to press on with capital expenditure during the slump, so *it is now advisable that they should postpone whatever new enterprises can reasonably be held back.*

> Keynes then admitted that it might be considered premature to abate efforts to increase employment so long as the figures of unemployment remained so high – i.e. around 11–12 per cent. He explained, however:

>> I believe that *we are approaching, or have reached, the point where there is not much advantage in applying a further general stimulus at the centre.* So long as surplus resources were widely diffused between industries and localities it was no great matter at what point in the economic structure the impulse of

an increased demand was applied. But the evidence grows that – for several reasons into which there is no space to enter here – the economic structure is unfortunately rigid, and that (for example) building activity in the home counties is less effective than one might have hoped in decreasing unemployment in the distressed areas. It follows that the later stages of recovery require a different technique. ...

We are in more need today of a rightly distributed demand than of a greater aggregate demand; and the Treasury would be entitled to economise else-where to compensate for the cost of special assistance to the distressed areas. (Hutchison, 1977, pp. 10–12; Hutchison's italics)

Possibly the most notable aspect of Keynes's thoughts is his recognition that the key issue in maintaining an economy on a sustainable growth path is a 'a rightly distributed demand'. Structural balance is the classical key to main-taining economic growth and full employment. There may well be occasions when the rate of change overwhelms an economy's ability to maintain its balance and therefore falls into a period of recession. But once it is understood that the issue is structural, not the level of aggregate demand or oversaving, the appropriate policy mix becomes more evident. Only a year after its publication did Keynes retreat from the policy advice found in *The General Theory*. There must have been many conversations that we will never know about inside Cambridge and out, with some of the most esteemed economists of his time, almost all of whom had been schooled in classical theory who well understood the fallacies that Keynes had published.

It was perhaps these conversations that convinced Keynes that he needed to revise the arguments he had published, perhaps in dismay at the ways in which what he had written had been interpreted and were being discussed. All he could do was counsel others, and then the war came with its different problems, and then the war came to an end and he was involved with Bretton Woods and the negotiations over the terms of post-war international economic arrangements. In the midst of all that, he did try to make clear that the version of Keynesian economics that had spread like wildfire from the moment *The General Theory* was published was not the version he endorsed.

FINAL THOUGHTS

This chapter has provided some of the more significant moments that led to the almost instantaneous acceptance of Keynesian macro across the economics world. The old joke, that new ideas in economics spread funeral by funeral, did not apply. There was an almost immediate adoption of Keynesian theory among economists, particularly among young economists, which pervaded the entire discipline almost from the very start. This was despite the fact, attested to by many who tried to read the book, that it was almost impossible to make sense of what Keynes was trying to say. There had been a Great Depression that by *The General Theory*'s date of publication had ended. The Great Depression, other than in the United States, had been brought to an end using the tried-and-true policies associated with classical theory. There had been cuts to spending and efforts to balance budgets, which had actually occurred in the United Kingdom in 1933. The New Deal had prolonged the Great Depression in the United States until the start of the 1940s. There was no reason to believe that Keynesian methods would succeed in a peacetime economy.

Yet, as this chapter has outlined, among economists, an interpretation of this new approach to dealing with the business cycle, which ever since has borne the name 'macroeconomics', had taken over the field. J.R. Hicks and Paul Samuelson laid the foundations, with many others helping to reinforce the pathway to the almost universally accepted argument that demand deficiency was the cause of recessions and that a public sector stimulus is the most effective cure. That was the message left behind by Hicks's IS–LM model and Samuelson's diagrammatic representation of an underemployment equilibrium where $I = S$, that is, savings equals investment.

We have since them been left with modern Keynesian macro, which has never generated a recovery, and with a policy of public spending that has never brought an economy robust economic growth and full employment. The alternative that has been swept away would be unknown to virtually all economists alive today. To the extent they know anything at all about the pre-Keynesian theory of the cycle, it would be entirely made up of elements of the straw-man version that has descended from the arguments discussed by Keynes and spread far and wide by Keynesians ever since. The result is an economics profession that has almost no actual idea why recessions occur or what needs to be done to bring them to an end.

8. The basis for Keynes's success: why was Keynes able to succeed?

The basic conceptual framework put forward in *The General Theory* was not novel. Others had argued that government spending was important and necessary to maintain economic growth and full employment. The general glut debate that was initiated by the publication of Malthus's *Principles* in 1820 had brought these issues to a head. And even while the economic mainstream rejected demand deficiency as an actual cause of recessions – for which it usually applied the term 'overproduction' – the concept retained a great deal of popularity beyond mainstream economic theory. Overproduction was, in particular, at the core of the Marxist theory of crises:

> For Marx, capitalist crises are crises of 'overproduction': too many commodities are produced than can be profitably sold, and too much capital has been invested in industry, in the attempt to claim a share of the available profits. (*Socialist Voice* [1983] n.d.)

The major advocates of demand deficiency had, in classical times, been Lauderdale, Malthus and Sismondi. Yet, by the time Keynes came to write *The General Theory*, the list of those he could enlist in his 'Brave Army of Heretics' was meagre indeed. As he wrote:

> Since the war there has been a spate of heretical theories of under-consumption, of which those or Major Douglas are the most famous. (Keynes, *Collected Writings* [1936] 1981, VII, p. 370)

There was indeed a spate of others, of whom Catchings and Foster may have been the most well known, particularly in the United States.[1] In England, J.A. Hobson was the most well known and certainly the most notorious. Hobson had been drummed out of the economics fraternity and had his career blighted because of his views on underconsumption. Silvio Gesell, who advocated 'stamped money', where actual currency would have a use-by date so that money would have to be spent in a timely manner, was also discussed by Keynes. There were thus others who considered demand deficiency as the cause of recessions, meaning that the overproduction argument remained in circulation. 'Under-Consumption Theories' were discussed by Haberler in his

Prosperity and Depression (1937, pp. 111–32). He begins his discussion by pointing out how inadequate they are as theories of the cycle:

> The cruder versions of the theory, which exist in innumerable varieties in all countries, will not be considered here, as their fallacy has been clearly demonstrated on various occasions. ... The under-consumption theory is a theory of the crisis and depression rather than a theory of the cycle. (Haberler, 1937, pp. 111–12)

There is also that rueful but still puzzled statement from Winston Churchill as treasurer in 1929, and well captured by Peden. It provides a reminder that public spending as a cure for unemployment did have a deep appeal well before *The General Theory* was published even without theoretical support among economists:

> Churchill pointed to recent government expenditure on public works such as housing, roads, telephones, electricity supply, and agricultural development, and concluded that, although expenditure for these purposes had been justified:
>
>> for the purposes of curing unemployment the results have certainly been disappointing. They are, in fact, so meagre as to lend considerable colour to the orthodox Treasury doctrine which has been steadfastly held that, whatever might be the political or social advantages, very little additional employment and no permanent additional employment can in fact and as a general rule be created by State borrowing and State expenditure. (Peden, 1996, pp. 69–70)

Thus, outside and beyond the economics community, there was a logic that appealed to many that public spending was a cure for unemployment and slow rates of economic growth. Until the publication of *The General Theory*, as far as the academic community and the bureaucracy were concerned, demand deficiency was the province of economic cranks, dwelling at the fringe. But with Keynes's renown and prestige, coupled with the state of mind created among both the general public and the economics community by the just-ended Great Depression, there was a willingness to consider such theories once again.

Nothing that is said below is original to me. That said, most of it, even for those who discuss any of this, are just peripheral issues, without any particular point to make other than that these were parts of the process that brought us to the economic theories we now find in our texts and to the specific ways we now address economic issues. Here, however, they are part of a larger story – how economic theory went off the rails; how we lost the policy sense and coherence of classical economic theory. That is the larger intent of this entire book. These are part of the stepping stones that helped create the entire pathway to where we are now.

KEYNES'S PRE-EMINENCE

Especially important among the mix of factors that allowed the Keynesian revolution to occur was Keynes's own personal renown as an authoritative public
figure and economist. He was the son of a Cambridge don and was educated at
Eton. He was a member of the Bloomsbury Group and associate of the elites.

He had become world famous with the publication in 1919 of *The Economic
Consequences of the Peace*. He had been the Treasury representative at the
Paris Peace Conference at the end of World War I. He had, however, resigned
in 1919 to write his tirade against the economic harm that he argued would be
created as a result of the Treaty's provisions. Although he had been wrong in
his economic assessment (see Mantoux, 1946), there were nevertheless a large
number who accepted that Keynes had been able to foresee the coming of the
Great Depression and had identified, at least in part, its cause.

Thereafter, he was a major public intellectual commenting on both economic and political matters. He wrote a number of books, which included collections of his more popular writings, *Essays in Persuasion* (Keynes, *Collected
Writings* [1931] 1981, IX) and *Essays in Biography* (Keynes, *Collected
Writings* [1933] 1981, X) in particular. It is worth mentioning in passing that
it was while putting together his 'Essay on Malthus', which was an expansion
of a speech he had been giving in and around Cambridge since before World
War I, that he ended up researching Malthus's economics in late 1932. It was
then that he discovered demand deficiency, an issue he had never previously
shown interest in or discussed. It was from these beginnings that he turned
his attention to devising a theoretical model that would account for the Great
Depression while also having a justification for the public works he had been
advocating even before the Great Depression began.

It was in his essay 'Can Lloyd George Do It?' (Keynes, *Collected Writings*
[1929] 1981, IX, pp. 86–125) in which he and Hubert Henderson, who was
his co-author and Cambridge colleague, had publicly advocated the use of
public spending to stimulate the British economy in the dull but not deeply
recessionary economic environment of the late 1920s. A passage from the text
will provide some flavour of what was to come in *The General Theory* in more
theoretical terms:

> A country is enriched not by the mere negative act of an individual not spending all
> his income on current consumption. It is enriched by the positive act of using these
> savings to augment the capital equipment of the country.
>   It is not the miser who gets rich; but he who lays out his money in fruitful invest-
> ment. (Ibid., p. 123)

In responding to the quote from Churchill above, they wrote:

> Some State expenditure he concluded, is inevitable, and even wise and right for its own sake, but not as a cure for unemployment.
>   In relation to the actual facts of to-day, this argument is, we believe, quite without foundation. (Ibid., p. 115)

It may be noted that Henderson's reaction to *The General Theory* was entirely hostile. In his view, the circumstances of the Great Depression were entirely of a different kind from the slump that had existed in 1929. The correspondence between Henderson and Keynes in 1936 lays out Henderson's views in no uncertain terms, which begins with a note from Keynes to his wife, following a seminar at Cambridge in which Henderson explained his criticisms of Keynes's theory of deficient demand. The correspondence is found in the *Collected Writings* ([1944–46] 1981, XXIX, pp. 218–31). In his final letter, which ended the correspondence, Henderson wrote:

> The chief impression conveyed by your book is that you hold that the main cause of unemployment in modern societies is a chronic deficiency of effective demand, assumed to be non-existent by the classical economists. ... I argue that an attempt to make effective demand permanently stronger would not in the long run reduce unemployment. (Ibid., p. 229)

Henderson, who had been Keynes's closest ally in 1929, had by 1936 become one of his strongest critics. Yet with all others who took a classical position, his views were dismissed by the rising Keynesian tide, while the views of the classical economists had even by then almost completely vanished. Even the pamphlet that both had co-authored has since then been almost entirely remembered as having been authored by Keynes alone.

In addition to Keynes's other activities, he was also at the time the general editor of the *Cambridge Economic Handbooks*, which provided another source of his authority as an economics commentator. And it is also worth noting that the assistant editor was Dennis Robertson, another close friend and Cambridge colleague, who was also ultimately to become another trenchant, but all but forgotten, critic of *The General Theory*.

Keynes had, moreover, been a prominent member of the Macmillan Committee that had been set up after the stock market crash in 1929 to examine the causes of the poor economic conditions of the time. Keynes was not only a member of the Committee, which was made up of a number of prominent economists of the time, but his testimony to the Committee was in part how he paved his way towards creating an environment in which *The General Theory* would gain virtually instantaneous acceptance. It was not, however, his arguments that mattered, but the prominence in which his critique of 'The Treasury

View' was to underpin his authority in criticizing the classical economics of his time. Keynes did endorse the role of public works, as did a minority of others on the Committee, in an addendum, but as he had not yet come across Malthus's arguments, Keynes did not blame the cause of the downturn on a deficiency of demand:

> The committee took evidence from many leading economists of the day ... on the subject of unemployment. It decided in favour of the so-called Treasury view that expenditure on public works was not the answer, in spite of the signing of Addendum 1 by some of its leading members. This addendum, which was signed by Keynes [and others] advocated a programme of public works and import restrictions. (Wikipedia, 2019d)

Part of the evidence that was provided to the Committee was from Keynes himself:

> Keynes dominated the proceedings of the Committee, both in examining witnesses and shaping the report. ...
> Keynes's efforts to shape the work of the Committee led him in February and March 1930 to spend five sessions elaborating his approach to monetary theory and policy. (Keynes, *Collected Writings* [1929–31], XX, p. 38)

It is again worth noting that his focus was on monetary theory, which was in part due to his academic work at the time in completing his *Treatise on Money*. The transcript of his testimony, along with the discussions in which Keynes was heavily involved, extends for almost 300 pages of the *Collected Writings* (ibid., pp. 38–311), yet none of it mentions demand deficiency. Nor was demand deficiency discussed in Addendum I of the report (ibid., pp. 283–309), even while it argued, in part, that public spending would increase employment. Orthodox economic opinion, in keeping with classical economic theory, did not accept that increased public sector expenditure was an effective remedy for unemployment, so that at the time it was more intuition than based on any actual theoretical position that was used to back such arguments. And while there was a contingent of economists who did see such a role for public spending in recessions, there was not as yet an economic theory that would justify such an approach, which was the conclusion accepted by the majority of the Committee who accepted the classical conclusion. Yet, the addendum to the report, which was signed by Keynes along with others, was part of the process in which the political and economic environment was being prepared for this change in mainstream theory when *The General Theory* was eventually published five years later.

And, in appreciating the influential role Keynes had played during the period prior to the publication of *The General Theory*, Keynes's continuous stream of articles in various political publications should not be forgotten, along with his frequent publications in newspapers and news publications. Keynes was a major public figure whom the English public in particular, but also internationally, looked to for advice on economic issues. His already existing influence and reputation made *The General Theory* the sensation it was to become.

THE TEMPER OF THE TIMES

Not only did it matter that it was Keynes who had brought demand deficiency to life within the mainstream, but also that the timing of the publication was crucial. Although Keynes came across Malthus in 1932, at the very depths of the Great Depression, and was working on crafting a theoretical foundation for public spending as a means to deal with recessions from that point on, the book was not published until 1936, by which time the Great Depression had ended. This, in its own way, may have assisted in the spread of Keynesian theory, since there would be no full-scale attempt to apply Keynesian policies until the 1960s. This time gap allowed aggregate demand to become entrenched within mainstream economic theory, while not having actually had the theory tested in the field.

What may be more noteworthy is that the Great Depression was brought to an end using classical economic tools everywhere (other than in the US where the Great Depression was prolonged until the 1940s, in spite of, or more likely because of Roosevelt's Keynesian-type policies). Even more telling was that the post-war recovery across the world was driven forward by the American economy, which boomed, even though the federal budget was balanced immediately the war came to an end. Thus, although Keynesian theory was finding its way among economists, in the US, due to his classical upbringing, along with his business background, the American president, Harry Truman, not only insisted on balancing the budget the moment the war had ended, but there was also the largest fall in the level of public spending as a proportion of total output to have ever occurred. The American economy went from massive wartime spending to a balanced budget within a year, where millions of service personnel suddenly found themselves 'unemployed' and in which huge wartime enterprises were completely shut down. Yet, in spite of the warnings given by Keynesian economists at the time – the Great Depression had only ended in the United States five years before – the result was the beginning of the most sustained period of economic growth in history, which lasted from the 1940s until the 1970s.

Yet, it was the memory of the Great Depression that became the embedded myth that helped promote the rise of Keynesian economics and the replace-ment of the classical theory of the cycle with Keynesian macroeconomics.

It was also the more centrally directed wartime economy that helped change public sentiment towards acceptance of a greater role for direct government intervention into the management of the economy. The exceptionally low rates of unemployment, which had been kept much lower than usual by the large numbers of working-age men who had entered the armed forces, was interpreted as providing an example of how government expenditure and employment could soak up the unemployment.

Even apart from the wartime example, there had also been a slow but definite shift in public sentiment towards a more interventionist form of government policy that was noted by Keynes himself in his 'End of *Laissez-Faire*' published in 1926:

> From the time of John Stuart Mill, economists of authority have been in strong reaction against all such ideas. 'Scarcely a single English economist of repute', as Professor Cannan has expressed it, 'will join in a frontal attack upon Socialism in general,' though, as he also adds, 'nearly every economist, whether of repute or not, is always ready to pick holes in most socialistic proposals'. Economists no longer have any link with the theological or political philosophies out of which the dogma of social harmony was born, and their scientific analysis leads them to no such conclusions. (Keynes, *Collected Writings* [1926] 1981, IX, p. 281)

The rise of 'socialism', however loosely it might be conceived, as an active political and economic force was becoming more evident, even beyond a recognition of an important role for governments in directing the economy. The revolution in Russia had made the communist system the new laboratory of a better world to come in many minds. As a recognition of the different mindset at the start of the twentieth century, and as a kind of indication of the mindset among the educated at the time, the following is the conclusion to Keynes's 'A Short View of Russia' that he wrote following his visit to Russia in 1925, only eight years following the communist takeover. Keynes clearly did not like what he saw, finding Russia under the Soviets oppressive and stifling. He was also clear that there were no economic lessons for capitalist economies to be found in the communist regime. Nevertheless, as a gauge of general attitudes to the new Russia held by many of those who would respond positively to *The General Theory* when it was published, the last two paragraphs of Keynes's booklet are instructive.

> Yet the elation, when that is felt, is very great. Here – one feels at moments – in spite of poverty, stupidity, and oppression, is the Laboratory of Life. Here the chemicals are being mixed in new combinations, and stink and explode. Something – there is just a chance – might come out. And even a chance gives to what is happening in

Russia more importance than what is happening (let us say) in the United States of America.

I think that it is partly reasonable to be afraid of Russia, like the gentlemen who write to *The Times*. But if Russia is going to be a force in the outside world, it will not be the result of Mr. Zinovieff's money. Russia will never matter seriously to the rest of us, unless it be as a moral force. So, now the deeds are done and there is no going back, I should like to give Russia her chance; to help and not to hinder. For how much rather, even after allowing for everything, if I were a Russian, would I contribute my quota of activity to Soviet Russia than to Tsarist Russia! I could not subscribe to the new official faith any more than to the old. I should detest the actions of the new tyrants not less than those of the old. But I should feel that my eyes were turned towards, and no longer away from, the possibilities of things; that out of the cruelty and stupidity of Old Russia nothing could ever emerge, but that beneath the cruelty and stupidity of New Russia some speck of the ideal may lie hid. (Keynes, *Collected Writings* [1925] 1981, IX, p. 271)

That Keynes would write his own theoretical work that mirrored in many ways the Marxist theory of the cycle, basing the contours of the cycle on periods of overproduction, added to the support for the arguments of *The General Theory* from a very influential cohort of economists, and the public in general. Such influences should not be overstated but should not be under-stated either. That it was the younger economists who responded positively to the emergence of Keynesian theory is part and parcel with the typically more leftwards political orientation of the young.

That Keynesian theory would provide a theoretical justification for more active policies to remedy policies of all sorts beyond high rates of unemploy-ment during recessions was the further attraction that would help entrench macroeconomics. The G of $C + I + G$ (see below) would allow for many further economic experiments in dealing with many issues that a more classi-cal approach would have warned economic policy makers about the dangers of. Deficits were no longer to be seen as an intrinsic danger to be eliminated as soon as possible. Instead, although it has taken time for the full flowering that has occurred in the twenty-first century, public spending has come to be seen just as legitimate a cause of growth as an equal level of private sector investment.

HIS RETURN TO TREASURY

And, as far as being able to influence the direction of government policy, Keynes was not just an outside influence, working in London and spending only a semester at Cambridge, but following the outbreak of war, he was asked to enter the British Treasury and oversee important aspects of its operation:

> In the Second World War, Keynes – by then the most eminent and famous econo-
> mist of his generation – entered the British Treasury as a 'demi-semi-official' (as he
> described his position). This post, his public stature, and the vast system of contacts
> with establishment figures that Keynes had acquired over the years, were to place
> him in a position of powerful influence. The 1941 budget was the first to be con-
> structed on the principles of Keynesian macro-management ideas, which became
> the Treasury orthodoxy.
>   Furthermore, in this triumphant return to the corridors of power, Keynes had
> been accompanied by a retinue of younger disciples such as James Meade and
> Richard Stone. These disciples, and particularly Meade, were to provide much of
> the impetus towards the further implementation of a Keynesian regime. From this
> intellectual milieu and bureaucratic powerbase emerged such famous milestones in
> British public policy as the 1942 Beveridge Report, and the 1944 White Papers on
> Employment Policy and Social Insurance. The year 1944 thus marks the birth of the
> Keynesian revolution in UK governmental policy. Since that time, Britain has had
> a Keynesian fiscal constitution: that is, there has been no constitutional restraint on
> governments to prevent them from running a budget deficit. (Burton, 1978, p. 33)

His publication, first as a series of articles in *The Times* in 1939 when the war broke out, and then as a separate publication published a year later titled, *How to Pay for the War* (Keynes, *Collected Writings* [1940] 1981, XXII, pp. 40–155), helped establish his mode of approach and his way of thinking. Britain was therefore the first to fall under Keynesian demand management techniques, with the United States taking up the same approach but not until after the war was over. It is noteworthy that in the United States, President Truman immediately returned the budget to surplus, which coincided with the beginning of the most sustained period of growth in history. Irrespective of what the future would bring, nonetheless Keynesian theory was advancing through the corridors of economic policy making, in part based on the example set by the UK.

EASE OF EXPLANATION – THE DIAGRAMMATIC APPROACH

Other changes were occurring that helped the advance of Keynesian theory, primary among them being the greater use made of static diagrams used to illustrate economic points. The proliferation of diagrams was facilitated by the improving print technologies that allowed such two-dimensional line drawings to spread widely within economic texts. What therefore helped make Keynesian economics clear, possibly even to Keynes himself, were the various diagrams that sprang up almost as soon as *The General Theory* was published that could be used to explain what Keynes meant. The book itself was noto-riously difficult to follow. Such early discussions assisted by diagrammatic representations were able to bring forward enough of Keynes's meaning to satisfy the interest in what he had meant without having actually to read the book. What made the transition so much easier were the various diagrams that sprang up that allowed others to form an understanding of what Keynes had meant, although not necessarily the meaning Keynes had himself intended.

The earliest of these diagrams is the IS–LM model, put together by J.R. Hicks and published in 1937. There is some controversy over whether Keynes personally accepted Hicks's diagram as a proper representation of his meaning. Whether he did or not, there is no question that the IS–LM diagram almost instantly entered the literature and has remained the workhorse rep-resentation of Keynes's core message. It fit the basic outline of *The General Theory* by focusing on the demand side, made aggregate demand the major element in creating growth, showed how an underemployment equilibrium could occur, brought the real and monetary sides of the economy together and demonstrated how an increase in public spending could lift the level of output and employment. It also did so in the same context as Keynes had done, by supposedly portraying the inadequacies of classical theory at the same time.

But what was most important was how easy the diagram was to explain. Rather than having to understand individual markets, the nature of production, the role of entrepreneurs, the adjustment of relative prices, the nature of money markets or any of the multitude of individual issues one would need to keep on top of if one were to understand the operation of an economy, the entire sequence of processes were brought together in one diagrammatic presentation that could be portrayed as explaining it all. Possibly more significant still was Paul Samuelson's 45-degree line and aggregate demand represented by $C + I + G$ (where C is total consumption, I is total private investment and G is total government expenditure). Without requiring any thought being given to what is actually happening within an economy when any of the variables are adjusted, these lines could be raised or lowered and the outcome read off the axes. The logic may have been superficial, but the outcome was straight-forwardly apparent. A fall in C or I could be compensated for by an increase in G, and thus both gross domestic product (GDP) and employment could be maintained or even increased.

To this was added the leakages and injections diagram, which in its simplest manifestation could be used to show that, in equilibrium, $I = S$, that is, invest-ment equals savings. Or when not in equilibrium, that the forces of just these two variables would shift the economy in the direction Keynes had said they would move.

The final addition to the stable of Keynesian diagrams were the aggre-gate demand–aggregate supply curves that became standard after inflation became a major issue in the 1970s. It added the aggregate supply curve to the picture and placed both aggregate supply and aggregate demand within a supply-and-demand curve apparatus that allowed for the simultaneous determination of both the price level and national output.

While there is more detail and breadth provided after these initial sets of instructions, they nevertheless remain the foundation for virtually all macroeconomics courses taught afterwards. Most economists never come to appreciate the extent to which such models fundamentally impair their ability to understand the operation of an economy, since there is no understanding provided of the adjustment process required to move from one position to another. Rather, they are taught that these represent the basic framework for understanding how an economy operates, with matters left at that. The aggregate demand curve shifts and the outcomes can just be read off the diagram. No actual examination of the economy is required, merely an examination of an aggregated set of data.

More importantly, virtually everyone who studies economics is instructed in these static Keynesian models as part of their introductory course in economic theory. This happens whether they go on to learn at a deeper level or never do another economics course again. In particular, it is the absorption of the lesson that economies are driven from the demand side, displayed in every diagram, that is the crucial factor, which can be manipulated to show the effects of changes in different parameters. The message learned – especially by those who never again spend another moment studying economic theory – is that recessions can be shortened, while economic growth and employment levels are increased, by additional public spending. This is a message that is only ever debated, let alone rejected, in a very small number of economic classrooms across the world.

THE PURPOSE OF THE GDP STATISTIC

The proliferation of economic data that has occurred since the publication of *The General Theory* was hastened by the absence of such data during the Great Depression. Although it is almost unimaginable today, there were no data measuring either the strength of the national economy overall, or the level of employment and unemployment, until the period after World War II. Although various proxies were used at the time, they were limited in scope and less comprehensive than the array of data that has become the norm. It was the very absence of such data in the midst of the greatest economic crisis in history that led to the enormous growth of national statistical collections that followed the war.

Although we have become used to the regular publication of data on GDP growth and the unemployment rate, neither existed in Keynes's own time.

While the unemployment rate peaked in 1933 at around 25 per cent in most countries, there were no official labour force statistics until after the war. Many of the numbers we use to examine the Great Depression were constructed only long after the event. There was the same lack of data measuring the national level of production. There were no GDP data collected or available. Like the labour force data, GDP data were first produced during the post-war period. Estimates of the size of the downturn are now calculated to have been a fall of between 30 per cent and 50 per cent in the level of output. Given the policies of the Hoover administration from the fall of the stock market at the end of 1929 – high taxes, massive increases in tariffs, no cuts to real wage levels, a huge fall in the stock of money – such figures are likely to be a reasonably accurate reflection of the times, but are still not necessarily comparable to modern data sets attempting to measure the same entities. How comparable they are with data sets of the same name published today is merely a matter of conjecture.

The single most important measure sought was designed to calculate the level of production across an economy. The concept behind the national accounts was originally designed by Simon Kuznets at the National Bureau of Economic Research during the 1930s, but while he laid down the structure, it was not his conceptual design that would be implemented. In its own way, the structure that was eventually adopted was basically a reflection of Keynesian theory. The aim was to produce data that could be related to employment creation on the assumption that the larger the level of output, the higher would be the level of paid employment.

The basic Keynesian theoretical framework in relation to employment was that the number of jobs would vary directly with the level of workplace production. The aim therefore was to measure the level of workplace production. This is an equation every economist will recognize:

$$Y = C + I + G + X - M,$$

where:
Y = GDP, output, national income, production, aggregate demand;
C = consumer demand;
I = private investment – the increment in the capital stock without adjustment for depreciation;
G = government spending;
X = exports;
M = imports.

Y represents the amount of output produced during some period of time, say a quarter or a full year. The aim is to provide an estimate of how much output is produced by the paid workforce during this period of time. Left out, therefore, was anything produced in the home. A restaurant meal was part of national output, while the same meal cooked at home was not. Of course, while the ingredients bought by the restaurant were netted out from the value added by the restaurant, these same ingredients were included in the accounts if they were bought for final use at home, so the data were at least partially inclusive of 'home production'. The aim was therefore to incorporate everything that required someone to be employed to provide, which would provide insights into the strength of the labour market. The underlying concept in the design of GDP was that the demand for commodities was in itself the demand for labour – a direct contradiction of classical theory.

Similarly, in dealing with G – government expenditure – there was no longer even a pretence that the goods and services produced by governments were necessarily value adding, or that the published figures were even a proximate measure of the value that had been created. Since only a proportion of what the government produced had been sold on the market, and even then the value of the resources used up in production were not accounted for, there was no measure of value added. Government spending was simply included without any attempt to calculate the actual contribution to the economy's overall productivity, or the amount of output that was added to the flow of useable product made available. Once again, the conception was that increases in GDP should be seen as an increase in employment-creating forms of activity, with government spending part of the process by which jobs were created. The proverbial digging holes and then refilling them would be shown as positive economic activity in the National Accounts.

Investment, represented by the letter I, was a measure of the increase in expenditure on capital goods, buildings and other forms of construction. No account is taken of the depreciation in capital assets that occurs during the period. Investment, as far as this measurement is concerned, can only be a positive figure. Again, depreciation may make an asset less capable of production, and reduce an economy's ability to produce in the future, but has no immediate or discernible effect on employment. And again, the value of the statistic crafted in this way was to strengthen the relationship between the measured level of investment expenditure and the level of employment in an economy.

Included in the measure of investment were changes in the level of inventories. 'Unintended inventory accumulation' was the theoretical process that allowed the national accounts to show the equality of saving and investment in money terms. Building inventories required labour, while consumption that came out of previously produced goods that had been held as stock would not add to jobs. The conceptual framework was thus designed to function as a means of measuring what a Keynesian believed was necessary for a government to do to increase the level of employment. Raising G in particular would become the first considered policy required to create jobs. Living standards were a secondary matter. Per capita GDP is a measure almost never discussed, which would be the case if even a rudimentary measure of how the average person was or was not benefitting from economic activity was of central importance in designing the statistic on production.

THE RELATIONSHIP BETWEEN KEYNESIAN THEORY AND THE MEASUREMENT OF GDP

But going back to the Keynesian equation of aggregate demand, it is important to note that it is an equation that comes in two forms. First, as a national accounting identity:

$$Y \equiv (C + I + G + X) - M$$

Written this way as an identity, it states that as a matter of definition, the level of GDP or domestic production (Y) can be calculated as the total of everything bought within an economy during some period of time minus the level of imports. As a matter of logic, if you take the total amount bought domestically and then subtract the total amount imported, the remainder must be the total amount produced domestically. The identity sign ($\equiv$) indicates there is no economic content in the expression.

　　Then there is the expression based on Keynesian theory:

$$Y = C + I + G + (X - M)$$

This is often now written: $Y = C + I + G + NX$, where NX represents net exports, that is, exports minus imports ($X - M$). Writing the expression in this way, with an equals sign and not an identity sign, turns the equation into a theory. It states that if you raise any of the elements on the right side of the equal sign, the level of GDP will consequently rise, and for that reason an increase in C causes an increase in Y. But note this. Y is not production but aggregate demand. There is a large degree of slippage between the national accounting estimate of production and this expression that is a totalling of the components that make up the elements of Keynesian aggregate demand. This has reinforced the conception that the elements of demand not only total up to the elements of production but are also the cause of their being the level that output has reached. But if production has any genuine meaning, it is an inventory of goods produced and services rendered during some period of time. One can say that an increase in consumption caused production to rise, but it leaves out the entrepreneur, the business, which was the actual cause of the rise in production. The actual sale to a final consumer at the end of the production process is far from the motivation for purchase and sale during the operation of an economy since the entire supply chain is omitted.

The unfortunate outcome of this overlap has been that the national accounting production data have reinforced the Keynesian notion of aggregate demand as the cause of the production that has been recorded. The categories used in statistical series throughout the world in every economy have been patterned to resemble the Keynesian theory that has grown up side by side. There would be virtually no economist working within either macroeconomics or statistical estimation who would appreciate the two entirely different meanings associated with what is an almost identical mathematical expression. This confusion is part of the reason Keynesian theory has managed to gain such widespread acceptance.

GOVERNMENT SPENDING

There is one further issue that has added to the complications when using national accounting data. This is the addition of government spending to the level of demand. Private sector goods and services are sold on the market, produced with goods and services that are also sold on the market. If the business makes a profit, then that production has been value adding. The economy has created more value than it has used up. For the public sector, there is no evidence that anything produced by government has added any value to the economy, and it is just as likely to have pulled the economy backwards. The inclusion of government spending straight into the national accounts renders the final total almost meaningless.

Going further, adding G to privately produced C and I allows a summation of two incompatible entities. Adding private and public sector expenditure as if they were both equally productive creates a false sense of what has taken place as far as the real economy is concerned. The digging of holes and refilling those holes has left no distributable product behind, but nevertheless shows up as a rise in GDP.

There is then the additional complication of the meaning of public sector infrastructure inside the national accounts. Suppose the government has chosen to support some project that will not be completed for seven years. Whatever is spent in Year 1 is automatically included within the national accounts and is therefore considered part of the nation's economic growth. Yet, nothing has been added other than in a completely notional sense. The economy is not only not more productive than it was, it is actually less productive, since all the resources used have disappeared but there is nothing available in return. It will be argued that a dividend will occur in six years' time when the project is completed. Perhaps, if the government has chosen well, when the project is completed the economy will eventually receive a positive return on the investment. But that will only occur then and only if the value that comes on stream is able to repay in added productivity for the value that has been used up. In the meantime, there is nothing to show for the expenditure as far as a more productive economy is concerned.

The benefit from the expenditure supposedly occurs in the jobs that have been created. No account is taken of the loss of value in relation to the alternate forms of investment that could have been undertaken instead, but were not because the government had employed those resources instead. There is nevertheless the belief that whatever else may have occurred in the first instance, jobs were created, and with the 'multiplier effects' due to those initial expenditures the economy will grow, since the workers on these projects will spend the money they earned in shops and on services. There is no explicit underlying concept representing the structure of production.

The original aim in creating national accounting data was to provide a measure of output – how much was being produced in one year relative to some previous period. The measure would provide an indication of the trend in the material well-being of a population. A second purpose might have been as a measure of the economy's productive output relative to its potential – how well the economy is performing in comparison with how well it is capable of performing. Instead, we have a measure that reinforces the Keynesian concept that an economy is driven from the demand side without providing much insight into the shift in the actual well-being of the population.

As an example of how misconceived the measure of GDP is, suppose one economy has grown by 10 per cent over the last year and another has grown by 1 per cent. From that statistic, it is impossible to tell which economy has the higher standard of living, which has a lower unemployment rate, or which has added to its productive potential for the year to come.

And let me point this out as well. How would one measure the growth in GDP that occurred over the period from 1900 till 1920? In just those 20 years, there was the introduction of the automobile, the airplane, the radio, the cinema, vaccines against many former deadly diseases, plus the introduction of electricity and the telephone into many homes, these along with a wide range of other innovations and inventions that added to human well-being. What measure could possibly have summarized these changes into a single number? Perhaps no such number exists. Yet, the number that is now produced worldwide is seen as the most important measure of economic well-being, when in reality its most important use has been to determine whether the economy will be able to add to the number of jobs available, but with this one additional side consideration – that it has helped to establish the Keynesian belief that an increase in aggregate demand will lead to an increase in employment.

GATHERING STATISTICAL DATA

Among the attractions of Keynesian theory is the relative ease with which data can be collected that are superficially able to be used to examine the outcomes of Keynesian policy. The core issues are aggregate demand and its relationship to the rate of unemployment. Along with data on the price level, most of the data needed to examine the consequences of a Keynesian policy are relatively easy to collect.

Not so for a classical model. A classical model is built around an assessment of the entire economic structure. The structure of production is a massive network of relationships between buyers and sellers, from primary producers through all stages of production, to sales, to the final buyer. Even then, the stock of assets owned by individuals, such as their cars and houses, have a major effect on real living standards going forward. The wealth of an economy is not determined by how much output it might generate at some moment in time but by the entire economy and its productive potential.

Not only is it the stock of productive assets that matters, but so too does the change in its stock of productive capital over time. Additions to that stock on the one hand are counterbalanced by the negative effects of depreciation. The value of that stock is in the end determined by the value of the output that it can assist in producing, so that an inventory at current prices is impossible to calculate with anything that could be remotely described as accurate.

Complicating these issues is the problem that, as time goes by, large parts of the existing capital stock are rendered valueless by the process of innovation. For more than 100 years, offices all over the world depended on the typewriter, yet there are virtually no typewriters left anywhere other than as curiosities and antiques. Whatever value they may once have had as part of a productive enterprise has vanished and been replaced via computerization.

Yet, if one is to determine how productive an economy is, the entire apparatus of the economy must be examined. It is not just the latest additions to final expenditure that matter, but the entire apparatus that includes the whole of the economy's infrastructure that had already been in existence before the period had commenced.

Keynesian theory, however, deals with final production, still a massive problem to estimate but far more manageable. For the private sector, once what to include has been determined, the calculations are theoretically straightforward. Estimates need to be made of the level of purchases by consumers, and to these may be added the level of expenditure by businesses on capital goods net of depreciation. It is a total of the investment goods bought during some period of time that is, in principle, available within the business accounts of every firm. There is no attempt here to diminish the difficulties involved, but only to explain that as challenging as this process is, the data are there and they can be collected, as they have been by statistical agencies across the world.

Net exports are possibly the easiest data to collect since every country monitors imports and exports and can be expected to have data covering both. Conversion to real estimates are also, relatively speaking, simple in principle.

Government spending is conceptually the most difficult to calculate, while in practical terms it is the easiest. The level of government outlays are known with reasonable precision since they are part of the annual budget estimates, which are then monitored throughout the year. How much governments spend is a known quantity. However, since the aim of the national accounts is to show value added, since public spending, unlike private expenditures, is not dependent on finding a buyer, there is nothing that guarantees that such public spending has created any value at all – in value-adding terms, that it is even positive.

Digging and refilling holes is the archetypal example of a non-value-adding form of public spending. The money is paid out, but no saleable product has been produced. Since the system of national accounts adds in government spending at cost, that is, all such spending is included as if it had been value adding, the data do not distort the underlying picture only when there are no major changes taking place in the pattern of public spending. As soon as there are such changes, interpreting increases in public spending as genuinely value-adding expenditure becomes overburdened with difficulty. The result is that such data are easy to manufacture but difficult to interpret. Adding together, as if they are equally relevant in assessing economic activity, private investment and government make-work activity provides sets of figures that are then used with little apparent concern.

Yet, the data are produced and seldom questioned even in relation to their superficial meaning, never mind in relation to their problematic origin. The purchase of a shovel, to take a trivial example, can be a consumption, investment or public expenditure. The shovel itself may have been produced more than a year ago, yet its purchase, irrespective of its intended use, will be recorded in the national accounts.

Such difficulties are experienced across the full range of statistical data. The labour market standard, which has existed since the 1940s, that one must work for merely one hour in a week to be counted as employed, obviously fails to capture many features of significance.

But, at the end of the day, as far as those who are assessing the data are concerned, the published data provide numbers with which to monitor policy outcomes. They are taken as published, accepted as both the right sets of data to examine and as an accurate enough set of figures on which policy can be based.

Economic ability is in many ways no longer judged in terms of how well a set of policies led to strong rates of growth and higher living standards, but how closely one's forecasts are to the published data sets when they are eventually released some time after the period in question has gone into history.

MATHEMATICS AND KEYNESIAN THEORY

A further attraction of Keynesian theory was the ease with which models could be constructed and then empirically tested. From the very start, economists were building models that explained in a series of equations how an economy worked. Keynes himself put together his $Z = D$ framework (see Chapter 4), which was almost immediately picked up on by others to structure Keynesian models.

Using such models and matching them with the emerging national accounting data made a natural fit for economists seeking to estimate various equations. Although computerization was only in its infancy, simple estimates of consumption functions, or the relationship between employment and output, could be readily worked up and assessed.

By the 1960s, with the emergence of vastly superior computer technologies, many began to construct large-scale Keynesian models that allowed data to be manipulated and theories tested. Even with the coming of monetarist theory, the interest was in trying different policy prescriptions and judging these against outcomes. The shifting of economics from a conceptual study to one based on mathematics and modelling was, in part, driven by the ease with which economic theory, and Keynesian theory in particular, could be modelled and judged.

The inaccuracy of such models ultimately meant that their use would diminish over time. Such models continue to exist but there is little public discussion of any such models, nor are their forecasts any longer seen as authoritative. But, inaccurate though such models may have been, the possibilities that they might have worked drew economists into testing the various aspects of Keynesian theory. Beyond that, the availability of so much data that conformed to Keynesian presuppositions meant that anyone with an interest in forecasting would be generally compelled to frame their work along Keynesian lines. Indeed, since the very definition of economic success has been framed in terms of various data-based outcomes associated with the Keynesian model – such as the multiplier or consumer demand and employment – Keynesian theory has become more deeply ingrained within the concepts of economists to the point where most economists would find it difficult to conceptualize economic problems in any other way.

POLITICS AND POLICY SIMPLICITY

Overwhelmingly, the great advantage that Keynesian economics provided was its intuitive simplicity. Everyone could understand the concept of recessions being caused by too little demand and too much saving. Since the Industrial Revolution, every succeeding period has been the most productive in human history. Whether in the time of Malthus, or a century later when Keynes was writing, the possibility that productivity had outrun the community's demand for goods and services has a plausibility that might have been valid. Although we teach economics as the study of scarcity, with the data showing variations in the amount of money left unspent (called 'saving') out of current money income received, there was an acceptance that a fall-off in demand could lead to recession. It seemed plausible that the demand for investment goods might fall short of the amount the community chose to save.

But, even more than the theoretical plausibility, there was the desire by governments to be seen to take action in the midst of a downturn. *The General Theory* had been published in 1936, well after the Great Depression had come to an end, so could not be tested at the time. It therefore had a theoretical appeal but had not been put to the test in the midst of an actual recession. In most of the world, the Great Depression had unmistakeably ended around 1933. No economy, with the possible exception of the United States, took an avowedly Keynesian-type approach to recovery, and no economy took so long to actually recover as the United States. From the mid-1930s on, other than the United States, no industrialized economy was any longer in recession.

Yet, the mythology that the Great Depression had been brought to an end in the US by the New Deal, and even more importantly, that it was the public spending that grew out of the coming of war at the end of the 1930s that ended the depression, reinforced the belief that such public spending created a positive economic environment for growth and employment. Even so, at the very top of the political and economic structures were politicians and economists who had been brought up on pre-Keynesian economic thought. The most devastating refutation of Keynesian theory came at the end of World War II, when US President Harry Truman immediately balanced the American budget and cut the immense amount of spending that had occurred during the war. Keynesians assumed that a return to the Great Depression was certain, yet the United States began an expansion that would continue for 30 years.

It is not possible to exaggerate the extent to which the circumstances at the end of the war have demonstrated how wrong Keynesian theory is. The millions who returned from the armed forces to civilian life were equivalent to a sudden upturn in mass unemployment. Each returned soldier was a newly unemployed person. Moreover, the various wartime industries immediately shut down. There was no further need for the tanks and artillery that had been the centre of production during the war. Those who had been working in various forms of war production experienced the equivalent of a shutting down of their industries.

Nevertheless, the American economy immediately returned to full employment as the millions of soldiers and displaced armaments producers found new work in the expanding enterprises of the time. The fluctuations in activity that did occur over the succeeding 30 years hardly amounted at any stage to a genuine recession, and certainly there was little concern, once the expansion began, of a return to recessionary conditions.

Yet, the actual circumstances of the economy did not disturb the development of Keynesian textbook theory. The publication of Lorie Tashis's Keynesian text in 1947, followed by the publication in 1948 of Samuelson's, and thereafter by many Samuelson clones, brought Keynesian theory into the heart of policy formation, if not immediately, then over time.

It was therefore for another generation to adopt Keynesian solutions to ancient economic problems, not the generation in which *The General Theory* had been published. Although overproduction and demand deficiency had long been recognized in classical times as the most common economic fallacy, this was a theory now backed with the authority of Keynes and the many freshly minted Keynesians who flooded from the universities. The combination of its superficial plausibility, the large increase in university attendance where many students took introductory courses in Keynesian macro whether intending to become economists or not, and the wish to find some means to ensure there was no repeat of the Great Depression, Keynesian fiscal policy became the policy of choice across the world. Although such policies have never worked, it remains the first instrument sought out when unemployment has risen higher than policy makers would like.

THE BUSINESS CYCLE JUSTIFICATION FOR DEFICIT FINANCE

The next extension of the Keynesian model virtually separated Keynesian theory from the business cycle. The original theory as argued by Keynes was that during recessions public spending should increase to create jobs, but that as soon as possible, not only should the spending be cut back, but surpluses should be run to eliminate the deficit that the previous public spending had created. The application of Keynesian theory has now proceeded so that there is no longer any recessionary justification required for the increase in public spending. All that is required is to argue that the outlays will create jobs. That other jobs in the private sector might therefore be crowded out is no longer even part of the debate. An increase in government spending is almost of itself justified by its job-creation effects. No examination over whether what is produced will create value-adding forms of output or whether the economy will subsequently grow, leading to increases in real incomes, seems necessary.

There remains some focus and discussion on deficits, perhaps enough that there will be some efforts to resurrect the theoretical critique that had once been mainstream among economists, to limit the level of public spending and rein in deficits. The warning that was attached to rising public spending during classical times was the concern over its inflationary effects. That was at a time when the word 'inflation' literally meant deficit finance. With the coming of Keynesian theory and the advocacy of deficit finance, the term came to mean only an increase in the price level.

Yet, it does appear that deficits were not always seen as the spectre of doom. The following, from an economic text written in 1901, provides an interesting comparison with more modern concerns, on the question of public expenditure and deficit finance. In leading to this conclusion, the issue of productive versus unproductive expenditure was raised, that is, would the expenditure pay for itself in subsequent revenues earned? In relation to whether there will be a positive return on funds outlaid, we find the following observation. The author was Joseph Shields Nicholson.

> The point is that unproductive expenditure of a nation must in the end involve increased taxation. All debt is an anticipation of revenue; and if the revenue is not obtained from production, it must be obtained from taxation. Accordingly, loans proposed for social benefit must always submit to two tests: *First*, Is State management necessary? *Secondly*, Is the object worth the cost in taxation? And how does it stand in the competition with other social objects? (Nicholson, 1893–1901, Vol. III, p. 410; original emphasis)

The one issue that was never mentioned is whether such expenditure would lead to a net increase in the level of employment. It would never have crossed Nicholson's mind, or the mind of any other classical economist, since it was a possibility that had been endlessly discussed and utterly rejected.

JOSEPH SHIELD NICHOLSON

A note here on Joseph Shield Nicholson, who will be referred to in the next chapter more extensively, and who will be referenced because even though having published his own three-volume text in 1901, more than 50 years after Mill's *Principles*, and when the name 'political economy' had gone out of fashion, he titled his text, like Mill's, *Principles of Political Economy*. There are, of course, differences between his own approach to many issues and Mill's, but there is never any doubt that they are on the same side of the fence, both economically and philosophically.

As noted by Wikipedia (2019b), 'In his principal work, *Principles of Political Economy* (three volumes, 1893–1901), [Nicholson] closely follows John Stuart Mill in his selection of material'. What the authors at Wikipedia, however, fail to understand, is that he also followed Mill in much of his approach to economic matters generally. Both sought a market system in which individual freedom was the underlying framework for both political and economic outcomes. He also followed Mill in recognizing an important role for government oversight of the economy. Unlike Mill, however, his text is as easy to follow for a modern reader as Mill's is now difficult.

NOTE

1. Catchings and Foster were among the 'leading pre-Keynesian economists in the underconsumptionist tradition, advocating similar issues to Keynes such as the paradox of thrift and economic interventionism. The two are now rarely mentioned in contemporary economics texts, standing as they do in the shadow of Keynes's *The General Theory*' (Wikipedia, 2019f).

9. Classical theory and the role of government

It is almost impossible any longer to know what a modern economist believes about the economic judgements found among economists prior to the publication of *The General Theory*. Possibly the most incorrect judgement still generally held is the belief that classical economists were strongly opposed to public spending in general, or to watching over the way in which individuals played out their economic roles, and that they instead insisted on an extremely limited role for government regulation or expenditure.

The term for the nightwatchman state is *laissez-faire* – leave things to the market to sort themselves out and allow businesses to manage their own affairs without government meddling. Nor should governments impress some kind of common good on the dealings between businesses and their customers or with their own employees. The main reason such beliefs have entered into the common mythology among economists is largely due to the premises upon which *The General Theory* was built. Keynes more or less argued that his predecessors had taken a hands-off view to the problem of recession. There was a view that matters were best left alone. Whether intentional or not, or whether that was the belief Keynes himself had harboured at the time – although he said otherwise in his 'End of *Laissez-Faire*' (1926) – the classical acceptance of a *laissez-faire* policy has been the conclusion that many have taken from their reading of Keynes in 1936. The classical conclusion that public spending would not cure unemployment was extended to a belief that there was virtually no role for government in the management on the economy.

This passage, quoted earlier, on Churchill as treasurer in 1929, captures much of what was the actual ethos of classical theory and policy on public spending:

> Churchill pointed to recent government expenditure on public works such as housing, roads, telephones, electricity supply, and agricultural development, and concluded that, although expenditure for these purposes had been justified:
>
>> for the purposes of curing unemployment the results have certainly been disappointing. They are, in fact, so meagre as to lend considerable colour to the orthodox Treasury doctrine which has been steadfastly held that, whatever might be the political or social advantages, very little additional employment and no

> permanent additional employment can in fact and as a general rule be created by
> State borrowing and State expenditure. (Peden, 1996, pp. 69–70)

There was, first, the view among economists that public spending would
have little if any positive effect on employment. This was 'the orthodox
Treasury doctrine' – Keynes's 'Treasury View'. Yet, second, there was also
a willingness to attempt to create employment through a series of public
expenditures, in this case on a series of projects that were intended to be value
adding and productive: 'housing, roads, telephones, electricity supply, and
agricultural development'. And third, here when it was tried, the practical
outcome supported the theoretical expectation. Public spending did not lead to
an increase in employment or a fall in unemployment.

But, whatever else they might have thought, classical economists had never
believed in public waste as a cure for unemployment. There had never been
a case for waste, but this changed with the coming of the Keynesian revolution.
This is from *The General Theory*:

> When involuntary unemployment exists, the marginal disutility of labour is neces-
> sarily less than the utility of the marginal product. Indeed it may be much less. For
> a man who has been long unemployed some measure of labour, instead of involving
> disutility, may have a positive utility. If this is accepted, **the above reasoning
> shows how 'wasteful' loan expenditure may nevertheless enrich the commu-
> nity on balance**. Pyramid-building, earthquakes, even wars may serve to increase
> wealth, if the education of our statesmen on the principles of the classical economics
> stands in the way of anything better. (Keynes, *Collected Writings* [1936] 1981, VII,
> pp. 128–9; bold emphasis added)

This is so outrageous that many Keynesians now attempt to argue that this
was stated more in the way of a joke than to be taken seriously. This was not,
however, intended as a joke. The point made was literally the point intended,
that if there were nothing better the government could think of, then anything
at all would do, wasteful or not. Keynes continues:

> It is curious how common sense, wriggling for an escape from absurd conclusions,
> has been apt to reach a preference for wholly 'wasteful' forms of loan expenditure
> rather than for partly wasteful forms, which, because they are not wholly wasteful,
> tend to be judged on strict 'business' principles. For example, unemployment relief
> financed by loans is more readily accepted than the financing of improvements at
> a charge below the current rate of interest; whilst the form of digging holes in the
> ground known as gold-mining, which not only adds nothing whatever to the real
> wealth of the world but involves the disutility of labour, is the most acceptable of
> all solutions. (Ibid.)

A bit of waste may, it seems, go a long way. The continuation of the above
passage – already quoted in Chapter 5 but repeated here for emphasis since the

notion is both entirely absurd but is also nevertheless the conceptual justification for a sizeable proportion of public spending to this day – has been taken as the archetypal advice that has been followed time and again by governments during recessions. Indeed, almost any public expenditure is now defended in the same way, whether during recession or in during normal periods of business conditions, as a means to create jobs. Anything at all will do:

> If the Treasury were to fill old bottles with banknotes, bury them at suitable depths in disused coalmines which are then filled up to the surface with town rubbish, and leave it to private enterprise on well-tried principles of *laissez-faire* to dig the notes up again (the right to do so being obtained, of course, by tendering for leases of the note-bearing territory), there need be no more unemployment and, with the help of the repercussions, the real income of the community, and its capital wealth also, would probably become a good deal greater than it actually is. It would, indeed, be more sensible to build houses and the like; but if there are political and practical difficulties in the way of this, the above would be better than nothing. (Ibid.)

The unit of account for all such expenditures is often the number of jobs created for whatever a government decides to spend money on. There is no regard paid to the projects and other activities that have been foregone by the private sector because the resources put to use by the government have become unavailable to others. And, of course, 'the help of the repercussions', the effects of the multiplier process, would extend and accelerate the process of economic growth. Naturally, better to do something value adding, suggests Keynes, but if nothing comes to mind then something else should be done. Gold mining is a complete waste of effort, he argued, but perhaps it is something since at least jobs are created. Wasteful expenditure has its value also in driving future production to meet the new demands of these formerly unemployed workers. Here is how the chapter ends:

> Ancient Egypt was doubly fortunate, and doubtless owed to this its fabled wealth, in that it possessed two activities, namely, pyramid-building as well as the search for the precious metals, the fruits of which, since they could not serve the needs of man by being consumed, did not stale with abundance. The Middle Ages built cathedrals and sang dirges. Two pyramids, two masses for the dead, are twice as good as one; but not so two railways from London to York. Thus we are so sensible, have schooled ourselves to so close a semblance of prudent financiers, taking careful thought before we add to the 'financial' burdens of posterity by building them houses to live in, that we have no such easy escape from the sufferings of unemployment. We have to accept them as an inevitable result of applying to the conduct of the State the maxims which are best calculated to 'enrich' an individual by enabling him to pile up claims to enjoyment which he does not intend to exercise at any definite time. (Ibid.)

The residual belief that has come down as a result of passages such as these was that, among economists prior to Keynes, the role of government was strictly limited, that an attitude of *laissez-faire* was universal, while the government's role was limited to times of war or for extreme emergencies of one kind or another.

CLASSICAL ECONOMISTS SAW A MAJOR ROLE FOR GOVERNMENT

The actual attitude to the government's role in economic management was discussed by J.S. Nicholson[1] in his three-volume *Principles of Political Economy*, published in 1901. In showing that economists had always had a strong view on the role of government in the management of an economy, he goes back to Adam Smith and *The Wealth of Nations*:

> The broadest survey of Adam Smith is sufficient to prove that he did not set up this system of minimum interference even as an economic ideal, and still less as the most general political ideal. At the very outset of his preliminary presentment of the 'of the obvious system of natural liberty' he introduces a most important qualifying clause. Every man is, indeed, on this system left perfectly free to pursue his own interest in his own way, but – mark the qualifications – only 'as long as he does not violate the laws of justice.' Thus the freedom of competition of the industry and capital of individuals is always subject to the limitations of these avowedly higher laws of natural justice. (Nicholson, 1901, pp. 178–9)

I will break off here to point out that the 'laws of natural justice' is one of those concepts that would have been absolutely straightforward to any educated person at the time this was written, but would likely be misread today, since, outside the study of law, the notion of 'natural justice' has no ready and automatic meaning. The point Adam Smith was making was that individuals have a right to be treated fairly, and therefore the government has a duty to ensure that fairness occurs. How that has unfolded since might be seen to include all sorts of restrictions on business, such as the abolition of child labour or limitations on hours of operation through to the imposition of a minimum wage. One man's imposition may be another man's sense of what may constitute 'natural justice'. What Adam Smith discussed was a vast open field in which governments may rightly act and ought to act. There is no doubt that governments have overstepped the bounds on many an occasion, but that economists had always believed that a government had a duty to find where those bounds were and then act on them, was universally accepted. The passage continues:

> And again, according to the system of natural liberty, the sovereign has – it is true – *only* three duties to attend to, but they are duties of the greatest importance, viz., protection against other States, the protection of every member of society from the injuries or oppression of every other member of it, and, finally, the duty of erecting and maintaining certain public works and institutions which it can never be the interest of any individual or small number of individuals to erect and maintain. (Ibid., p. 179; original emphasis)

Summing up, this is where Nicholson saw things in 1901:

> Thus, according to the actual teaching of Adam Smith, if competition leads to injustice or oppression, the State ought to intervene, and if self-interest is inadequate to provide various institutions for the satisfaction of actual needs, the State ought to provide for their erection and maintenance. (Ibid., pp. 179–80)

It is, however, worth pointing out that even while seeing a role for governments, he was hardly of the view that the responsibility was being placed in the most judicious of institutions. One could only wish that modern economic texts have passages such as the following to keep everything in the proper perspective:

> The assumption that government is all-wise and all-powerful is so far removed from the truth as to be of little use even for the purposes of abstract reasoning. With the best intentions, governments may ruin their legislation by ignorance and their administration by feebleness. And very frequently the intentions are not the best, if by best we mean that the public interests, with the due regard to the future as well as the present, are always dominant. The government, even of the most democratic states, must be formed of persons who are themselves liable to errors of judgment and errors of passion. And to a considerable extent they are supposed to carry out the mandate of their electors. The electors are open to all kinds of persuasion, as well as to the persuasion of justice and reason. … In the most advanced democracies, laws are still made and unmade in the interests of powerful classes and sometimes against the interests of considerable minorities. Officials are still appointed for all sorts of reasons apart from merit and efficiency, and are not removed, or removed, on a similar diversity of excuses. (Nicholson, 1901, p. 249)

One cannot quote the whole of Nicholson, but it is as engaging today as Mill's *Principles* is now formidable. Yet, they both speak from the same script, with Nicholson frequently referring to Mill's *Principles*, even with Mill's first edition having been published more than half a century before his own book had been published. And in his views on the role of government, he was doing no more than following Mill, who did much to outline just how crucial government was in the management of an economy. And in this, both Nicholson and Mill had been speaking for the entire classical tradition.

J.S. MILL ON THE ROLE OF GOVERNMENT

What ought to alert anyone to the major role that classical economists had invested in governments in overseeing an economy are the near-200 pages out of the 1000 pages found in Mill's *Principles* ([1871] 1921, pp. 795–979). This is the opening paragraph of Chapter 1 of Book V: 'On the Influence of Government'. The paragraph has been divided not just into its constituent sentences to provide clarity, but even some sentences have been subdivided. Commentary is provided between these broken sentences of what was originally a single paragraph. This is how Mill began:

> One of the most disputed questions both in political science and in practical states-manship at this particular period relates to the proper limits of the functions and agency of governments.

Mill notes that the question of the proper role and limits of government action within an economy have long been in dispute:

> At other times it has been a subject of controversy how governments should be constituted, and according to what principles and rules they should exercise their authority; but it is now almost equally a question to what departments of human affairs that authority should extend.

The debate has not completely ended, but is now really about what governments should do and under which circumstances what they do is done, not whether they should do anything at all. This is a debate that is likely to intensify rather than to roll back:

> And when the tide sets so strongly towards changes in government and legislation, as a means of improving the condition of mankind, this discussion is more likely to increase than to diminish in interest.

When the occasion arises that there are large numbers who wish to see the powers of government used to help improve the living conditions of the population, there is certain to be even more such pressures for governments to use what powers they have to achieve these ends. 'Impatient reformers' believe that taking hold of government is the quickest way to achieve their ends. They are therefore tempted to use these powers in ways that 'stretch' their right to do so 'beyond due bounds':

> On the one hand, impatient reformers, thinking it easier and shorter to get possession of the government than of the intellects and dispositions of the public, are under a constant temptation to stretch the province of government beyond due bounds ...

And then there is the fact that populations have become used to governments using their powers for all kinds of reasons other than in ways that provide benefits to the public:

> while, on the other, mankind have been so much accustomed by their rulers to interference for purposes other than the public good ...

Or there are governments who, though attempting to assist the public, have taken actions that actually do not assist the public at all:

> or under an erroneous conception of what that good requires ...

The result is that there are so many poorly designed proposals, even by those whose sincere aim is to benefit the population. This they will do even if they fail to understand that such changes cannot be achieved unless the population is already onside with those proposals, which requires prior public debate:

> and so many rash proposals are made by sincere lovers of improvement, for attempting, by compulsory regulation, the attainment of objects which can only be effectually or only usefully compassed by opinion and discussion ...

The result of these rash proposals or these misdirected attempts to improve the lot of individuals is that there are some who have written off the role of government action in improving living conditions right from the start:

> that there has grown up a spirit of resistance *in limine* [that is, from the very beginning of a debate even before there has been any discussion] to the interference of government, merely as such, and a disposition to restrict its sphere of action within the narrowest bounds.

Because of their different histories, in Continental Europe, there has been far too much left to the role of governments. In England, in contrast, there has been too little:

> From differences in the historical development of different nations, not necessary to be here dwelt upon, the former excess, that of exaggerating the province of government, prevails most, both in theory and in practice, among the Continental nations,

while in England the contrary spirit has hitherto been predominant. (Mill, *Principles* [1871] 1921, pp. 794–5)

This is a debate that has never disappeared and that probably never will. This transcends what governments should do, who should pay, how governments should finance their programmes, and what is the role of deficits. There have been different answers at different times and in different political constituencies. The level of communal prosperity makes a difference to the answers given, as does the prevailing political morality and cultural tradition. But that there will always be calls upon the government to do something, and often calls to do more than they already do, of this there is little doubt.

THE MEANING OF *LAISSEZ-FAIRE*

The meaning of *laissez-faire* is probably no different today than it was in the middle of the nineteenth century: as far as the economy was concerned, in a *laissez-faire* environment, a business would be permitted to do whatever it wished to earn a profit as long as it stayed within the law.

The term *laissez-faire* is said to have come from a meeting in 1681 between Colbert, the French Minister of Finance, and a group of French business people. Colbert had asked what the government could do to help French industry and the reply received was, '*Laissez-nous faire*', which basically meant, 'Leave us alone' or perhaps, 'Leave it to us'. The connotations that have stemmed from this have been taken to mean that a government should do nothing to help, but also do nothing to impede the operation of a business, leaving a business free to make all the rules for its own operation.

It is safe to say that no government has ever left businesses completely on their own, permitted to do anything they wished in pursuit of profit. It is also very unlikely that anyone with any actual influence over policy has ever suggested that an open-ended *laissez-faire*-type arrangement be put in place. The practical question has always been, what should or should not be done by governments, and what difference do such regulations make? Once the market began to demonstrate the abundance that could flow from the economic system that had evolved almost entirely on its own, there was a wish to ensure that the flow of goods and services would continue, but in a way that kept all negative externalities to a minimum.

It is also safe to say that there has never been a political community in which a large proportion of the community did not distrust business. Whether it is a butcher's thumb on the scale, or large-scale financial fraud, the amount of money involved has always made people suspicious of business. Protection for consumers and employees has always been sought from governments.

Protection by businesses from the fraudulent practices of other businesses has also been perennially sought.

The actual issues during the classical era revolved around what ought to be done. The Industrial Revolution had created an entirely new system of commercial relations that had never existed before. The classical economists, in explaining the operation of this entirely new economic system that was coming into existence before their eyes, also had to think through what the rules of the game ought to be. It is what helped to make classical economic theory as philosophical as it was, since these questions could not, and cannot, be answered by reference to an economic model in the way modern economic theory is discussed.

THE LIMITS OF *LAISSEZ-FAIRE*

The final chapter of Mill's Book V was Chapter XI: 'Of the Grounds and Limits of the *Laisser-Faire* or Non-Interference Principle'. Mill's aim was to provide a demarcation between the legitimate role for governments and what would constitute going beyond its just limits, especially if the economic system was to provide the bounty it appeared to be able to provide:

> The supporters of interference have been content with asserting a general right and duty on the part of government to intervene, wherever its intervention would be useful. (Mill, *Principles* [1871] 1921, p. 941)

Mill points out that there are, however, some, which he calls 'the *laissez-faire* school', who generally limit the usefulness of government intervention to protecting individuals and the owners of property 'against force and fraud' (ibid.). This does not, in Mill's view, go any way near far enough, 'since it excludes … some of the most indispensable and unanimously recognized of the duties of government' (ibid.).

Mill then lists all the reasons that others might object to a stronger role for government, and the list is as comprehensive as one could wish, other than it assumes an open society in which individuals are free to produce. The possibility of a Marxist state in which the government would take upon itself the entire responsibility for organizing production and distribution across an entire economy was unimaginable to Mill. Had Mill lived to see the Russian Revolution, there is no doubt his reaction would have been at least as strong as J.S. Nicholson's, who in 1921, just as the communists began governing in Russia, published his scathing *The Revival of Marxism*. In his chapter on the

'Marxian Theory of Value', he draws directly on Mill's *Principles*. There he states, following Mill:

> The normal price of a thing is that price which, under the normal conditions of demand, year in and year out, suffices, when split up, to remunerate the varied agents of production. (Nicholson, 1921, p. 77)

This is merely the economic consideration, and thus leaves aside how reprehensible Mill would have found the totalitarian absence of liberty. A welfare state within a democratic order is not in any sense a command economy run by a central committee.

That said, within the confines of a market economy in which entrepreneurial judgement is the driving force in the determination of economic outcomes, there is no single principle that determines what might not be undertaken by a government. The keyword is expediency. Mill was very clear on this. In summing up 'The Functions of Government in General' he makes clear that there is nothing a government might not end up doing in the particular circumstances of some time and place:

> Enough has been said to show that the admitted functions of government embrace a much wider field than can easily be included within the ring-fence of any restrictive definition, and that it is hardly possible to find any ground of justification common to them all, except the comprehensive one of general expediency; nor to limit the interference of government by any universal rule, save the simple and vague one, that it should never be admitted but when the case of expediency is strong. (Mill, *Principles* [1871] 1921, p. 801)

This is the very opposite of *laissez-faire*.

FREEDOM OF SPEECH AND ECONOMIC PROSPERITY

But there was one prohibition that Mill thought of as a particularly pernicious activity of governments that he condemned outright. This was the suppression of freedom of speech, which has major negative consequences for an economy:

> The notion, for example, that a government should choose opinions for the people, and should not suffer any doctrines in politics, morals, law, or religion, but such as it approves, to be printed or publicly professed, may be said to be altogether abandoned as a general thesis. It is now well understood that a régime of this sort is fatal to all prosperity, even of an economical kind: that the human mind when prevented either by fear of the law or by fear of opinion from exercising its faculties freely on the most important subjects, acquires a general torpidity and imbecility, by which, when they reach a certain point, it is disqualified from making any considerable

advances even in the common affairs of life, and which, when greater still, make it gradually lose even its previous attainments. ...

Yet although these truths are very widely recognized, and freedom both of opinion and of discussion is admitted as an axiom in all free countries, this apparent liberality and tolerance has acquired so little of the authority of a principle, that it is always ready to give way to the dread or horror inspired by some particular sort of opinions. Within the last fifteen or twenty years, several individuals have suffered imprisonment, for the public profession, sometimes in a very temperate manner, of disbelief in religion; and it is probable that both the public and the government, at the first panic which arises on the subject of Chartism or Communism, will fly to similar means for checking the propagation of democratic or anti-property doctrines. In this country, however, the effective restraints on mental freedom proceed much less from the law or the government, than from the intolerant temper of the national mind; arising no longer from even as respectable a source as bigotry or fanaticism, but rather from the general habit, both in opinion and conduct, of making adherence to custom the rule of life, and enforcing it, by social penalties, against all persons who, without a party to back them, assert their individual independence. (Mill, *Principles* [1871] 1921, p. 940)

The danger occurs not where, in his example, communism is discussed but where it cannot be discussed. Free markets are made to work and can only work where free speech exists. Where free speech is suppressed, and free thought suppressed along with it, the economy will be less productive, often much less productive, than it otherwise would have been.

NOTE

1. For more on Joseph Shield Nicholson, see his Wikipedia entry. He was certainly eminent in his own time: 'In 1880 Nicholson became Professor of political economy at Edinburgh University. ... He was the first President of the Scottish Society of Economists, serving from its creation in 1897 until 1903' (Wikipedia, 2019b).

10. Austrian economic theory and the classical economic tradition

Although Carl Menger initiated the marginal revolution with the intent to find a unified theory of value, the names now most closely associated with the Austrian school are Friedrich Hayek and Ludwig von Mises. And while both are seen from a distance as almost one and the same, up close they were quite different from each other. There are many ways to highlight their differences, but here their approaches will be compared through their attitudes to John Stuart Mill, since both specifically identified themselves with the classical liberal tradition.

Where it matters is in the social aims an economist might hold. The essence of Mill's approach to economic theory was to attempt to answer the question, what ought to be done to create the greatest amount of good for the greatest number of people? Uppermost in his mind was the question of what can be done to raise the living standards and economic well-being of the individual members of the community. Yet, while he called himself a 'socialist', it was the kind of socialism that by today's standards would have had him grouped among the most market-oriented political theorists of the present day. In particular, he would find modern macroeconomic theory, and the policy matrix that accompanies its Keynesian basis, completely false. While he saw a definite role for government involvement in the economy, the basic framework was that everything that can be left to the market should be, while also understanding that not everything can be left to the market. He saw a clear but limited role for government regulation.

Hayek's approach is similar to Mill's (and I would say to my own). Hayek discusses the economics prior to the publication of Menger's *Principles of Economics* in 1871, noting that this was only 'a mere twenty-three years since the **great restatement of classical economics** by John Stuart Mill' (Hayek, 1992, pp. 96–7; bold emphasis added). He continues:

> It is important for proper appreciation of Menger, that we do not underestimate what had been achieved before. It is misleading to think of the preceding period, 1820–1870, as simply dominated by Ricardian orthodoxy. At least in the first generation after Ricardo there had been plenty of new ideas. Both within the body of classical economics as finally expounded by John Stuart Mill and even more outside it there had been accumulated an array of tools of analysis from which later

generations were able to build an elaborate and coherent structure of theory after the concept of marginal utility provided the basis of the unification. If ever there was a time in which a quasi-Ricardian orthodoxy was dominant, it was after John Stuart Mill had so persuasively restated it. Yet even his *Principles* contain very important developments which go far beyond Ricardo. (Ibid., p. 97)

The point was that Mill had provided much of the raw material that the marginalists had been able to consolidate into a more unified whole. Hayek stops to state that:

It is indeed quite difficult to understand how a scholar of the penetration and transparent intellectual honesty of John Stuart Mill could have singled out what was so soon felt to be the weakest part of his system for the confident assertion that 'there is nothing in the laws of value which remain for the present or any future writer to clear up; the theory of the subject is complete'. (Ibid., p. 98)

That Mill, the greatest utilitarian scholar of his generation, had no interest in making utility the core of his own theory of value may have been a conundrum to Hayek, although it might also have suggested that utility had been considered by Mill but then rejected. Yet, the core point here is that there is no question that Hayek had a profound and extremely high regard for the economics of Mill, self-proclaimed 'socialist' though he may have been. This is opposite to the attitude taken by Mises.

The economics of Mises is astonishingly detailed and profound. But what makes his approach so austere is its narrow focus on economic issues almost entirely outside the social and political arena. Hayek, like Mill, was continuously thinking through how economic conditions could be improved using as many arms of policy as possible, while always understanding the limits that are placed on the various possibilities available by the fundamental laws of economic theory that rule out various approaches as unlikely to be successful. Hayek did not take a *laissez-faire* approach but was clear that a number of policy options that many others might adopt would in actual fact make economic conditions worse. His opposition to such policies was thus not based on a blanket opposition to government action in general, but on an understanding of the kinds of government actions that would inevitably fail wherever adopted. Mises, on the other hand, thought that only an absolutely rigid adoption of market-based economic theory was acceptable. And unlike Mill, who even in 1848 could see how economic policies would be constrained by popular pressures to alleviate economic hardships and to use governments to temper economic outcomes, Mises accepts no compromise with the hard-edged views of how a market economy must operate. Here he discusses his views of John Stuart Mill in his *Liberalism in the Classical Tradition* (Mises, 1985):

> John Stuart Mill is an epigone of classical liberalism and, especially in his later years, under the influence of his wife, full of feeble compromises. He slips slowly into socialism and is the originator of the thoughtless confounding of liberal and socialist ideas that led to the decline of English liberalism and to the undermining of the living standards of the English people. Nevertheless – or perhaps precisely because of this – one must become acquainted with Mill's principal writings:
>
> *Principles of Political Economy* (1848)
> *On Liberty* (1859)
> *Utilitarianism* (1862)
>
> Without a thorough study of Mill it is impossible to understand the events of the last two generations. For Mill is the great advocate of socialism. All the arguments that could be advanced in favor of socialism are elaborated by him with loving care. In comparison with Mill all other socialist writers – even Marx, Engels and Lassalle – are scarcely of any importance. (Mises, 1985, p. 195)

An indication of how adamantine Mises's political judgements are may be recognized in the following comment from the Preface he wrote for *Liberalism* in 1962:

> In England the term 'liberal' is mostly used to signify a program that only in details differs from the totalitarianism of the socialists. (Ibid., p. xvi)

At any rate, no actual socialists have ever cited Mill as the source of their views on how an economy ought to be managed. Yet Mises's concerns over the drift of economic theory and government policy remain a vivid warning of how dangerous economic theory has become, both economically and politically.

THE NATURE OF AUSTRIAN THEORY

Austrian economic theory is rightly associated with the marginal revolution. At the start of the 1870s, there were three virtually simultaneous revolutionary documents that found their way into the economic literature in their approach to economic analysis, led by William Stanley Jevons in England, Léon Walras in Switzerland and Carl Menger in Austria. The essence of this shift was to place marginal utility at the centre of economics as the core element of its theory of value.

There should, however, be no doubt that utility was already deeply embedded within economics and among economists. The philosophical tradition to which John Stuart Mill personally belonged was utilitarianism, for which he was possibly the single most important advocate. That he, and indeed every economist, understood that the demand side of an economy was ultimately driven by consumer assessments over which products put on the market by entrepreneurs would provide them with utility, and that their buying decisions would be determined by personal assessments related to which products would provide them with the greatest utility per unit of currency spent, added no new insights into the operation of a market economy. This was seen as both obvious and also of no particular theoretical significance, since the level of utility is not a measurable quantity. As even a cursory reading of the classical literature on supply and demand would show, no deeper incursion into the theory of marginal utility was required to understand how a market economy worked.

It has been argued that the theory of marginal utility was given its impetus into the mainstream as part of the response to Marxist writings – in particular, following the publication of the first edition of Marx's *Capital* in 1867. Marxist economic theory, and especially its theory of capitalist exploitation, was derived from the labour theory of value, which had by then long departed from mainstream economic analysis. Nevertheless, as Marxist socialism had been gathering momentum, particularly on the continent, there was a wish among some economists to finally kill off Marxist theory by pointing out that there is a demand side to an economy that rendered Marxist analysis completely invalid, while relative prices were not determined by the cost of labour, but required the incorporation of other elements on the cost side of a production function.

Whatever may have been the reason that marginal utility caught on at that particular moment, there is no question that it did, becoming over time the textbook expression of the theory of value. It was one of the ways in which economics shifted from a theory that dealt with empirical relationships, since business costs are actually quantifiable, to one in which abstract, non-quantifiable entities were substituted. Production costs are visible and known to those who make business decisions. The level of utility is an abstract entity that cannot be measured, which therefore also means that marginal utility, the measure at the centre of marginal apparatus, can never itself be anything other than an abstraction. The unreality of marginal utility is a large part of the reason that indifference curve analysis was introduced, although again there is no actual ability to measure any of the elements in the analysis. It, too, is fully abstract, with no actual direct relationship to what occurs either within a business environment or among those who are making consumption decisions. It did not need such analysis to demonstrate that an increase in relative price would shift demand towards the product whose price has fallen, or that an increase in income would lead to an increase in demand for at least some products.

More consequential was the shift of the focus of economic theory from the supply side of the economy to the demand side. Although there was no intention to ignore supply considerations, but merely to add in a more theoretical conception of demand, what occurred instead was the introduction of an utterly abstract, totally unquantifiable entity that had no measurable existence, but which placed the focus on analysis on the demand side of the economy. There might be additional utility in buying more, and there may be diminishing marginal utility the more of some particular product one had, but all that was obvious. The diamond–water paradox[1] of value was not actually a paradox. It did not need a statement from economic theory to show that some objects have prices well beyond any bare necessity in relation to a buyer's future existence.

VALUE IN USE VERSUS VALUE IN EXCHANGE

Indeed, the introduction of utility virtually ended the distinction that had existed since at least from the time of Adam Smith, between value in use versus value in exchange. Water in most instances has a very low price – a low value in exchange – but is essential for life, and thus has a very high value in use. Mill discusses the value of a music box for sale in the middle of a modern city versus the value of that same music box for someone who is about to set off into the Canadian wilderness. Price at that stage is divorced from the object's original cost of production, but hardly needs economic theory to explain why the price would have become as high as it then might become. Yet, for all that, marginal utility became embedded, with the supply side of the economy for all practical purposes omitted from the discussion.

Menger discusses the transition in the nature of the conceptualization of value in use in an appendix in his *Principles* and underscores its interchangeability with utility and its undoubted presence within English classical theory:

> Like Adam Smith, David Ricardo, Thomas Robert Malthus and John Stuart Mill employ 'value in use' as synonymous with 'utility.' Indeed, Robert Torrens and J.R. McCulloch even employ the term 'utility' instead of 'value in use.' Among recent French writers, the same thing is done by Frédéric Bastiat. Lord Lauderdale and N.W. Senior recognize utility as a prerequisite of exchange value, but not as use value, which is a concept they repudiate altogether. What is understood in England by the concept exchange value is best illustrated by the following passage from John Stuart Mill: 'The words Value and Price were used as synonymous by the early political economists, and are not always discriminated even by Ricardo. But the most accurate modern writers, to avoid wasteful expenditure of two good scientific terms on a single idea, have employed Price to express the value of a thing in relation to money; the quantity of money for which it will exchange ... the value or exchange value of a thing [we shall therefore understand] its general power of purchasing; the command which its possession give over purchasable commodities in general'. (Menger, [1871] 1976, pp. 307–8; references in the passage have been removed; square brackets in the original)

Utility was an inevitable inclusion within the theory of exchange but was not placed at the centre of the theory of value, which was largely determined by production costs.

FURTHER CONSEQUENCES OF THE INTRODUCTION OF MARGINAL UTILITY

There was also an important element of mathematization of economic theory within the shift to marginal utility. Whether or not any of it could be measured, one could nevertheless construct various equations and come to conclusions about the logic of choice between alternate products. The elaboration of the concept in pages of mathematical jargon had an attraction, which helped shift the nature of economic theory away from its philosophical base and towards economics-as-physics.

Going further, the shift towards utility helped shift economic theory from its macroeconomic focus on the economy as a whole, to a microeconomic focus on individual buyers. Until the marginal revolution, economic theory concentrated on the entire economy, with the individual elements brought into the picture as needed to complete the explanation. This was now reversed. The economy was disaggregated into its individual final consumer elements, with the picture of the full economy seen as the aggregation of the individual components. The supply side merely followed along where the demand side had led.

Going further still, no consideration was given to the fact that an economy is dynamic, with hardly a day going by without significant change in supply-side conditions, and with no year going by without major disruption in the array of products up for sale, or in the technologies being used to produce. The static picture of individuals buying products, choosing between X and Y, as if the products were some kind of permanent fixed set of entities, was not just abstract but incoherent. The picture presented about the nature of the actual economy provided no overlap with the actual shifts that inevitably take place as economies adjust.

Sitting beneath the theory as it was conceived in the 1870s were most if not all the classical presuppositions found in Mill and his contemporaries, including Say's Law, which was specifically endorsed by Jevons (Kates, 1998, p. 82). The aim was to provide a clearer conception of the demand side of the economy, to provide a counterpart to the production costs that were crucial in determining what was supplied to the market and the prices at which goods would be sold. And embedded within the supply side was the entrepreneur/capitalist who would determine what to produce and the inputs to combine during production.

Utility maximization is, however, calculable, even in principle, only in a static environment in which there are no changes in the products brought to market that would disturb any of the existing relative price relationships. Nothing is expected to happen that might enlighten purchasers of an alternative array of goods or services in which some other product or service is preferable. It answers a question that no one is really interested in because the answer is uninteresting. Utility provides the obvious answer to what we already know: why do individuals buy one set of goods and services rather than another? And the answer is based on: (1) this is how much money someone has; and (2) these are the particular goods and services that will provide the most satisfaction in total, given how much money a buyer has available to spend. It moves the economic debate not a step further towards answering questions about how an economy should be structured so that individuals can end up with more real purchasing power, or how new and better products and services can be made available to the market.

AUSTRIAN ECONOMICS AND *LAISSEZ-FAIRE*

Yet, if a modern economist is asked to outline the views of classical economists, the likelihood is that a caricature will be built around the arguments found within modern Austrian economic theory. What has made this confluence even stronger is that Austrian economic theory is seen as a facet of a libertarian political philosophy, which is as close to a *laissez-faire* approach as found in the modern world. It has no relationship to classical economic theory or to classical teachings on the role of the state in managing a market economy, but how would a modern economist know?

This cannot be emphasized enough. The Austrian tradition, especially given how it has evolved since the nineteenth century, is entirely different from the classical tradition in the English-speaking world. The brew that brings together the marginal revolution, Austrian economic theory and libertarian philosophy, although separate strands, have left as a residual a belief that these are all related to one another, and that these are in some sense representative of the attitudes and beliefs of the classical economists. The likelihood of there being a broader understanding of how false this presumed relationship is, appears unlikely. Yet, it should be stated for the record.

The two major representatives of the Austrian tradition found in economic discussions are Friedrich Hayek and Ludwig von Mises. Their views are the examples of the classical tradition that modern economists would most likely look towards if they sought an understanding of the English classical school. Peter Boettke has argued that this is more a matter of the circumstances that surrounded the contemporary debates that were of most importance at the time, that many of those we associate with the Austrian tradition fled Europe prior to World War II:

> The Austrian school by the 1950s is no longer viewed as just a scientific body of thought, but instead link closely with the *laissez-faire* argument and there's a lot of reasons for that, that are tied sociologically to the fact that the Austrians in the 1930s and 40s – in particular again Mises and Hayek – are embroiled in two major debates.
> One of those debates is with the market socialists and the other debates are with Keynes and the interventions of the Keynesian school. So the Austrian school gets identified that way and that sort of has stuck. (Boettke, 2015)

Opposition to both Keynesian economics and the socialist economies of Eastern Europe after they were overrun by the Soviets would have meant that the issues they were involved with were highly politicized in a free-market direction. Certainly, to oppose Keynesian public spending, never mind Soviet-style central planning, would place an economist well within the more free-market side within any public debate.

It is still, however, necessary to repeat the central conclusion of this chapter: if one wishes to understand the English classical tradition in economic theory, and especially the role of government regulation, then one must read classical English authors. No substitutes will do. If you wish to understand the economics of Mill and his contemporaries, you must read Mill and his contemporaries.

HAYEK AND *THE ROAD TO SERFDOM*

The slant that is brought to economic analysis by Austrian theory is nevertheless towards the *laissez-faire* end of the political spectrum. A large part of the reason that there is little appreciation of the strong support for a major role for government among classical economists is that most economists today associate the classical attitude to government intervention with the Austrian deep reluctance to entertain a role for government regulation and the provision of public welfare.

The principal text that someone outside the Austrian tradition might be aware of from the Austrian school is Friedrich Hayek's *Road to Serfdom*, published in 1944 at the end of World War II, just as the Soviet Union was about to begin its political domination of Eastern Europe, a domination that continued until the start of the 1990s. This is a linkage that goes straight to Keynes. Within the economics profession of the 1930s, Hayek had been Keynes's major adversary, although this opposition almost entirely consisted of his criticisms of Keynes's *Treatise on Money*. Hayek famously said nothing upon the publication of *The General Theory*, nor did he enter into any of the debates over Keynesian economic theory until the Great Inflation of the 1970s. His eventual public adoption of an anti-Keynesian position was consistent with his past economic thinking, although there is reason to believe that he viewed public spending during the Great Depression favourably (see Kates, 2015a, pp. 52–3).

It is his *Road to Serfdom* that has made Hayek's approach to economic management appear particularly *laissez-faire*. It was written at the end of World War II, which had been waged against a totalitarian centralized economy, even while the Soviet Union was allied against Nazi Germany which was itself a totalitarian centralized economy. This was all the more relevant for its time, given that the war machine of the Allies had been centrally managed. It is irrelevant whether Hayek has been misrepresented, or whether this was a moment in history when world sentiment appeared to be moving in a centrally managed direction. The residual belief is that Hayek had represented the minimalist position of a public sector role in directing or managing an economy. The book, when read today, can be more clearly seen for what it is – as an argument against central planning. This was all the more on his mind since the war economies of the democracies had been managed in a very much centralized fashion. Statements such as the following might lead one to believe that Hayek was going much further than just restating the principles of the classical economists:

> For at least twenty-five years before the specter of totalitarianism became a real threat, we had progressively been moving away from the basic ideas on which Western civilization has been built. That this movement on which we have entered with such high hopes and ambitions should have brought us face to face with the totalitarian horror has come as a profound shock to this generation, which still refuses to connect the two facts. Yet this development merely confirms the warnings of the fathers of the liberal philosophy which we still profess. We have progressively abandoned that freedom in economic affairs without which personal and political freedom has never existed in the past. (Hayek, 1944, Chapter 1, n.p.)

Yet, he also made his position on *laissez-faire* quite clear:

> There is nothing in the basic principles of liberalism to make it a stationary creed; there are no hard-and-fast rules fixed once and for all. The fundamental principle that in the ordering of our affairs we should make as much use as possible of the spontaneous forces of society, and resort as little as possible to coercion, is capable of an infinite variety of applications. There is, in particular, all the difference between deliberately creating a system within which competition will work as beneficially as possible and passively accepting institutions as they are. Probably nothing has done so much harm to the liberal cause as the wooden insistence of some liberals on certain rough rules of thumb, above all the principle of *laissez faire*. (Ibid.)

There may be no more in the arguments presented by Hayek than are found in the arguments of any of the classical economists. That is, even according to Hayek there is a significant role for an active government policy, but it must be tempered with an understanding of the role of markets that must be allowed to undertake the largest part in shaping an economy in new directions. If anything, Hayek was arguing against others who were seen to have taken a much more strident position against a major role for government. To those who were inclined to take a much more interventionist approach, even the moderate position taken by Hayek may have sounded overly restrictive. Arguing for a limited use of public direction in an economy, and finding Keynesian macro, especially as it was then developing, a major mistake in policy formation and theory, would have meant that, for many, Hayek would have been seen as representing an extreme position. In actual fact, he may have been stating nothing different from the view any classical economist might have stated had they been in his place. Skidelsky is exactly right: 'The state, Hayek says, should provide a social safety net' (Skidelsky, 2006, p. 102). That is far from the Hayek as usually portrayed, but it is an accurate portrayal of his views. His close association with Mises would have helped emphasize that view.

MISES AND *HUMAN ACTION*

Ludwig von Mises's *Human Action* is an austere no-frills explanation of not just how a market economy works, but also why only a market economy can work. There are the members of a community who have material desires they would like satisfied and personal services they would like to engage. Most of what individuals want is dependent on what has already been produced and sold in the past, of which they have personal knowledge, although some of those desires are for goods and services that have only recently been made available.

There are also individuals who earn their own living by running businesses that produce these goods and services in the hope that others will buy them, and in so doing pay enough in total amongst all purchasers to cover the costs of production.

There are also entrepreneurs who run businesses that produce inputs that are used within other businesses. Ultimately, however, all production is focused on satisfying the demands of final consumers. It is in this sense that consumers call the shots. What people are willing to pay for determines what will be produced, since only those enterprises that produce goods and services that earn a profit can stay in business.

But what people will be willing to pay for is an unknown that can only be discovered if an entrepreneur makes the decision to produce some good or service and put it on the market at some particular price. Only then can it be discovered whether whatever has been produced can be sold at a profit. Once it has been determined that a profitable enterprise can be established to produce these particular goods and services, many other firms may then follow and try to produce the same product or even better versions.

This is how the market works through the trial-and-error efforts of entrepreneurs to find products that can be sold at a profit. If a community is content never to change any of the products it chooses to buy, and there are never any interruptions or changes in the supply conditions for the inputs used in production, the economy can enter a steady state that can repeat the same routine endlessly. But since in the real world there are new innovations taking place all the time, and changes in the supply conditions for inputs, a steady-state outcome is an impossibility.

Therefore, to ensure an economy continually improves the products produced, and can adjust to new conditions in the supply of inputs, a market mechanism is essential. No other mechanism will work if a community is intent on improving its standard of living or wishes to accommodate changes in the conditions of supply.

The question then is whether there is any role for government oversight and regulation in such an economy. And while it is clear that Mises is reluctant to state that there is such a role for governments because of the principle of give-them-an-inch-and-they-will-take-a-mile, he does accept that government does indeed have such a role nevertheless. This is from *Human Action*:

> There are certainly cases in which people may consider definite restrictive measures as justified. Regulations concerning fire prevention are restrictive and raise the cost of production. But the curtailment of total output they bring about is the price to be paid for avoidance of greater disaster. The decision about each restrictive measure is to be made on the ground of meticulous weighing of the costs to be incurred and the prize to be obtained. **No reasonable man could possibly question this rule**. (Mises, [1949] 1963, p. 748; bold emphasis added)

There ought to be no doubt from this passage that there are circumstances for which government regulation is warranted. It is a cost–benefit calculation in which regulations are laid down. These regulations have a cost in lost production, but in which there is a positive return in the prevention of an even more costly outcome whose probability of occurrence has been reduced.

Mises's reluctance to state in a more fulsome way that such regulations have a role in economic management is based on his no doubt correct judgement that from the example of this unquestionable positive use of government regulations to diminish the possibility of a much more costly outcome has been a thin edge of the wedge to justify an enormous and monstrous regulatory regime across all the economies of the world. If anything has occurred, the meticulous examinations that now occur are to determine if there is absolutely no possible harm that might occur if some regulation is not introduced and enforced. The weight of evidence has now been placed on those who wish to reduce such regulations where outcomes with a small probability of occurrence are not made the basis for such rules. The principle should therefore not be seen as a blanket ban on government regulation per se, but as the need for those who wish to impose such regulations to demonstrate that the potential risk is large and that the market would not be expected to provide its own cure if left on its own to work things out.

Individuals who, for example, wish to build houses in the middle of flood plains that are expected to flood only once every 50 years should be permitted to do so, but are also told that if they do, they must cover the cost of insurance themselves and not expect a government to make good any losses they might endure because of flood damage. And while there is need for licensing for doctors and electricians, since no consumer can be expected to research into the competencies of individuals who declare themselves a doctor or electrician, there is no need for regulation in endless other occupations, with hairdressers perhaps the most notorious example of regulatory overkill.

But there is a further issue in relation to regulation. Within political debate, to argue that no regulations are ever justified will instantaneously lose the public debate. No one will accept that the market can be left to itself without any oversight and regulation. Finding the balance is important. But not to recognize an important social function of regulation by governments, especially by governments under popular control, is to throw the baby of good economic management out with the bathwater of heavy-handed control.

Yet, it is just this reluctance to accept the role of government regulation that makes the purist position so detrimental to the defence of the market. A market outcome is not necessarily a moral outcome. The classical approach, which gave an imprimatur to regulation and public provision of infrastructure along with various public services, did so with an emphasis on the need to limit such expenditures, while leaving to the market anything that could be undertaken by entrepreneurs. Mises, in his reluctance to endorse the role of governments, may therefore have created the impression that an extreme *laissez-faire* approach is the only alternative to the more expansive approach that has actually been adopted everywhere. Mises's position is not in any case the position that had been adopted by classical economists.

AUSTRIAN THEORY OF THE CYCLE

The Austrian theory of the cycle sits entirely within the classical framework. While it is the only version of classical business cycle theory to survive the Keynesian revolution, it is important to appreciate that it was merely one version of the classical theory of the cycle. Haberler, in his *Prosperity and Depression* (1937), includes the Austrian theory of the cycle in Chapter 3 among those he classified as 'Over-Investment Theories'. Such theories, of which there were many versions, depend on expansion of credit during the up phase of the cycle, which leads to an extension of investment programmes that eventually lead to a situation where there are insufficient real resources available to complete all the projects that had been begun at the trough of the cycle. The 'inflationary' 'artificial extension of credit' eventually leads to a downturn as a significant proportion of the various investment programmes are unable to be brought to completion. Among the Austrian theories of the cycle, Haberler discusses Hayek's approach in particular, opening the section with this introduction:

> Great pains have been taken to explain this process in terms of relative prices and of supply and demand for particular types of goods. To Professor HAYEK we owe the most elaborate analysis. (Haberler, 1937, p. 45)

Haberler's discussion continues for five pages (ibid., pp. 45–9). It is from Hayek's approach that the modern version of the Austrian theory has been derived. The following is a modern discussion that brings the nature of the theory into a modern setting:

> Most of Hayek's work from the 1920s through the 1930s was in the Austrian theory of business cycles, capital theory, and monetary theory. Hayek saw a connection among all three. The major problem for any economy, he argued, is how people's actions are coordinated. He noticed, as Adam Smith had, that the price system – free markets – did a remarkable job of coordinating people's actions, even though that coordination was not part of anyone's intent. The market, said Hayek, was a sponta- neous order. By spontaneous Hayek meant unplanned – the market was not designed by anyone but evolved slowly as the result of human actions. But the market does not work perfectly. What causes the market, asked Hayek, to fail to coordinate peo- ple's plans, so that at times large numbers of people are unemployed?
>   One cause, he said, was increases in the money supply by the central bank. Such increases, he argued in *Prices and Production*, would drive down interest rates, making credit artificially cheap. Businessmen would then make capital investments that they would not have made had they understood that they were getting a distorted price signal from the credit market. But capital investments are not homogeneous. Long-term investments are more sensitive to interest rates than short-term ones, just as long-term bonds are more interest-sensitive than treasury bills. Therefore, he concluded, artificially low interest rates not only cause investment to be artificially high, but also cause 'malinvestment' – too much investment in long-term projects relative to short-term ones, and the boom turns into a bust. Hayek saw the bust as a healthy and necessary readjustment. The way to avoid the busts, he argued, is to avoid the booms that cause them. (Library of Economics and Liberty, 2019)

There are many features of Hayek's theory that might assist in making sense of the cycle but there are others that do not. It is just one version of the more generalized classical approach that was based on structural disequilibrium.

RELATIONSHIP TO KEYNESIAN THEORY

There is one other issue that might be noted, and that is the general refusal to take Keynesian economics on directly. Austrians do, of course, stand apart from Keynesians in how they understand the operation of an economy. Yet, there is a strange reluctance to criticize modern macroeconomic theory, and especially to take on the concepts related to aggregate demand deficiency in anything other than an oblique way.

This is not to suggest that the Austrian theory of the cycle is not intrinsically hostile to Keynesian macro, or to doubt that modern macroeconomic policy is alien from Austrian policy. It is that even though this is so, there is little direct criticism of the underlying Keynesian theory beyond pointing out how a Keynesian policy may go off the rails and create inflationary pressures.

The crucial issue relates to the question of whether an economy can and does go into recession because of a deficiency of aggregate demand. Mises wrote two brief articles in the 1950s on Say's Law that he described as obviously true. But neither he nor virtually any of the major Austrian economists have attempted a defence of Say's Law in the kind of way that might undermine the structure of modern macroeconomic theory.

NOTE

1. The supposed contradiction that, although water is on the whole more useful than diamonds, in terms of survival, diamonds nevertheless command a higher price in the market.

11. An overview of classical economic theory

UNDERSTANDING THE OPERATION OF AN ECONOMY AS UNDERSTOOD BY THE CLASSICS

Although there are many elements that separate the operation of an economy as understood by classical economists versus the operation as understood by economists since that time, the most important difference overall was the classical focus on the supply side of the economy and, in particular, the outstanding importance of value added in making sense of events.

Let us turn first to value added, which is discussed in no modern text that I know of in any detail, with tremendous loss to the ability of economists to understand what is going on. No matter what an economy produces, it must put to use some of its existing resource base in creating that production. Everything produced, whether a consumer good or whether productive investment, requires the drawing down on the economy's existing resource base, whether it is natural resources, labour time, capital goods, or entrepreneurial and managerial effort – the land, labour, capital and entrepreneur of classical theory. Yet, far from this being trivially true and understood by all, the significance of the absolute necessity to employ various 'factors of production' in whatever is being produced is almost invariably ignored as too unimportant to raise in discussing both the mechanism of production and the reasons why this mechanism occasionally breaks down. It is one of those presuppositions that seem too obvious to mention.

Here is what must therefore be understood as just a preliminary. These factors of production have value, since their existence has required the use of economic resources. Moreover, almost every productive resource has alternative uses and other forms of output, towards which they could be applied in bringing them to the market. Their value, which should be understood as their *relative* value in comparison with every other resource available for productive use, is determined in relation to the goods and services they are used to produce. Their value thus comes as a by-product in the unfolding of the economy as a whole. The relative value of the steel being produced, for example, is dependent on the cost of mining iron ore, building and maintaining a steel plant, the wages and other related costs associated with the employment of labour, and with the return to those who have decided to attempt to earn their own living by producing steel. It is also in part determined by the value of what else steel is being used for as an input as part of domestic production, along with its value as an exported good. The structure of demand helps determine the structure of supply.

This same principle is involved in producing everything. The production of everything requires the combination of an entrepreneur, natural resources of one kind or another, labour and physical capital. There must also be a price mechanism that determines the relative cost of each of these resources in a way that allows the relative price of every good or service to be determined so that the final output reflects the intensity of demand for each product, as well as the scarcity of the inputs that have been used during production. This can only occur within a market system where relative prices are determined through supply and demand. This is where value added comes into the story. Production must add value, which means that the value of the goods and services produced must exceed the value of the resources used up.

Only if there is a price mechanism in which relative prices are determined by the market so that the value of each and every input and the value of output can be measured, is it even possible for mutually consistent production decisions to be made. Only in this way is it even possible to measure whether value-adding activity has occurred. Without the market in place, every economic decision maker is flying blind. Without the market mechanism determining the relative costs of each and every input, there is no means to keep production costs to a minimum. In fact, there is no means to determine in a realistic way any of the production costs anywhere in the economy.

Once it is understood that only value-adding activities can make an economy grow and allow individuals to increase their incomes and wealth over time – and there are always many activities that are non-value-adding, either through choice, as in welfare expenditures, or through error where businesses are running at a loss – only then can it be understood that it is essential to manage an economy so that individual enterprises are run in such a way that the outcome is a higher level of value created relative to the value of the resources used up in production. And the only way that can occur is if enterprises are operated by individual entrepreneurs who personally care about whether their businesses are creating value, because each individual entrepreneur's own income will depend on whether their business is able to earn a profit. There is no faking such entrepreneurial concern through the employment of a public servant. Only actual entrepreneurs with their own personal incomes on the line, worry about revenues versus costs. No public servant ever does, or if some do, this is a concern that is eaten away through time.

The economy is thus not driven from the demand side by the wishes of buyers – the great conceptual error of the marginal revolution reinforced then by the Keynesian revoultion – but from the supply side, that is, by entrepreneurs, according to whose judgement a particular form of good or service is estimated as likely to earn for themselves a profitable return.

All this presupposes the existence of a moral and political order in which individuals are permitted to open businesses and run them for a profit; where profit making is not resented by the population at large; where individuals are content to earn their living as wage earners; where governments do not tax excessively, or more generally, plunder value-adding businesses; where government-determined forms of output overwhelm market-determined production decisions; where regulation is kept to a necessary minimum; where it is widely understood that everyone's prosperity is dependent on allowing businesses to function as best they can and earn profits; where competition is recognized as the ideal economic environment where producers of better products are allowed to drive other producers from the market; where the price mechanism is allowed to operate without government interference; where tariff walls and other impediments to trade do not limit import competition.

CLASSICAL THEORY OF THE CYCLE

The major shift in the nature of economic theory came with the advent of Keynesian economics following the publication of *The General Theory* in 1936. The major change, which has persisted ever since, was to reorient the theory of the cycle from the supply side of the economy to the demand side. The introduction of aggregate demand as the driver of the economy has made economic policy virtually incoherent ever since. No Keynesian stimulus has ever led an economy from recession to recovery.

The core to understanding the nature of recession in classical terms is an understanding of the structure of production. Modern macro is built around aggregate final demand by various classifications of purchasers: consumer demand for goods and services; private sector purchases of capital goods; government expenditure on literally anything at all; and the net purchases of domestically produced goods and services by buyers in foreign countries. In all this, the vast hinterland of input-producing businesses and industries is ignored. These are never introduced into macroeconomic analysis other than on occasion. No discussion occurs in relation to the structure of the economy.

The classical theory was based on a recognition that purchases by the ultimate buyers of goods and services is the tip of the economic iceberg. Out beyond the production and sale of goods and services is the vast array of producers who never sell to final purchasers. These are producers of goods such as raw steel and crude oil and services such as business consultancies and architectural firms. These make up the vast bulk of economic activity in an economy.

Most of the businesses within this hinterland of producers may never sell a single item directly to a final purchaser, but the entire economy is dependent on the accurate ability of these producers to provide precisely the inputs needed by other businesses. An economy depends not just on their existence, but on their ability to fulfil the productive needs of all other economic agents. Their production must match as closely as possible the specific requirements of business, and in doing so, there are tremendous competitive pressures to remain the specific firms that others will purchase from. There is simply no means to map the interconnecting sales of these supplying firms to the businesses that buy their inputs from these suppliers. It is here more than anywhere that the spontaneous self-adjustment processes of the economy come into their own.

And it is here that the market mechanism shows its mettle. To say that a particular way of doing something is the *least-cost* means of production means specifically that if the least-cost approach is adopted, this approach uses up a smaller proportion of the economy's resource base so that there are more resources left over, available to produce other goods and services. The more costly a process – that is, the more resources it uses up – the fewer additional goods and services that can be produced. Ensuring that the least-cost approach is adopted is essential to ensure that living standards in general can rise at the fastest rate. And this applies to labour as much as it does to each of the other inputs into the production process.

Crucially, the ferocious competition that exists among suppliers is to be the least-cost producer. This does not, of course, mean to run at a loss, but to be the producer best able to fulfil the input specifications at a lower price while still earning a profitable return. But unless the market mechanism is available to direct producers towards production techniques that use fewer resources per unit of output, there is no possibility whatsoever for the economy to find the least-cost approach to producing the goods and services the economy supplies.

The fantastically complex network of producers, which includes the providers of final goods and services but also every other producer as well, is what is known as 'the structure of production'. Their interrelationships constitute the production side of the economy in its entirety, with each individual enterprise contributing to the whole. What, however, must be emphasized is that these are each individual businesses that exist and can only exist if they are able to sell to others who seek what they produce, and which must themselves be able to provide others with what they seek and need at prices low enough, but of a quality high enough, to attract buyers to them. There is, therefore, a continuous process as existing businesses expand or contract and new businesses enter the market while others leave. This is a structure that is continuously in the midst of change.

The miracle of the market is that these businesses can coordinate their operations as well as they do in what is an incredibly decentralized and uncoordinated melange of independent enterprises. Individual business owners must find their own way with no central planning agency to direct their efforts. That it operates as efficiently as it does is what needs to be recognized. That the process may on occasion break down, where more than the normal proportion of firms contract or leave the market at one and the same time, also resulting in higher than usual levels of unemployment, should not be thought of as anything other than an almost certain occurrence that must take place from time to time. These occurrences are described as recessions, or if particularly deep and prolonged, as depressions. Explaining why there are more placid times, but also occasionally economic downturns, is what constituted the classical theory of the cycle.

RECESSIONS AS THE CONSEQUENCE OF BREAKDOWN IN THE STRUCTURE OF PRODUCTION

Recessions were correctly understood by classical economists as the consequence of a breakdown in the structure of production. To understand why the recession occurred required an understanding of why the structure of production no longer fully meshed. Something had occurred that interrupted the flow of output from one producer to another. Either final demand had radically shifted, which meant that the hinterland of suppliers no longer represented the productive requirements of the economy, or the actual supply chain had itself been transformed through changes in the hinterland itself. In one way or another, disruptions to the structure of production caused firms to close or contract before the additional resources that had become free from their previous uses could be absorbed.

More completely, the disruptions to the structure of production were more often than not the consequence of changes in prevailing credit conditions, or if not themselves the initial cause of recession, these changed credit conditions had occurred simultaneously with actual changes in the supply chain conditions of the economy.

Yet, within the theory of the cycle, one specific possible cause of recession was ruled out – that the economy's level of production had grown so rapidly that the level of aggregate demand could not rise as quickly, so that goods and services could not be sold. The preferred expression used among classical economists was to deny that overproduction was ever a possible cause of recession, with the phrase demand deficiency used on occasion as the equivalent. The great irony is that modern mainstream Keynesian macroeconomic theory was a fallacy among classical economists. They were obviously in no doubt that recessions could and did occur; they nevertheless denied absolutely that such recessions were ever caused by a deficiency of aggregate demand.

Recessions in classical times were associated with higher than normal levels of unemployment. If businesses were closing down at abnormally high rates, the number of individuals who were unemployed and were seeking work was also abnormally high. Yet, the most important means to return the economy to full employment was to allow the economy to adjust and take whichever measures that would allow that readjustment to occur as rapidly as possible.

And in understanding how unemployment could be reduced, the core principle that had existed since early in the classical period was stated by John Stuart Mill as the fourth of his *fundamental* propositions on capital: 'demand for commodities is not demand for labour'. The level of employment was unrelated to the level of aggregate demand and, therefore, attempting to lower unemployment through an increase in the demand for goods and services was impossible. The principal Keynesian policy of raising aggregate demand to create jobs and lower unemployment was denied absolutely by classical economic theory as a means to achieve this end. It was a policy only occasionally attempted prior to the publication of *The General Theory*, a policy that has never succeeded on any occasion in which it has ever been attempted. Classical economists within the mainstream understood the errors embedded in any such attempt to increase the number of jobs within an economy.

THE CYCLE AND UNEMPLOYMENT

The Keynesian revolution did many things to both policy and theory but what may ultimately have proven to have had the greatest effect has been the shift from viewing an economy as the source of the goods and services we consume to becoming the arena in which jobs are created. Jobs were once the by-product of economic activity. It has now been almost reversed, where the purpose of economic growth is to create jobs. It is an important part of the muddle into which economic policy has fallen.

There is no doubt that the loss of jobs is an important consequence of recession. But, in the classical understanding, the jobs have been lost because the specific tasks these previous job holders had undertaken did not return enough profit to their employer to cover the cost of their wages. It had nothing to do with aggregate demand. It was everything to do with the job, and the business that had originally offered that job, being no longer capable of earning a positive return on the work the employee was hired to fulfil. The one essential consequence was that the job had to be vacated and the employee forced to find another place of employment. Pumping up aggregate demand, especially where the jobs newly created also do not provide a positive return on the wages paid, rather than being a cure for unemployment, makes the underlying problem worse.

To a modern Keynesian, even the phrase 'structure of production' has no serious meaning and provides no additional understanding to an economist trying to analyse the problem. For a classical economist, however, job creation schemes through increased public spending, which are typically introduced as part of a 'stimulus package', only lead to a future slowing of the economy's rate of growth and must prolong the adjustment process. This would have been completely obvious to any properly instructed classical economist. It is an outcome that is more than invisible to a modern economist raised on demand deficiency. It is an outcome that is actually incomprehensible. Although no stimulus package has ever achieved its ends, when economists try to work out what went wrong, the one place that is never examined is the stimulus itself. The absence of value-adding production as part of a stimulus package is never recognized as diminishing an economy's ability to employ at the going wage rate.

MORE DETAIL

Of fundamental importance in seeing the economy as classical economists would have seen it, is to understand that a classical economist thought of the entire economy as one vast store of resources that could be used either to produce for present enjoyment or else be used to generate additional productive capital. A classical economist was, moreover, continuously aware of an economy's legacy from the past. Nothing bought in the present was the instantaneous result of some immediate decision to buy, but was, instead, the end point of some long, drawn-out process that went back in time, encompassing the entire array of labour and inputs that had been essential for the particular good or service to become available to purchase.

The transport networks across every city in the world are, just to take one example, an inheritance from the past. The underground in London, the metro in Paris and the subway in New York have each been in existence for more than a century, but once built are there and essential to the value-adding processes of the economy. Even so, there are massive additional amounts of labour and capital that must be continuously applied in maintaining these networks and updating the technologies so that additional drawdowns from the existing economic infrastructure are continuously being poured in. Thus, when passengers purchase their tickets in the morning, the cost of the fares is almost entirely unrelated to the vast array of capital involved in allowing passengers to reach their final destinations.

This inheritance exists not just within transport networks but throughout an entire economy. The term 'investment' refers only to the capital that has just been produced. Ignoring the masses of capital that already exist creates a major misunderstanding of what has allowed the economy to function and that allows individuals to buy what they buy. Everything purchased in a modern economy is based on the existence of a vast array of the capital inherited from the past, along with a multitude of skilled labour whose past training is equally essential to the operation of the economy in allowing this stock of capital to be put to use. This vast agglomeration of capital and labour encompasses virtually the entire economy, which is supplemented by only the trivial additions that happen to be made during some period of time, such as a week, a quarter and even across an entire year. In the modern world, just spending a day at the beach can require an enormous amount of capital (such as the car in which one drives to the beach and the roads on which these cars are driven), along with a large number of working people. For virtually everyone, these are near invisible as productive agents in permitting us to enjoy the living standards that are just taken for granted, as part of just how things are. A single journey on a city's transport network and its cost is perhaps a consumption item, but is in no way a representation of the actual value embedded within the entire network.

There is also the entrepreneur who plays the pivotal role in shaping the economy, first through managing an enterprise, then through determining the business's future direction, and finally through innovation that brings new products and new structural changes to the enterprises they run. Rather than seeing the economy as a largely static self-organizing structure, an economist intrinsically understood that present outcomes are the result of purposeful decisions by individuals embedded within the economy who based their decisions on the outcomes they expected to follow from their taking the paths they took.

The central challenge was the creation of wealth, which presupposed the creation of capital embedded within a business enterprise. There were, of course, periods of depressed economic circumstances just as there were periods of rapid growth and prosperity. The cycle was an unfortunate fact of life, but was inevitable given that all economic decisions are made in advance of an unknown future, which meant that economic decisions often turned out to be wrong. And when the existence of the system of money and credit creation was brought into the story that allowed for investment in products and forms of capital that would not in the end bring a positive return on the funds laid out, there was never any doubt that downturns were inevitable.

Core to the adjustment process was the price mechanism. The market mechanism would throw up prices that would become the background against which production decisions, and then consumption decisions, would be made. Movements in relative prices were the key to ensuring that resources were used economically, that goods and services were produced as cheaply in relation to the economy's resource base as possible.

The labour market would also adjust to circumstances, with wage rates shifting in relation to the supply and demand conditions as they prevailed. In good times, there was only frictional unemployment, as individuals sought out the best jobs available while employers sought out the best workers they could afford to undertake the tasks they needed done. During periods of economic downturn, many people would be thrown out of work, which everyone recognized as a catastrophic occurrence for which there was no remedy other than the adjustment processes of time. The one supposed remedy – public works – was often attempted even though classical economic theory specifically concluded that such an approach could not succeed. In John Stuart Mill's words, 'demand for commodities is not demand for labour'. In modern terms, an increase in public spending would not lower the unemployment rate, just as it never has.

MARGINAL REVOLUTION

The first of the so-called revolutions in economics was the 'marginal revolution'. Although Mill's statement on value has been ridiculed ever since by those who came after, it is difficult to see in which way he was wrong. As he wrote, obviously tempting fate:

> Happily, there is nothing in the laws of Value which remains for the present or any future writer to clear up; the theory of the subject is complete: the only difficulty to be overcome is that of so stating it as to solve by anticipation the chief perplexities which occur in applying it. (Mill, *Principles* [1871] 1921, p. 436)

Prices are determined in the market by supply and demand. For those goods or services for which there are no supply constraints on production, *relative* prices are determined according to their relative production costs. Where there is scarcity that constrains market supply, there is a premium that pushes the price level higher. The same will occur if businesses are able to create a monopoly position. Marshall discussed Jevons's misunderstanding of his marginalist predecessors in a long footnote, of which this was only a small part:

> [Jevon's] success was aided even by his faults. For under the honest belief that Ricardo and his followers had rendered their account of the causes that determine value hopelessly wrong by omitting to lay stress on the law of satiable wants ['diminishing marginal utility' in modern terms], he led many to think he was correcting great errors; whereas he was really only adding very important explanations. He did excellent work in insisting on a fact which is none the less important, **because his predecessors, and even Cournot, thought it too obvious to be explicitly mentioned,** viz. that the diminution in the amount of a thing demanded in a market indicates a diminution in the intensity of the desire for it on the part of

individual consumers, whose wants are becoming satiated. (Marshall, [1920] 1947, p. 101n.; bold emphasis added)

The bit in bold is emphasized because it highlights the role of presuppositions that often make it difficult to understand an earlier generation of economic writings. Marshall points it out from the perspective of his own time looking back at an even much earlier time.

Yet, the great discontinuity occurs less with the introduction of marginal utility, but with the loss of the classical presuppositions that were the basis for utility to become explicitly the basis for price determination. And then, more importantly, this loss of comprehension was emphasized with the introduction in the 1930s of the diagrammatic representations of equilibrium where marginal revenue equalled marginal cost. The shift to a rigid but quite sterile conception has been embedded within economic theory ever since.

That every economic decision going forward is dependent on some kind of cost–benefit analysis by the decision maker is undeniable. One might even say that marginal cost is being weighed up against marginal benefit. But formal presentation of a demand curve, whose slope and position are never known, and the marginal revenue curve derived from it as the core of the theory of the firm, reduces the value of economic instruction rather than enhances it. The straightforward fact is that no firm has ever set its price for any product in such a formal way. Not because they would not if they could, but because they cannot.

The supposed lesson is that a firm attempts to maximize its profits by (notionally?/actually?) choosing a price where the expected addition to revenue of producing one additional unit of output of a specific product will be equal to the expected addition to costs of producing that one additional unit of production. No time dimension is considered; no concerns about the erratic behaviour of markets are introduced. It is just a flat, static, non-dynamic presentation of a process that never occurs, which is supposedly a representation of the market process. The framework makes an understanding of the market mechanism seem extraordinarily mechanical and rigid. Nothing of the crucial importance of entrepreneurial calculation is included. It is an empty, useless exercise in logic that makes the dynamics of the market less comprehensible. The classical approach to understanding the operation of markets is so vastly superior that it is shameful that economic theory has instead chosen to go down this barren path.

KEYNESIAN REVOLUTION

Since the publication of *The General Theory*, almost no discussion of the supply side is considered in examining the way an economy works. Since job numbers are, according to Keynesian theory, related to the level of demand for final goods and services, the interest is in the latest set of activities and not the density or structure of the infrastructure that lies behind. The nature of the economy taken as a whole is virtually ignored. An economy with 10 per cent growth is seen as, in some important sense, doing better than an economy with 2 per cent growth, since the larger the economy's growth rate the faster the growth in employment is expected to be. Other considerations are placed into the background.

Eventually, the supply side was introduced as the mainstream presentation in the aggregate supply–aggregate demand framework when a wage explosion occurred simultaneously with an oil boycott in the 1970s, so that it could no longer be realistically denied that supply-side considerations were also important for understanding why an economy might go into recession. But even then, it was only on the demand side that a policy to return to full employment could be implemented. And even then, it was *aggregate* supply that was introduced into the analysis. There was still no element of the structure of production and how the meshing of the supply chain of the economy was essential to understanding the operation of an economy and why it might from time to time enter recession.

The Keynesian grip on policy has, in fact, transcended its original purpose to explain the cause of recessions and to frame policies to restore full employment. There is now an equivalence given to the I and G in the $C + I + G$ (total consumption + total private investment + total government expenditure) equation, so that increases in private investment and government spending on 'infrastructure' are seen as equivalent in their effects on employment and economic growth and well-being.

THE CLASSICAL FRAMEWORK

To help explain the core difference between the classical and modern frameworks, the most basic of all diagrams, the production possibility curve (PPC), is used below (Figure 11.1) to contrast the nature of classical and modern economics. A PPC is usually presented at an early stage of an introductory economics course. Typically, it picks two products and shows some kind of trade-off between them in relation to the quantity of each that can be produced with the resources available, such as the guns and butter example used by Samuelson ([1948] 1998, pp. 17–21). The more produced of one of these products, the less that can be produced of the other. The diagram is, however, more profound than it is usually taken to be, since, if properly constructed and conceptualized, it allows one to understand more completely the point classical economists had been trying to make.

The diagram having become a staple in modern theory (cf. Mankiw, 2007, pp. 24–7, who uses cars and computers), it therefore has an unassailable presence even though it is by nature vague and imprecise. Importantly, what must be appreciated is that the two axes of a properly designed diagram must represent two kinds of products whose combined output between them exhausts the entire economy's ability to produce. Examples might include goods on the one hand and services on the other. Or it might show privately produced products and government-produced products on each of its two axes. But, whatever might be chosen, any combination on the PPC itself cannot be exceeded. To produce more of one necessitates a fall in production of the other.

At the very core of classical thought was the recognition that all production uses up some part of the resource base available. It made no difference whether what was produced was purely for current consumption or whether this was production of new capital goods that were intended to raise productivity levels at some future date. All production drew down on the existing productivity of the economy. Most importantly, until the flow of new productive capital could occur, even those activities devoted towards future production were seen as a drawing down with no return until there actually was a return.

In Figure 11.1, the vertical axis shows forms of output that draw down on the resource base with no attempt made to replace what has been drawn down.[1] Here shown are purchases by final users – designated by the standard C for consumer demand – and purchases by governments – designated by the traditional G for government spending. Their combined production uses up resources, but what is produced is not intended to contribute to production at some future date. Resources are drawn down, products are either consumed or services rendered, but the economy is now less capable of producing since the resources have been used up while nothing has been created to replace what has been used up.

The horizontal axis represents all forms of drawing down on the economy's resource base that are directed towards producing forms of output that will add to the economy's productive base in the future. These are referred to as 'investment', shown in the diagram as I_{C+G}, which is the investment counterpart of $C + G$, while I_C is the investment counterpart of C on its own. While public investment is included, the infrequency that public investment is tested by its market return makes its inclusion problematic, but can be included nowhere else. These are products (or services such as education) that are intended to leave the economy able to produce an even greater flow of output at some stage in the future, but also include resource use to replace and maintain productivity worn down during the production process.

In the PPC shown, consumer outlays, government spending plus investment (which is defined to include investment by the public sector) exhaust the economy's ability to produce. Either because of institutional limitations, or because

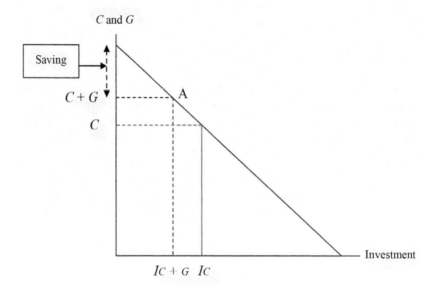

Figure 11.1   Production possibility curve: C, I and G

the economy cannot produce more than its potential, it is, as already noted, not possible to produce more than some combination on the curve itself, which is what point A represents.

The value of the PPC diagram is that it brings the interior of the economy into focus, which, in modern theory, is generally ignored. Inside the PPC is everything within an economy that can be used to satisfy human needs, either directly, as with consumption goods such as a loaf of bread, or indirectly, such as a tonne of iron ore.

Some of what is found within an economy is used to produce consumer goods (flour and ovens to bake bread) or are already consumer goods (such as actual loaves of bread on a supermarket shelf). And some of those existing resources are being used to produce capital goods that will eventually be used in the production process either to produce more capital or consumer goods. But what matters most of all is the structure of production – the interconnected web of commercial relationships that exist across the economy. These are businesses with their capital and employees. These are the purchase and sale between the various firms that produce inputs for the production of other inputs. These are the infrastructures that provide the connecting rods between the various economic entities. And these are the producers of final goods and services.

All these are what is represented by the interior of the PPC. It is this hinterland of 'factors of production' – a vestigial concept carried over from classical times – whose existence and configuration determine what will be produced and how much of each particular item. Directing resources to their particular uses are entrepreneurs, but also to some extent, the government. These internal relationships between the various inputs are configured according to the price signals that are determined in the market for each of the inputs used. The final output produced, that is, the C, I and G shown on the axes, is determined by the decision makers found within the interior of the economy. The outcome of these decisions is shown on the axes in the form of the goods and services bought by consumers, investors and governments: C, I and G.

Modern macroeconomic theory almost entirely ignores the structure of production, focusing only on the production of final goods and services. A modern economist looks at what is represented by the outer edge of the diagram, but seldom attends to what is represented by the interior. Modern theory argues that the higher the level of C, I and G, the higher will be the level of employment. The causation is seen to go from expenditure to production, that is, from the periphery to the interior.

This is the reverse of the causation as seen by a classical economist. It was the productivity of the economy that determined the flow of consumer and government goods and services, as well as the additions to capital. Jobs were a derived demand that would flow from the need to employ individuals to undertake the required production. During periods not classified as recessionary, individuals would prepare themselves for employment and the wages system would adjust to ensure as many employees as possible were engaged. The circumstances that existed during recessions are discussed below.

SAVING AND INVESTMENT

To a classical economist, the central question was how to increase 'the wealth of nations', that is, how to increase living standards. The answer would be that, in relation to the diagram, it was necessary to increase the area under the PPC by moving it up and to the right. The more investment there was, the more it might move, but even under the best of circumstances, it would move outward only very slowly.

The crucial issue was that of saving. In a modern macroeconomic model, saving is enumerated in money terms and is seen as a negative, an absence, a failure to spend. National saving is defined as current money income in total less total money spent on consumption in the current period. Figure 11.1, although conceived in classical terms, can be used to explain modern macroeconomic reasoning. Saving can be seen as the difference between the level of unproductive demand, that is $S = Y - (C + G)$, with Y, as usual, representing total income, which is found where the PPC curve meets the vertical axis. The level of saving is then equal to the level of investment, which is here shown as I_{C+G}.[2]

But this does not quite get to the Keynesian conception. But this does not quite get to the Keynesian conception. First, the PPC is entirely conceived in real terms. The units on the axes are actual products, the billions of items produced in an economy, from bread to bakeries. $C + G$ *is* made up of actual items of consumer goods and services plus government purchased goods and services. Saving in Keynesian macro is one step further removed from this diagram since it is entirely denominated in money terms. $\$S = \$Y - (\$C + \$G)$ is a near representation of the modern concept. Perhaps complicating these issues further, saving is frequently restricted to $Y - C$, with G net of transfers not entirely defined one way or the other, perhaps intrinsically conceived of as being as productive as business investment. It is possible that to make sense of modern economic theory properly, the horizontal axis should be $I + G$. With the vertical axis restricted to consumption alone, saving is shown as $Y - C$ as in the original Keynesian model. It is unclear where government spending fits into the notion of savings in a modern macroeconomic model.

Saving in classical terms, however, represented the resource base used to produce investment goods, while also providing workers with their food and shelter. Saving was identically equal to investment, since saving was by definition resources used to build capital goods. Yet, this was more than a tautology, since it emphasized the trade-off between those forms of activity that added nothing to productivity in comparison with those that did, with decisions to save and invest driving the overall outcome.

Understanding the role of saving as the building up of real productive assets, as well as providing the consumer goods that workers will buy and use before their own activities result in the production of consumable goods and services, is a necessity if one is to understand how an economy functions. A town in a war zone, or caught short because of some natural disaster, soon discovers how important the real stock of provisions available is.

In sum, the PPC diagram captures with a great deal of subtlety the meaning of saving and investment in classical times. An economy's inheritance from the past, its resource base, can either be sold for immediate consumption or used as inputs into adding to the economy's capital stock. Saving, when understood as a proportion of the productive apparatus of the economy applied to building an economy's productive capacities, is then exactly equal to the level of investment. That segment of the entire productive part of the economy not aimed toward improving the future productivity of the economy is used to provide consumer products or government services in the present. All, however, draw down on the productivity of the economy.

In terms of the diagram, classical economic policy was directed at expanding the area under the curve, not raising the level of spending as represented by the final outputs produced. The contrast with modern economic theory could not have been more complete. In modern macroeconomics, it is the total expenditure on *C*, *G* or *I* that supposedly determines the size of the economy, which in turn determines the level of employment. It is the expenditure found on the periphery of the diagram that determines what takes place internally, and most importantly, determines how large the productive triangle is. In a classical model, it was the reverse. The triangular area under the curve determined the economy's potential level of output, with various economic and political circumstances determining the distribution of what was produced among *C*, *I* and *G*.

Gross domestic product (GDP) measures, which are also estimated in terms of *C* + *I* + *G*, could be used as an estimate of the success of the economy as long as the proportion of expenditure on *G* was a constant. The rate of growth in the triangular area would be roughly reflected in the increases in final demand. It was Keynesian economics that turned this measure of economic activity into a theory of production, so that higher levels of demand would in theory lead to higher levels of output. A classical economist would, however, have understood that the causation was from the interior of the economy to the periphery and not the other way around as modern macroeconomics now argues.

THE BASIS FOR ECONOMIC GROWTH IN A CLASSICAL MODEL

The ability of the economy to produce in a classical model is determined by the stock of existing factors of production, which is represented by the area beneath the PPC. While it might be true to say that some of the inputs that are used during some period of time are produced during that period of time, overwhelmingly what determines the ability of the economy to produce is the vast array of already existing capital assets plus the available skilled labour that are deployed in the production process. That some of these productive capabilities are utilized to generate inputs during the period – such as the use of an already existing electricity-generating capacity to produce a flow of power during the period itself – does not distract from the fact that virtually the whole of an economy's productive capacity is in place at the start of a production period. The notion that the various inputs, such as the labour that happens to exist with the skill set it possesses, are anything more than the inheritance from the past and not some newly sprung productive capacity unrelated to the economy's prior production practices, is to recognize that every economy is dependent on its past for its ability to produce in the present. It is also a reminder that future production is importantly determined by what exists in the present. Spending on some capital project that is still incomplete at the period's end is still counted as part of output even though the economy has depleted some of its resource base but has as yet added nothing to the economy's ability to produce or consume.

All production draws down on the existing resource base. All production uses up some of the existing asset base beneath PPC. What is produced may then be classified into two branches: output that is used by its buyers without any expectation that it will add to the future flow of goods and services; and output that is intended to increase the future flow of goods and services. This second branch of production is referred to as *investment*. The resources that have been used to produce this investment are the proportion of the nation's resources that have been saved and are the nation's *savings*. If one recognizes that the combined asset base plus labour time that have been applied to produce for the future is that proportion of the nation's resources that has been saved (that is, not used to produce consumption goods for present purposes), it will be seen that saving and investment are identical, without this equality being in any sense a truism.

In Figure 11.2, saving and investment are not calculated as a proportion of total output, and therefore found on the axes, but are an area of the total available productivity of the entire economy and are thus represented by an area beneath the PPC. In the diagram, it appears that it is exactly the proportion of the economy above $C + G$, but that is just an approximation. It is whatever it is and could be more or less than the area shown. It is the conception that is crucial.

It is recognition that the amount of saving is that proportion of the entire economy's resource base that is devoted to increasing the future productivity of the economy. It is, moreover, made up of bricks and mortar, food and clothing, capital assets and labour time. It is the proportion of the economy's productive base that is devoted to increasing the economy's future productive base. And the more successful an economy is, the further the PPC will move away from the origin. The greater the area under the PPC, the greater the capacity of the economy to produce.

The level of investment on the horizontal axis is not replicated in the modern statistical measure of investment in GDP. It is the sum total of economic activities that not only are intended to raise future productivity but will actually achieve that end. Some of that expenditure is replacement investment for the capital used during the period. C and G both require a drawing down of the economy's productive base, as does investment. Maintaining the capital base is a necessary element in merely allowing an economy to stay where it is.

Beyond replacement, there is then the development of the economy's capital base, which is made up of additions to capital, conceived as a stock of

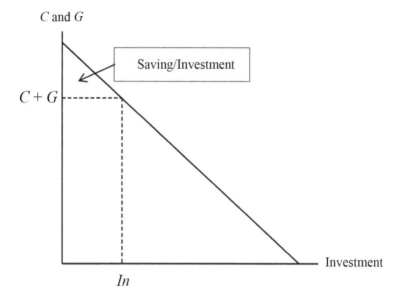

Figure 11.2   The point of steady-state neutral investment

newly produced capital assets, plus the improved technology that is built into new capital based on innovation and the application of new knowledge to the capital stock. Within such expenditure there are forms of investment that will never lead to an overall improvement in the economy's productivity. Mistakes are common and ultimately resources will have been drawn down on the economy's existing capacity without completely replacing what has been drawn down. At the same time, some of this improvement in the underlying capacity of the economy is provided by governments, whether in investments such as building drainage systems or providing new roads. Many such government projects, however, though offered up as investment projects never lead to an increase in the ability of the economy to produce larger volumes of output. The distinction made here is thus conceptual in that all that are classified as forms of investment are projects that actually succeed in achieving future improvements in output. The stress in this conception is in the outcome rather in attempting to find some objective measure that can separate investments that do cause the PPC to move outwards versus those that do not. It might just be noted in passing that investment expenditures that are wholly funded by private entrepreneurs rather than in part or in whole by governments are more likely to cause the economy to expand.

Somewhere on the division between $C + G$ and the level of I there is a point, here designated as *In*, which is the point of neutrality between a level of capital investment that will shift the PPC outward and where it will instead shift the curve inwards. A sufficiently rapid level of capital investment will shift the curve out. Too little investment, which does not even allow sufficient investment to replace what has been used up, will cause the curve to shift inwards. At *In*, the level of investment will leave the economy exactly as productive as it had previously been.

It has only been since the middle of the eighteenth century, with the advent of the market economy and entrepreneurial decision making, that our economies have been able to improve living standards on an almost annual basis. Year by year, the additions to the capital stock and its improvement have more than balanced the level of productivity that has been drawn down during production. From a classical perspective, economic growth is an entirely supply-side phenomenon, driven by the provision, year by year, of a more productive capital stock. There is no necessity for it to continue, but the broad framework of what must occur if growth is to follow was made plain by classical economists who had conceived the mechanism in an entirely different way from those who believe that the underlying drivers are increases in aggregate demand.

THE CLASSICAL THEORY OF THE CYCLE

The classical theory of the cycle was built around an understanding that the individual actions of a large number of producers, especially in an environment in which money and credit were the intermediary between buyers and sellers, would from time to time lead to economic crises and a downturn in activity. Business decisions, being made typically in advance of the circumstances in which those decisions would be expected to earn a return, could not be perfectly meshed with the economic outcomes that would actually occur.

Monetary and financial disruption was seen as a major potential for destabilization. Disruptions in the market for credit were of surpassing importance. What has been described as 'irrational exuberance' was often the cornerstone of the downwards phase of the theory of the cycle. But other forces might also on occasion add to the instability. These might include cataclysmic events such as wars and natural disasters. Just as important were government decisions or international phenomena that themselves disrupted markets (such as, for example, the OPEC oil boycott of the 1970s). But whatever might be the cause, a large number of business decisions turning out badly could lead to a downturn in activity. The classical theory of the cycle was a well-developed feature of economics prior to the publication of *The General Theory* (see Haberler,

1937). Let us therefore use the PPC diagram to explain the nature of recession and the recovery process in classical theory.

Figure 11.3 shows an economy in non-recessionary times with the economy at point A on the PPC. There is therefore as much as possible being produced, there is full employment (that is, no cyclical unemployment) and all resources are being used as efficiently as possible. The level of consumption plus public spending is $C + G$, while the level of investment is $I_{(C+G)fe}$, the subscript *fe* indicating full employment.

The economy goes into recession for any number of possible reasons, none of which are related to a deficiency of demand. This being a classical model, the economy did not slow because consumers suddenly out of nowhere decided to save and not spend. The coming of recession is shown by the shift of the economy from point A to point R. There may be some inwards movement of the curve itself due to some of the economy's capital base having become unemployable, but since the PPC represents the economy's potential and not the actual circumstances of the recession, the inwards movement is generally of little significance at the earliest stage of the recession.

The fall in output is understood as a consequence of some major distortion in the structure of production. There may be a period in which the actual circumstances are disguised by ongoing levels of economic activity. But with the structure of supply no longer conforming to the structure of demand, and therefore with some of the capital stock now uneconomic, and some areas of employment no longer contributing to profitable outcomes, a crisis had finally occurred that has revealed the fact that the existing economic structure can no longer support the level of incomes being distributed. A significant proportion of the economy may have appeared to be financially sound until that moment because there are financial assets that can be drawn down, and individual personal economies that can be undertaken to allow the situation to limp along.

The clearest sign of recession is the large drop in investment, shown in the diagram by the fall from $I_{(C+G)fe}$ to $I_{(C+G)r}$, with the subscript *r* indicating recession. With the onset of recession, there are higher than normal levels of unemployment. The level of consumption and government expenditure typically remains the same, with the fall in C perhaps even compensated by a rise in G. The economy therefore moves to point R, at a point showing a fall in investment but no significant change in consumer and government spending. And wherever point R might be relative to the two axes, in a recession it must be inside the PPC. The policy question then becomes, what can be done to return economic activity to its former level and, most importantly, reduce the level of unemployment as quickly as possible?

The Keynesian macroeconomic perspective is to assume that the problem has been an increase in saving. That is, a sudden fall off in aggregate demand has caused the downturn. The assumption is that the PPC is where it had

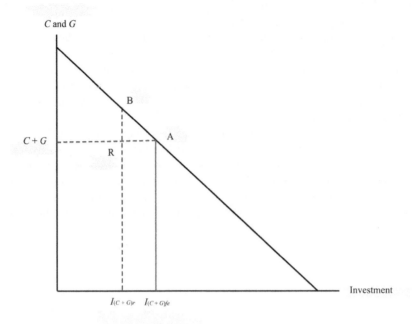

Figure 11.3   An economy in recession

originally been so that the community need only increase its expenditures and
the economy will return to full employment. No problem with the underlying
structure of production is brought into the story. There is a fall in expenditure
but the specific goods and services as well as the investment goods that the
economy would produce at full employment have not changed. As far as the
desired composition of output is concerned, or in terms of the actual structure
of supply, nothing of significance is different. The assumption would be that
the major problem was a fall in confidence ('animal spirits'). No consideration
would be given to the possibility that the economy needs major readjustment,
and more importantly, that increasing public spending to absorb unspent
savings would impede the return to full employment over the longer term.

Whatever might be the underlying set of considerations, the policy response
would be an increase in public spending, increasing the level of *G*. The
economy would be directed towards outcome B. A successful policy, at least
according to modern macroeconomic theory, would thus return the economy to
full employment, but with a reduced level of investment and a higher level of
C + *G*. The fall in investment would not necessarily diminish living standards
at that particular moment, although it might. More long term, however, the fall

in productive investment would inevitably reduce the economy's long-term potential rate of growth and could even lead it into a decline.

In contrast to modern forms of policy, given the importance of value-adding investment in creating economic growth, classical policy was aimed at shifting the economy from R back to A. There would be a number of policy changes that might be adopted, such as seeking to lower real wages, reducing taxation or lowering rates of interest. But, the overall approach was to allow the structure of the economy to adjust to the new circumstances so that wages and prices could move to their full employment market-clearing levels while the economy adjusted to a more productive structure of production that the recession had itself indicated was needed.

The policy that would not be adopted would be to raise public spending (G) to shift the economy from R to B. The crucial imperative would be the restoration of the level of productive investment. Even if the shift from R to B could be effected, the longer-term consequences would have been recognized as a reduction in the economy's long-term rate of growth. At point B relative to point A, $C + G$ is greater while productive investment is lower. A smaller proportion of the nation's resources are being used in growth-creating ways.

But, more importantly, for a classical economist, the economy was in recession because the structure of production was misshapen. The structure of supply no longer matched the structure of demand, and this referred to more than just final demand. The entire structure of production across the economy, which incorporated the structure of value-adding supply from the most basic inputs through to final output, was not properly aligned.

Any effort to reward businesses for producing in markets in which they could not earn a profitable return without either direct or indirect government subsidies only meant that the economy would continue to underperform. All production would continue to draw down on the resource base. Subsidizing wasteful forms of production would mean that the recovery process would be increasingly dominated by forms of production that would never repay their costs in further growth. The capital structure of the economy would therefore not improve as rapidly as it might have, and might well end up in a situation where there was not even sufficient investment to restore the capital that had been used up in production. The PPC would move inwards towards the origin. The economy would no longer be as productive as it had previously been. Living standards would fall while even the labour market might stagnate. Recovery would be postponed rather than hastened.

The inevitable outcome of such misdirected production was a fall in real earnings. If the economy did end up at point B and full employment, it would only have occurred if real wages had contracted since the economy was less productive than it had previously been.

A SUMMARY STATEMENT

Here are some of the insights highlighted by this approach. It is taken from an article that was part of a symposium I led on the economics of John Stuart Mill (Kates, 2015c):

1. While the ultimate aim of all economic activity is to create consumer goods and services, to do so requires a vast hinterland of productive inputs that constitute overwhelmingly the largest part of the economy.
2. Resources are used up irrespective of whether or not what is produced is intended to be consumed in the present or to be used to increase the future flow of output.
3. Value added is the single most important concept in understanding economic growth. For an economy to grow, value-adding activity must occur across the economy even if particular individual activities do not themselves create added value. In a stationary economy, value created is equal to the value used up.
4. Economic growth occurs only when more value is created than is used up.
5. Economic activities that do not at least replace the value that has been used up slow an economy down. If across an economy more value is used up than replaced, the economy will contract.
6. Productive investments take time, often requiring many years before the requisite outlays are repaid in addition to the economy's flow of goods and services.
7. Productive investments are almost invariably the consequence of entrepreneurial judgement.
8. Unproductive activity in the classical sense draws down on existing resources in creating utility but leaves nothing tangible in return that can contribute to future rates of growth.
9. The level of productive investment cannot be increased by increasing the level of non-value-adding forms of public spending – an economy cannot be made to grow by wasting its resources in forms of production that do not repay their production costs.
10. Recessions are caused by distortions in the structure of production that occur within the interior of the economy.
11. Recessions may on occasion be the result of attempts to produce more than the economy is capable of producing, leading to unexpected input shortages, bottlenecks and increased costs.
12. The most frequent, but not the only cause of the distortions that lead to recession are disorders that occur within the monetary and financial system.

13. A Keynesian stimulus will not only never work, it will make things worse since it will almost invariably divert resources from productive uses to unproductive.

14. Even worse, a Keynesian stimulus, working as it almost invariably does by producing non-value-adding forms of output, will create commercial pathways within the economy (a structure of production) that cause resources to be used in ways that are difficult to reverse without further economic disruption.

15. National saving is made up of resources, not money.

16. National saving is literally the use of resources to improve the underlying productivity of the economy.

17. Thinking of saving as money amounts will make a sound grasp of the underlying realities impossible.

18. Recessions are never caused by decisions to save – both the owners of capital and the owners of labour are always keen to have the resources they own earning an income.

19. Allowing resources to find their best uses through adjustments in relative prices must be the single most important element of policy, not only during recessions but also in every phase of the cycle.

20. Unemployed resources need time to find their most productive uses, which is as true for unemployed capital as it is for unemployed labour.

21. There are various policies governments may adopt to hasten the adjustment process during recessions, which may include small increases in public spending.

22. Business tax cuts and commercial interest rate reductions are likely to be a useful positive approach in dealing with recession.

23. The one policy governments should never adopt is to attempt to end a recession by replacing private sector expenditure with public expenditure.

24. There is no such thing as a multiplier process.

25. There is no such thing as a general glut.

All these are discussed in more detail at textbook length in the third edition of my Free Market Economics: An Introduction for the General Reader (2017), which is John Stuart Mill's Principles of Political Economy written for the twenty-first century.

NOTES

1. The PPC shown is a straight line in this presentation since there is no reason to presume resources are more productive in one form of production than in any other. This is all the more so since in classical theory whether some asset is an item

of capital is not intrinsic to the object itself, but is dependent on the decision of its owner. Providing a curved PPC would not change the argument in any way.

2.   Anyone who has done an introductory course in economics is aware of the conceptual framework that underlies the production possibility curve's construction and why the equation shown represents total saving in real terms. Y is total output where all available resources are fully employed. This can occur at any point along the production possibility curve. In relation to $S = Y - (C + G)$, Y in this case is where the production possibility curve meets the vertical axis and is the maximum level of consumption plus government spending possible where only consumer goods and public goods are being produced. The difference between the level of output, Y, and the level of $C + G$ represents saving (S), which in classical terms represents the amount of productive inputs available for productive investment shown along the horizontal axis.

12. Afterword

I will only say it here at the very end, although it ought to be clear from the text. I have written a book that more or less states that pretty well the whole of mainstream economic theory is worthless in devising policy. Virtually none of it will assist anyone in making decisions on how to make an economy prosper. It may be great for writing aimless papers that end up published in major journals, and it may provide cover for governments wishing to waste enormous sums of money on projects that take their fancy, but there is nothing I can see that throws light on how an economy works or what to do to make an economy grow more rapidly.

What makes this more astonishing to me than anything else is that, try as I might to discover others who understand this as well, there are virtually no others I can find. There are some, but they are very few and very far between. When I set out on this journey into the economic theories of the past, everything they wrote from the mid-nineteenth century onwards until the marginalists took over seemed so obvious to me that I could hardly believe there would be any difficulty in getting others to see it as well. When every stimulus package after the Global Financial Crisis failed to deliver a recovery, I assumed there would be some kind of revolt against the structure of modern theory. Yet, the mainstream that more or less solidified into its present structure in the 1930s has been left untroubled by its colossal failures.

That said, I will end by dedicating this book to my grandchildren: Matilda, Eve, Louis, Henry and Ada, with one more still to come at the time this is being written; to their parents, Benjamin and Debbie, Joshua and Beatrix; but most of all to my wife, Zuzanna, who puts up with a lot so that I can find the time to do the reading and the writing that has finally ended up in the book before you.

Bibliography

Bagehot, W. 1873. *Lombard Street: A Description of the Money Market*. Accessed January 2019 at https://oll.libertyfund.org/titles/bagehot-lombard-street-a-description-of-the-money-market.

Beveridge, W.H. 1944. *Full Employment in a Free Society*. London: George Allen & Unwin, Ltd.

Boettke, P. 2015. 'The Austrian tradition in economics'. *Libertarianism.org*. Interview with Trevor Burrus [podcast]. Accessed October 2019 at https://www.libertarianism.org/media/free-thoughts/austrian-tradition-economics.

Boulding, K.E. 1945. *The Economics of Peace*. New York: Prentice Hall.

Burton, J. 1978. 'Keynes's legacy to Great Britain: "folly in a Great Kingdom"'. In J.M. Buchanan, J. Burton and R.E. Wagner (1978), *The Consequences of Mr Keynes*. London: The Institute of Public Affairs, pp. 26–55.

Canlorbe, G. 2016. 'Say's Law, between Classical, Keynesian and Austrian interpretations. Conversation with Dr. Steve Kates conducted by Grégoire Canlorbe'. *Man and the Economy*, 3(2), 267–97.

Clay, H. 1916. *Economics: An Introduction for the General Reader*. 1st edition. London: Macmillan.

Clay, H. 1942. *Economics: An Introduction for the General Reader*. 2nd edition. London: Macmillan.

Colander, D. and Landreth, H. 1997. 'Political influence on the textbook Keynesian revolution: God, man, and Laurie Tarshis at Yale'. Accessed September 2019 at https://community.middlebury.edu/~colander/articles/Political%20Influence%20on%20the%20Textbook%20Keynesian%20Revolution.pdf.

DeLong, B. 2006. 'Krugman's intro to Keynes's General Theory'. *Brad DeLong's Grasping Reality* [blog]. Accessed September 2019 at https://delong.typepad.com/sdj/2006/03/krugmans_intro_.html.

Dillard, D. 1948. *The Economics of John Maynard Keynes: The Theory of a Monetary Economy*. New York: Prentice Hall.

Ebeling, R. 2015. 'Assessing Böhm-Bawerk's contribution to economics after a hundred years'. Liberty Fund online discussion. *Online Library of Liberty*. Accessed December 2019 at http://oll.libertyfund.org/pages/lm-bawerk.

Ely, R.T. and Hess, R.H. 1937. *Outlines of Economics*. 6th edition. New York: Macmillan.

Feser, E. 2006. *The Cambridge Companion to Hayek*. Cambridge, UK: Cambridge University Press.

Haberler, G. von. 1937. *Prosperity and Depression: A Theoretical Analysis of Cyclical Movements*. 1st edition. Geneva: League of Nations.

Haberler, G. von. 1939. *Prosperity and Depression: A Theoretical Analysis of Cyclical Movements*. 2nd edition. Geneva: League of Nations.

Haberler, G. von. 1941. *Prosperity and Depression: A Theoretical Analysis of Cyclical Movements*. 3rd edition. Geneva: League of Nations.

Hansen, A.H. 1936. 'Mr. Keynes on underemployment equilibrium'. *Journal of Political Economy*, **44**(5), 667–86.

Hansen, A.H. 1953. *A Guide to Keynes*. New York: McGraw-Hill.

Harris, S.E. (ed.). 1947. *The New Economics: Keynes' Influence on Theory and Public Policy*. New York: Alfred A. Knopf.

Hayek, F.A. von. 1944. *The Road to Serfdom*. Accessed October 2019 at https://en.wikiquote.org/wiki/The_Road_to_Serfdom.

Hayek, F.A. von. [1971] 2013. *The Collected Works of F.A. Hayek. Vol. 13: Studies on the Abuse & Decline of Reason: Text and Documents*. Edited by Bruce Caldwell. Chicago, IL: University of Chicago Press.

Hayek, F.A. von. 1979. *The Counter-Revolutions of Science: Studies on the Abuse of Reason*. Indianapolis, IN: Liberty Fund.

Hayek, F.A. von. 1992. *The Fortunes of Liberalism. Vol. 4: The Collected Works of F.A. Hayek*. Edited by P.G. Klein. Chicago, IL: University of Chicago Press.

Hicks, J.R. 1932. *The Theory of Wages*. London: Macmillan.

Hicks, J.R. 1937. 'Mr. Keynes and the "classics": a suggested interpretation'. *Econometrica*, **5**(2), 147–59.

History of Economic Thought. 2019a. 'John Stuart Mill: 1806-1873'. Accessed August 2019 at https://www.hetwebsite.net/het/profiles/mill.htm.

History of Economic Thought. 2019b. 'Responses to the *General Theory*'. Accessed April 2019 at http://www.hetwebsite.net/het/essays/keynes/responses.htm/.

Hoover, K. 2007. 'New classical macroeconomics'. In *Liberty Fund Encyclopedia: Government Policy, Macroeconomics, Schools of Economic Thought*. Accessed March 2020 at https://www.econlib.org/library/Enc/NewClassicalMacroeconomics.html.

Hutchison, T.W. 1953. *A Review of Economic Doctrines, 1870-1929*. New York: Oxford University Press.

Hutchison, T.W. 1977. *Keynes v. the Keynesians: An Essay in the Thinking of J.M. Keynes and the Accuracy of Its Interpretation by His Followers*. London: The Institute of Economic Affairs.

Hutchison, T.W. [1979] 1981. 'The limitations of general theories in macroeconomics'. In T.W. Hutchison, *The Politics and Philosophy of Economics: Marxians, Keynesians and Austrians*. Oxford: Basil Blackwell.

Hutt, W.H. 1960. 'The significance of price flexibility'. In H. Hazlitt (ed.), *The Critics of Keynesian Economics*. Princeton, NJ: D. van Nostrand Company.

Hutt, W.H. 1963. *Keynesianism – Retrospect and Prospect: A Critical Restatement of Basic Economic Principles*. Chicago, IL: Henry Regnery Company.

Hutt, W.H. 1974. *A Rehabilitation of Say's Law*. Athens, OH: Ohio University Press.

Hutt, W.H. 1979. *The Keynesian Episode: A Reassessment*. Indianapolis, IN: Liberty Press.

Kates, S. 1998. *Say's Law and the Keynesian Revolution: How Macroeconomic Theory Lost Its Way*. Cheltenham, UK and Lyme, NH, USA: Edward Elgar Publishing.

Kates, S. 2003. *Two Hundred Years of Say's Law: Essays on Economic Theory's Most Controversial Principle*. Cheltenham, UK and Northampton, MA, USA: Edward Elgar Publishing.

Kates, S. 2009. 'The dangerous return of Keynesian economics'. *Quadrant*, March 2009. Accessed February 2020 at https://quadrant.org.au/opinion/qed/2009/02/the-dangerous-return-to-keynesian-economics/.

Kates, S. (ed.). 2010a. *Macroeconomic Theory and its Failings: Alternative Perspectives on the Global Financial Crisis*. Cheltenham, UK and Northampton, MA, USA: Edward Elgar Publishing.

Kates, S. 2010b. 'Influencing Keynes: the intellectual origins of the general theory'. *History of Economic Ideas*, **18**(3), 33–64.

Kates, S. 2010c. 'The history of economic thought and public policy: Say's Law, Keynesian economics and the Global Financial Crisis'. In Ó. Dejuán, E. Febrero and M.C. Marcuzzo (eds), *The First Great Recession of the 21st Century: Competing Explanations*. Cheltenham, UK and Northampton, MA, USA: Edward Elgar Publishing.

Kates, S. 2010d. 'Why your grandfather's economics was better than yours'. *Quarterly Journal of Austrian Economics*, **13**(4), 3–28.

Kates, S. 2011a. *Free Market Economics: An Introduction for the General Reader*. 1st edition. Cheltenham, UK and Northampton, MA, USA: Edward Elgar Publishing.

Kates, S. (ed.). 2011b. *The Global Financial Crisis: What Have We Learnt?* Cheltenham, UK and Northampton, MA, USA: Edward Elgar Publishing.

Kates, S. 2013. *Defending the History of Economic Thought*. Cheltenham, UK and Northampton, MA, USA: Edward Elgar Publishing.

Kates, S. 2014a. 'The dangerous return of Keynesian Economics – a five year review'. *Quadrant.* March 2014. Accessed November 2019 at https://quadrant.org.au/magazine/2014/03/dangerous-return-keynesian-economics-five-years/.

Kates, S. 2014b. *Free Market Economics: An Introduction for the General Reader*. 2nd edition. Cheltenham, UK and Northampton, MA, USA: Edward Elgar Publishing.

Kates, S. 2015a. 'Mill's fourth fundamental proposition on capital: a paradox explained'. *Journal of the History of Economic Thought*, **37**(1), 39–56.

Kates, S. 2015b. 'Steven Kates replies: why the history of economics needs defending'. *Journal of the History of Economic Thought*, **37**(1), 145–50.

Kates, S. 2015c. 'Liberty matters: reassessing the political economy of John Stuart Mill'. Online symposium on the economics of John Stuart Mill. *Online Library of Liberty*. Accessed November 2019 at https://oll.libertyfund.org/titles/liberty-matters-reassessing-the-political-economy-of-john-stuart-mill-july-2015.

Kates, S. (ed.). 2016a. 'The hundredth anniversary of Clay's *Economics*: the best introduction to economics ever written'. *History of Economics Review*, **64**(1), 27–41.

Kates, S. 2016b. *What's Wrong with Keynesian Economic Theory?* Cheltenham, UK and Northampton, MA, USA: Edward Elgar Publishing.

Kates, S. 2017. *Free Market Economics: An Introduction for the General Reader*. 3rd edition. Cheltenham, UK and Northampton, MA, USA: Edward Elgar Publishing.

Kates, S. 2019. 'The dangerous persistence of Keynesian economics'. *Quadrant.* March 2019. Accessed November 2019 at https://quadrant.org.au/magazine/2019/03/the-dangerous-persistence-of-keynesian-economics/.

Kent, R.J. 2005. 'Keynes and Say's Law'. *History of Economics Review*, **41**, 61–76.

Keynes, J.M. [1919] 1981. *The Collected Writings of John Maynard Keynes. Vol II: The Economic Consequences of the Peace*. Edited by Donald Moggridge. London: Macmillan.

Keynes, J.M. [1925] 1981. 'A short view of Russia'. In *The Collected Writings of John Maynard Keynes. Vol. IX: Essays in Persuasion*. Edited by Donald Moggridge. London: Macmillan.

Keynes, J.M. [1926] 1981. 'The end of *laissez-faire*'. In *The Collected Writings of John Maynard Keynes. Vol. IX. Essays in Persuasion*. Edited by Donald Moggridge. London: Macmillan.

Keynes, J.M. [1929] 1981. 'Can Lloyd George do it?'. In *The Collected Writings of John Maynard Keynes. Vol. IX: Essays in Persuasion*. Edited by Donald Moggridge. London: Macmillan.

Keynes, J.M. [1929–31] 1981. *The Collected Writings of John Maynard Keynes. Vol. XX: Activities 1929-1931. Rethinking Employment and Unemployment Policies*. Edited by Donald Moggridge. London: Macmillan.

Keynes, J.M. [1930] 1981. *The Collected Writings of John Maynard Keynes. Vols V and VI: A Treatise on Money 1 and 2*. Edited by Donald Moggridge. London: Macmillan.

Keynes, J.M. [1931] 1981. *The Collected Writings of John Maynard Keynes. Vol. IX: Essays in Persuasion*. Edited by Donald Moggridge. London: Macmillan.

Keynes, J.M. [1933] 1981. *The Collected Writings of John Maynard Keynes. Vol. X: Essays in Biography*. Edited by Donald Moggridge. London: Macmillan.

Keynes, J.M. [1936] 1981. *The Collected Writings of John Maynard Keynes. Vol. VII: The General Theory of Employment, Interest and Money*. Edited by Donald Moggridge. London: Macmillan.

Keynes, J.M. [1939–45] 1981. *The Collected Writings of John Maynard Keynes: Vol XXII: Activities 1939-45: Internal War Finance*. Edited by Donald Moggridge. London: Macmillan.

Keynes, J.M. [1940] 1981. *How to Pay for the War*. Book reproduced in *The Collected Writings of John Maynard Keynes. Vol XXII: Activities 1939-45: Internal War Finance*. Edited by Donald Moggridge. London: Macmillan.

Keynes, J.M. [1944–46] 1981. *The Collected Writings of John Maynard Keynes. Vol XXIX: The General Theory and After – A Supplement*. Edited by Donald Moggridge. London: Macmillan.

Keynes, J.M. 1946. 'The balance of payments of the United States'. *The Economic Journal*, **56**(222), 172–87.

King, J.E. 2014. *The Microfoundations Delusion: Metaphor and Dogma in the History of Macroeconomics*. Cheltenham, UK and Northampton, MA, USA: Edward Elgar Publishing.

Krugman, P. 2006. 'Introduction'. In J.M. Keynes, *The General Theory of Employment, Interest and Money*. London: Palgrave Macmillan.

Kuhn, T.S. 1962. *The Structure of Scientific Revolutions*. Chicago, IL: University of Chicago Press.

Library of Economics and Liberty. 2019. 'Friedrich August Hayek: 1899-1992'. Accessed October 2019 at https://www.econlib.org/library/Enc/bios/Hayek.html.

Lucas, R. 2003. 'Macroeconomic priorities' [Presidential address delivered at the 115th meeting of the American Economic Association, 4 January 2003, Washington, DC]. *American Economics Review*, **93**(1), 1–14.

Malthus, T.R. 1820. *Principles of Political Economy*. London: John Murray.

Mankiw, G. 2007. *Principles of Economics*. 4th edition. Mason, OH: Thomson South-Western.

Mantoux, E. 1946. *The Carthaginian Peace or the Economic Consequences of Mr Keynes*. Oxford: Oxford University Press.

Marshall, A. [1890] 2013. *Principles of Economics*. Basingstoke: Palgrave Macmillan.

Marshall, A. [1920] 1947. *Principles of Economics – An Introductory Volume*. 8th edition. London: Macmillan.

McCracken, H.L. 1933. *Value Theory and Business Cycles*. New York: Falcon Press.

Menger, C. [1871] 1976. *Principles of Economics*. Translated by J. Dingwall and B.F. Hoselitz. Auburn, AL: Ludwig von Mises Institute.

Mill, J.S. [1843] 1967. *A System of Logic, Ratiocinative and Inductive: Being a Connected View of the Principles of Evidence and the Methods of Scientific Investigation*. 2 vols. 8th edition. London: Longmans, Green & Co.

Mill, J.S. [1844] 1974. 'Of the influence of consumption on production'. In J.S. Mill, *Essays on Some Unsettled Questions in Political Economy*. Clifton, NJ: Kelley.

Mill, J.S. [1859] 1998. *On Liberty*. In *On Liberty and Other Essays*. Edited by J. Gray. Oxford: Oxford University Press.

Mill, J.S. [1871] 1921. *Principles of Political Economy with Some of their Applications to Social Philosophy*. New impression of the new 7th edition of 1909. Edited with an introduction by Sir W.J. Ashley. London: Longmans, Green, & Co.

Mises, L. von. [1949] 1963. *Human Action: A Treatise on Economics*. 4th revised edition. San Francisco, CA: Fox and Wilkes.

Mises, L. von. 1985. *Liberalism in the Classical Tradition*. New York: The Foundation for Economic Education.

Newcomb, S. 1886. *Principles of Political Economy*. New York: Harper & Bros.

Nicholson, J.S. 1893–1901. *Principles of Political Economy*. 3 vols. London: Adam & Charles Black.

Nicholson, J.S. 1921. *The Revival of Marxism*. London: John Murray.

O'Brien. D.P. [1975] 2004. *The Classical Economists Revisited*. Revised edition. Princeton, NJ: Princeton University Press.

Peden, G.C. 1996. 'The Treasury view in the interwar period: an example of political economy'. In B. Corry (ed.), *Unemployment and the Economists*, Cheltenham, UK and Brookfield, VT, USA: Edward Elgar Publishing.

Pigou, A.C. 1932. *The Theory of Unemployment*. London: Wiley.

Pigou, A.C. [1933] 1999. *A.C. Pigou Collected Economic Writings. Vol. 8: The Theory of Unemployment*. Basingstoke: Palgrave Macmillan.

Pigou, A.C. 1936. 'Mr. J. M. Keynes' General Theory of Employment, Interest and Money', *Economica*, **3**(10), 115–32.

Pigou, A.C. 1951. *Keynes's 'General Theory': A Retrospective View*. London: Macmillan.

Ricardo, D. 1951–73. *The Works and Correspondence of David Ricardo*. 11 vols. Edited by P. Sraffa with the collaboration of M.H. Dobb. Cambridge, UK: Cambridge University Press.

Ricardo, D. [1819–21] 1973. *The Works and Correspondence of David Ricardo. Vol. VIII: Letters, 1819-June 1821*. Edited by P. Sraffa with the collaboration of M.H. Dobb. Cambridge, UK: Cambridge University Press.

Robinson, J. 1937a. *Introduction to the Theory of Employment*. London: Macmillan.

Robinson, J. 1937b. *Essays in the Theory of Employment*. London: Macmillan.

Robinson, J. [1942] 1966. *An Essay on Marxian Economics*. London: Macmillan.

Romer, D. 1996. *Advanced Macroeconomics*. New York: McGraw-Hill.

Ryme, T. 1990. *Keynes's Lectures, 1932-35: Notes of a Representative Student*. Ann Arbor, MI: University of Michigan Press.

Samuelson, P.A. 1946. 'Lord Keynes and the General Theory'. *Econometrica*, **14**(3), 187–200.

Samuelson, P.A. [1948] 1964. *Economics: An Introductory Analysis*. 6th edition. International Student Edition. New York: McGraw-Hill.

Samuelson, P.A. [1948] 1998. *Economics: The Original 1948 Edition: An Introductory Analysis*. New York: McGraw-Hill.

Schumpeter, J.A. [1946] 1947. 'John Maynard Keynes 1883-1946. *The American Economic Review*, Vol. 36, No. 4 (Sep., 1946), pp. 495–518'. Reprinted in S.E.

Harris (ed.), *The New Economics: Keynes' Influence on Theory and Public Policy*. New York: Alfred A. Knopf.

Skidelsky, R. 2006. 'Hayek versus Keynes: the road to reconciliation'. In E. Feser (ed.), *The Cambridge Companion to Hayek*. Cambridge, UK: Cambridge University Press.

Smith, A. [1776] 1976. *An Inquiry into the Nature and Causes of the Wealth of Nations*. Edited by E. Cannan. Chicago, IL: University of Chicago Press.

Socialist Voice. [1983] n.d. 'Marxist theory of crises'. *Marxists.org*. Accessed September 2019 at https://www.marxists.org/history/etol/newspape/socialistvoice/marx19.html.

Sweezy, P. [1946] 1964. 'A ten-years-after review of *The General Theory*'. In R. Lekachman (ed.), *Keynesian Economics: A Report of Three Decades*. New York: St Martin's Press.

Tarshis, L. 1947. *The Elements of Economics: An Introduction to the Theory of Price and Employment*. Boston, MA: Houghton Mifflin.

Taussig, F.W. 1896. *Wages and Capital: An Examination of the Wages Fund Doctrine*. New York: D. Appleton & Company.

Taylor, F.M. 1925. *Principles of Economics*. 9th edition. New York: The Ronald Press Company.

Wikipedia. 2019a. 'Financial crisis of 2007–08'. Accessed January 2019 at https://en.wikipedia.org/wiki/Financial_crisis_of_2007%E2%80%9308.

Wikipedia. 2019b. 'Joseph Shield Nicholson'. Accessed September 2019 at https://en.wikipedia.org/wiki/Joseph_Shield_Nicholson.

Wikipedia. 2019c. 'Lorie Tarshis'. Accessed August 2019 at https://en.wikipedia.org/wiki/Lorie_Tarshis.

Wikipedia. 2019d. 'The Macmillan Committee'. Accessed September 2019 at https://en.wikipedia.org/wiki/Macmillan_Committee.

Wikipedia. 2019e. '*On Liberty*'. Accessed September 2019 at https://en.wikipedia.org/wiki/On_Liberty#Economy.

Wikipedia. 2019f. 'William Trufant Foster'. Accessed September 2019 at https://en.wikipedia.org/wiki/William_Trufant_Foster.

Wikipedia. 2020a. 'Arthur Cecil Pigou'. Accessed February 2020 at https://en.wikipedia.org/wiki/Arthur_Cecil_Pigou.

Wikipedia. 2020b. 'Alvin Hansen'. Accessed February 2020 at https://en.wikipedia.org/wiki/Alvin_Hansen.

Wilson, T. 1943. 'Review of *Keynesian Economics* by Mabel F. Timlin'. *The Economic Journal*, **53**(210/211), 224–6.

Wikipedia is sometimes denigrated as faulty and potentially erroneous. I have nevertheless included a number of passages from Wikipedia entries, but only where what is found in Wikipedia corresponds with the results and conclusions from my own research.

Index